how to be a
GOURMET COOK
on a
HAMBURGER BUDGET

Ruth & Alan Hinden

Thank You for helping build the Las Vegas Temple.

Ruth Hinden
Alan W. Hinden

Published in the United States by RBH Publishing Enterprises, a division of Advertising Unlimited, Ltd., 4528 West Charleston Boulevard, Las Vegas, Nevada 89102.

Printed in the United States of America.

Typeset by Word Processing Professionals, Burbank, California.

First Printing: March, 1982

ISBN: 0-939842-03-3

HOW TO BE A GOURMET COOK
ON A HAMBURGER BUDGET

Preface v
How We "Cooked Up" This Book vii

BUDGET GOURMET TIPS 1
    Tricks to Becoming a Wise Consumer 2
    Budget Tips for Your Entertaining Dollar 5
    Tricks to Better Nutrition 5
    Substitution of Ingredients 6
    Measuring Table of Equivalents 11
    Basic 4 Chart 13
    Can Size Equivalents 14

MAIN DISHES 15
    Meaty Tips 16
    Meat Planovers 17
    Fish Planovers 17
    Pasta Planovers 18
    Rice Planovers 18
    Bean Planovers 18
    Egg Planovers 19
    Cheese Planovers 19
    Beef Dishes 20
    Ground Beef Dishes 31
    Pork Dishes 55
    Sausage Dishes 60
    Ham Dishes 63
    Chicken and Turkey Dishes 69
    Fish Dishes 90
    Tuna and Salmon Dishes 94
    Miscellaneous Meat Dishes 99
    Pasta Dishes 103
    Rice Dishes 109
    Bean Dishes 111
    Egg and Cheese Dishes 114

VEGETABLES, SALADS AND SIDE DISHES 121
    Tips for Buying Vegetables and Fruits 122
    Vegetable Planovers 122
    Vegetables 124
    Salads 131
    Miscellaneous 135

DESSERTS 137
    Fruit Planovers 138
    Cookie and Cake Planovers 139
    Fruit Dishes 140
    Cakes 150
    Pies and Torts 165
    Cookies 175
    Dessert Breads 180
    Cheesecakes 182
    Refrigerator and Gelatin Desserts 184
    Frozen Desserts 189
    Rice - Pasta 192
    Pudding 194
    Miscellaneous Desserts 196

BREADS AND CEREALS 201
    Bread Money Saving Ideas 202
    Bread Planovers 202
    Breads and Cereals 203

MISCELLANEOUS 206
    (Sauces, Gravies, Dressing, Jelly,
    Punch, Syrup)

INDEX 215

What is the determining factor between a gourmet meal and a plain old everyday meal? I contend that the way the meal is prepared and served - with flair and imagination makes the difference. Money doesn't have to be the factor. Imagine these elegant meals - Plum Glazed Chicken on Wild Rice, Crepes Frangipane or Turkey Manicotti - don't you get the feeling of a fine gourmet restaurant? Yet, each of these are easy on the budget.

France has long been considered the culinary leader in the world, yet, if you study French cooking, you'll discover their love for sauces gives their meals that special flair. Simple sauces can be the difference between common and gourmet main dishes, side dishes and desserts.

You'll be excited to learn how people all over the North American continent serve gourmet meals without spending big dollars. Company coming? You're to furnish the dessert for a get-together? You will find so many recipes to fit these and all your other cooking needs; contributed by budget conscious cooks from all over the United States and Canada.

Any dish can be dressed up for company or special occasions with a garnish. Try a little whipped cream on pies and gelatin desserts. Slivered nuts, sliced olives and other things of that sort on casseroles and slices of fruit with meats.

An important idea to remember is that recipes are guides. Use the good ideas here to develop your own specialities. Casseroles can be easily altered to fit your likes and food on hand. Most recipes do not have to be exact with the exception of cakes and cookies which require the correct proportion of dry and liquid ingredients and baking soda/powder. You can experiment with spices and herbs to change the taste of the dish. They should not change the consistency.

I make almost all my foods from "scratch". This not only saves me money, but I feel that home prepared meals are more nutritious and wholesome than packaged ones. For this reason, I have included a list of substitutes on pages 6 to 10. For example, if a dish calls for packaged cheese sauce, I use the recipe for cheese sauce on page 207. If a recipe calls for canned soups, you can use the recipes on page 10.

v

As members of the Church of Jesus Christ of Latter Day Saints (the Mormons), we do not use or recommend the use of alcoholic beverages that have not had the alcohol cooked out during the preparation of the recipe. We also do not use or recommend the use of coffee or tea. If you feel as we do that these substances can be harmful to your body, you can use the following substitutes: 1 cup of 7-Up or other type of lemon-lime soda for 1 cup of alcohol plus rum or brandy flavoring if desired. Cocoa or chocolate can be used for coffee in dry form or with water added according to recipe directions. The taste will be changed somewhat with these substitutions.

The recipes without a name below them are from our special recipe file or from Ruth's mother, LaBerta Altermatt.

Alan and Ruth Hinden

ACKNOWLEDGMENTS:

Illustrations by Rosina Shore.
Color photography by Ron Strobelt.
Cover by Alan W. Hinden
Typesetting by Shirley Price

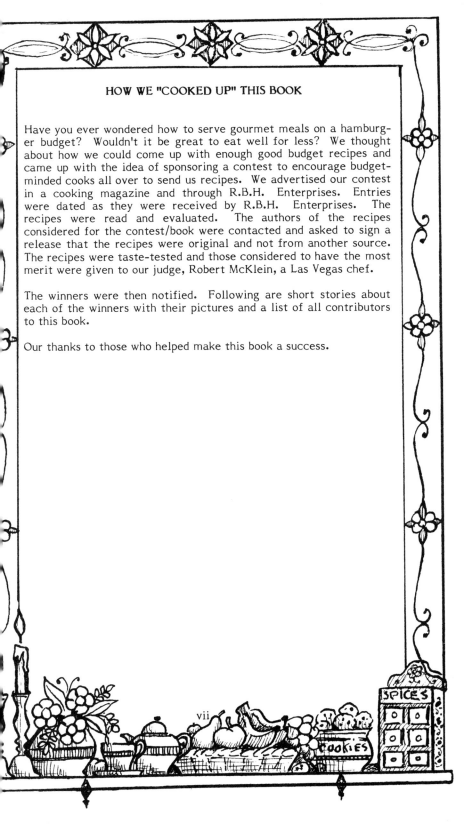

HOW WE "COOKED UP" THIS BOOK

Have you ever wondered how to serve gourmet meals on a hamburger budget? Wouldn't it be great to eat well for less? We thought about how we could come up with enough good budget recipes and came up with the idea of sponsoring a contest to encourage budget-minded cooks all over to send us recipes. We advertised our contest in a cooking magazine and through R.B.H. Enterprises. Entries were dated as they were received by R.B.H. Enterprises. The recipes were read and evaluated. The authors of the recipes considered for the contest/book were contacted and asked to sign a release that the recipes were original and not from another source. The recipes were taste-tested and those considered to have the most merit were given to our judge, Robert McKlein, a Las Vegas chef.

The winners were then notified. Following are short stories about each of the winners with their pictures and a list of all contributors to this book.

Our thanks to those who helped make this book a success.

FIRST PLACE $300.00 WINNER
MRS. ELVIRA GIBBONS
PLUM GLAZED CHICKEN ON WILD RICE (Page 72)

"You have given me that special feeling of joy! It feels great!," was the response we received when Elvira Gibbons found that she was the first place winner of our gourmet cooking on a hamburger budget contest.

Elvira is a widow who lives in North Sydney, Nova Scotia with her daughter. She told us that she has always lived within five miles of her birthplace. Her small town of about 8,000 people is very friendly and she loves the feeling of being able to exchange greetings with friends on the street. She is the mother of two sons and a daughter and has eleven grandchildren.

Elvira loves to cook. Christmas is an extra special time because she loves to prepare home baked gifts for her friends and family. She is always cooking or baking something.

Elvira spends a lot of time writing to penpals throughout the world. She also enjoys entering contests. In 1979, she won a new car which she sold to the dealer and used part of the money for a cruise ship trip through the Carribean. "It was my only long distance trip and I was like a child at Christmas," she reported.

She is a member of the Sydney Mines Senior Citizens Club and the Ladies Auxiliary of the Canadian Legion, Branch #8. Being a member of these two groups gives her the opportunity to enjoy another of her joys in life which is dancing. She also enjoys walking a few blocks to play bingo with friends (sometimes she even wins a little).

Her greatest joy, however, is the hugs and kisses from her grandchildren.

SECOND PLACE $100.00 WINNER
MRS. EDNA (CLYDE) PRANGE
CREPES FRANGIPANE (Page 196)

Edna was born on a farm north of Hoxie, Kansas. She lived there almost half of her life. Most of the time she walked to a parochial school two-and-a-quarter miles from her home. When she first started attending school, the grades were divided into two groups. Grades 1-4 were taught by the pastor and grades 5-8 were taught by his daughter. When the pastor accepted a call to a different parish, the school became a one classroom school. It had no modern conveniences.

Edna started cooking and baking as a child. She remembers the first time her mother asked her to make bread. She was very nervous since her mother did not use recipes and used homemade yeast. However, she followed her mother's directions and she recalls it turned out "fit to eat". When she started to relax, she found that she enjoyed cooking very much. In fact, cooking, baking and crafts are her hobbies. Edna's parents moved off the farm to Lincoln, Nebraska to live near two of her sisters. Edna moved with them. She met her husband through his relatives from his hometown of Firth, Nebraska. The Pranges have two children, Bruce, age eighteen and Lori, also a recipe contributer, age fourteen.

Edna likes to use almonds in cooking and set out to create an exotic crepe dessert using almonds. She developed the filling from her favorite vanilla cream recipe, adding ground almonds and almond extract. Powdered sugar, whipped cream and grated chocolate seemed to top it off nicely. She had created a winner! The name "Frangipane" comes from the name of the Marquis Frangipania, a Major General under Louis XIV of France.

ix

THIRD PLACE $50.00 WINNER
KAREN COLMER
TURKEY MANICOTTI (Page 104)

Karen is twenty-eight years old and single. She lives with her father (retired from Sears Roebuck in Champaign, Illinois) and mother (a homemaker). She has two older sisters. Karen works at Collegiate Cap and Gown in Champaign, where she has been employed for the past nine years. Her hobbies are cooking, baking, sewing, crocheting, and flower arranging.

Karen started to cook when she was small by helping her mother in the kitchen. Between her mother and grandmother, she learned a lot about cooking and baking. They also taught her to sew and crochet.

In her senior year of high school, she took an occupational course and worked in "The Blossom Shop", a flower shop in Farmer City, Illinois. This was where she learned to arrange flowers.

She graduated from Mansfield High School in 1971. Her class was the last class to graduate from there. The next year the school was consolidated with Farmer City, seven miles west of Mansfield.

In December 1977, Karen won a turkey and a $20.00 gift certificate for groceries with her cooking entry in a local newspaper cooking contest. Her entry was Santa's Whiskers cookies. She also has a Certificate of Merit from the Wilton Method of Cake Decorating for a six week course she completed in 1981.

Karen helps her parents raise a good-sized garden every summer and then helps with the canning. She has liked to cook and bake for as long as she can remember. To be able to prepare something that looks and tastes good for her family or friends is one of her greatest joys.

x

CHEF AND CONTEST JUDGE
ROBERT MC KLEIN

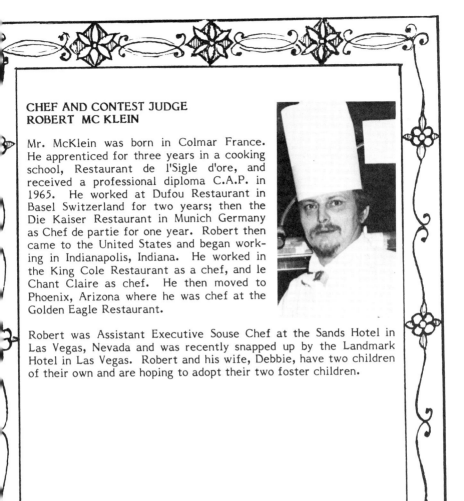

Mr. McKlein was born in Colmar France. He apprenticed for three years in a cooking school, Restaurant de l'Sigle d'ore, and received a professional diploma C.A.P. in 1965. He worked at Dufou Restaurant in Basel Switzerland for two years; then the Die Kaiser Restaurant in Munich Germany as Chef de partie for one year. Robert then came to the United States and began working in Indianapolis, Indiana. He worked in the King Cole Restaurant as a chef, and le Chant Claire as chef. He then moved to Phoenix, Arizona where he was chef at the Golden Eagle Restaurant.

Robert was Assistant Executive Souse Chef at the Sands Hotel in Las Vegas, Nevada and was recently snapped up by the Landmark Hotel in Las Vegas. Robert and his wife, Debbie, have two children of their own and are hoping to adopt their two foster children.

TO

Milton and Helen

J. L. and LaBerta

OUR PARENTS

LIST OF CONTRIBUTORS

Adams, Lil
  Gettysburg, SD
Allen, Mrs. James (Eleanor)
  South Bend, IN
Amendola, Faye
  New Haven, CT

Anderson, Muriel
  Pleasant Valley, NY
Arnet, Joyce
  Winnipeg, Manitoba Canada
Awalt, Caroline M.
  Huntington, CT

Baker, Jean
  Chula Vista, CA
Behrens, Vivian
  Franklinville, NJ
Belair, Betty
  Cumberland, RI
Biller, Mary A.
  Willard, OH
Blatter, Esther
  McClusky, ND
Bond, Dolie
  Carlsbad, NM
Bossen, Mary P.
  Davenport, IA

Boyer, Mrs. Charles
  Fremont, OH
Bradley, Carol
  Fort Dodge, IA
Brennan, Betty Ann
  Faribault, MN
Brown, Amelia
  Pittsburg, PA
Brown, Mrs. D. C.
  Pittsburg, PA
Brown, Marie
  Wilson, NC

Camenisch, Marge
  Joliet, IL
Cantrell, Grace F.
  McKenney, VA
Cherry, Jim
  Pittsfield, IL

Colmer, Karen
  Mansfield, IL
Conejo, Adela
  Seguin, TX
Cunningham, Joyce
  Alliance, OH

Davis, Maxine
  Centralia, IL
Denitto, Dorothy
  Sykesville, MD
Dietz, Katherine E.
  Grosvenordale, CT

Doria, Theresa
  Butler, PA
Douvier, Mrs. Frank
  Freeport, MN

Ede, Mrs. Gordon
  Invermere, BC Canada
Edgecomb, Margaret E.
  Bar Mills, ME
Edmonds, Ava Gail
  Wellford, SC

Ellingson, Mrs. Stanley
  Wolverton, MN
Eudy, Mrs. John
  Des Moines, IA

xiii

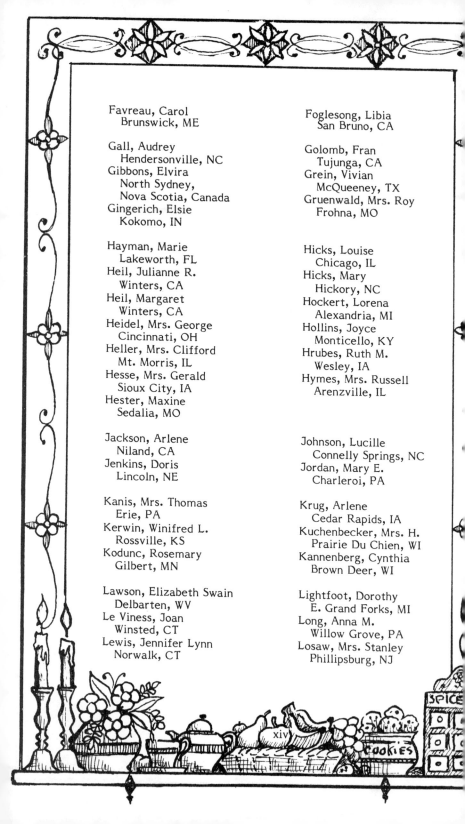

Favreau, Carol
  Brunswick, ME

Foglesong, Libia
  San Bruno, CA

Gall, Audrey
  Hendersonville, NC
Gibbons, Elvira
  North Sydney,
  Nova Scotia, Canada
Gingerich, Elsie
  Kokomo, IN

Golomb, Fran
  Tujunga, CA
Grein, Vivian
  McQueeney, TX
Gruenwald, Mrs. Roy
  Frohna, MO

Hayman, Marie
  Lakeworth, FL
Heil, Julianne R.
  Winters, CA
Heil, Margaret
  Winters, CA
Heidel, Mrs. George
  Cincinnati, OH
Heller, Mrs. Clifford
  Mt. Morris, IL
Hesse, Mrs. Gerald
  Sioux City, IA
Hester, Maxine
  Sedalia, MO

Hicks, Louise
  Chicago, IL
Hicks, Mary
  Hickory, NC
Hockert, Lorena
  Alexandria, MI
Hollins, Joyce
  Monticello, KY
Hrubes, Ruth M.
  Wesley, IA
Hymes, Mrs. Russell
  Arenzville, IL

Jackson, Arlene
  Niland, CA
Jenkins, Doris
  Lincoln, NE

Johnson, Lucille
  Connelly Springs, NC
Jordan, Mary E.
  Charleroi, PA

Kanis, Mrs. Thomas
  Erie, PA
Kerwin, Winifred L.
  Rossville, KS
Kodunc, Rosemary
  Gilbert, MN

Krug, Arlene
  Cedar Rapids, IA
Kuchenbecker, Mrs. H.
  Prairie Du Chien, WI
Kannenberg, Cynthia
  Brown Deer, WI

Lawson, Elizabeth Swain
  Delbarten, WV
Le Viness, Joan
  Winsted, CT
Lewis, Jennifer Lynn
  Norwalk, CT

Lightfoot, Dorothy
  E. Grand Forks, MI
Long, Anna M.
  Willow Grove, PA
Losaw, Mrs. Stanley
  Phillipsburg, NJ

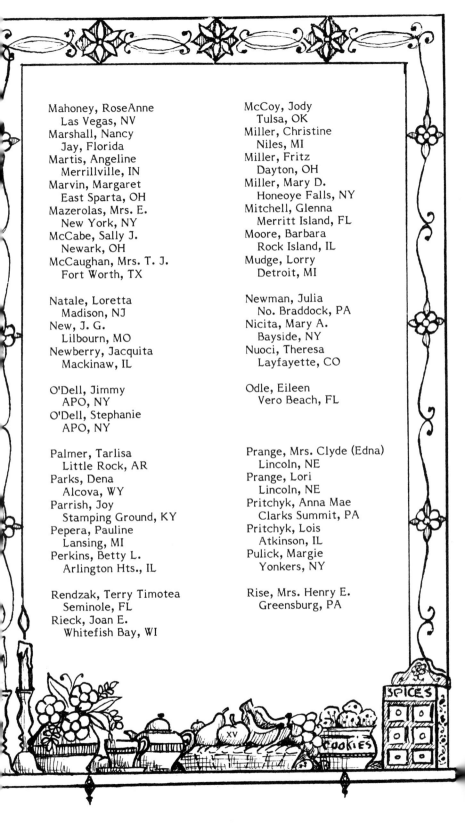

Mahoney, RoseAnne
  Las Vegas, NV
Marshall, Nancy
  Jay, Florida
Martis, Angeline
  Merrillville, IN
Marvin, Margaret
  East Sparta, OH
Mazerolas, Mrs. E.
  New York, NY
McCabe, Sally J.
  Newark, OH
McCaughan, Mrs. T. J.
  Fort Worth, TX

Natale, Loretta
  Madison, NJ
New, J. G.
  Lilbourn, MO
Newberry, Jacquita
  Mackinaw, IL

O'Dell, Jimmy
  APO, NY
O'Dell, Stephanie
  APO, NY

Palmer, Tarlisa
  Little Rock, AR
Parks, Dena
  Alcova, WY
Parrish, Joy
  Stamping Ground, KY
Pepera, Pauline
  Lansing, MI
Perkins, Betty L.
  Arlington Hts., IL

Rendzak, Terry Timotea
  Seminole, FL
Rieck, Joan E.
  Whitefish Bay, WI

McCoy, Jody
  Tulsa, OK
Miller, Christine
  Niles, MI
Miller, Fritz
  Dayton, OH
Miller, Mary D.
  Honeoye Falls, NY
Mitchell, Glenna
  Merritt Island, FL
Moore, Barbara
  Rock Island, IL
Mudge, Lorry
  Detroit, MI

Newman, Julia
  No. Braddock, PA
Nicita, Mary A.
  Bayside, NY
Nuoci, Theresa
  Layfayette, CO

Odle, Eileen
  Vero Beach, FL

Prange, Mrs. Clyde (Edna)
  Lincoln, NE
Prange, Lori
  Lincoln, NE
Pritchyk, Anna Mae
  Clarks Summit, PA
Pritchyk, Lois
  Atkinson, IL
Pulick, Margie
  Yonkers, NY

Rise, Mrs. Henry E.
  Greensburg, PA

XV

SPICES

COOKIES

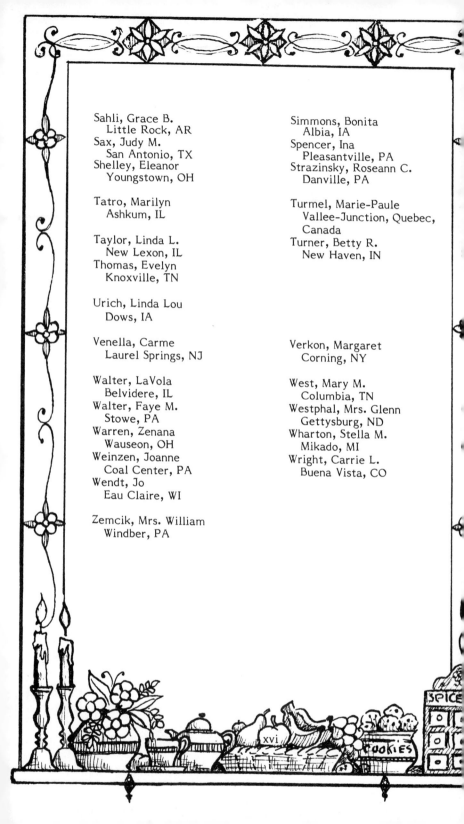

Sahli, Grace B.
  Little Rock, AR
Sax, Judy M.
  San Antonio, TX
Shelley, Eleanor
  Youngstown, OH

Tatro, Marilyn
  Ashkum, IL

Taylor, Linda L.
  New Lexon, IL
Thomas, Evelyn
  Knoxville, TN

Urich, Linda Lou
  Dows, IA

Venella, Carme
  Laurel Springs, NJ

Walter, LaVola
  Belvidere, IL
Walter, Faye M.
  Stowe, PA
Warren, Zenana
  Wauseon, OH
Weinzen, Joanne
  Coal Center, PA
Wendt, Jo
  Eau Claire, WI

Zemcik, Mrs. William
  Windber, PA

Simmons, Bonita
  Albia, IA
Spencer, Ina
  Pleasantville, PA
Strazinsky, Roseann C.
  Danville, PA

Turmel, Marie-Paule
  Vallee-Junction, Quebec,
  Canada
Turner, Betty R.
  New Haven, IN

Verkon, Margaret
  Corning, NY

West, Mary M.
  Columbia, TN
Westphal, Mrs. Glenn
  Gettysburg, ND
Wharton, Stella M.
  Mikado, MI
Wright, Carrie L.
  Buena Vista, CO

BUDGET

TIGHTFISTED

BUYING "CENTS"

GROCERY LIST

BUY IN SEASON

SALES

BULK

SOUP

GOURMET TIPS

TRICKS TO BECOMING A WISE SHOPPER

Planning is probably the most important aspect of menu planning on a budget. By planning, one avoids waste of foods and time. It is wise to plan a week's menus at a time. Plan to use all the food purchased. I call foods that are left "planovers" rather than leftovers since they can be used to simplify future meals during the week. This book contains many great recipes for the remainder of that pot roast, baked potatoes, vegetables, etc. that are left from one meal or the extra quantity cooked for planned future meals. "Planovers" are great money and time savers.

A shopping list is a must. Failing to buy items you need for recipes can be disasterous to your budget. The amount of time and money wasted is one factor, but another is that people tend to buy "impulse" items whenever they visit the store. Therefore, it is wise to stay out of stores as much as possible or learn to be in very good control of your spending.

After your menus are planned, list the ingredients you will need to purchase for each recipe. Check supplies on hand so you will not get food items that you already have. List the amounts that will be needed for the recipe. In this way, you will not buy too much or too little. Plan leftovers into meals as you make your plans.

Another way I keep my budget in line, but still enjoy the more expensive foods on occasion, is to "ration" the costly foods. I give everyone only so much steak, ham, etc. Other foods are provided in the meal so they will have plenty to eat. I don't put more than the portion I want eaten in one meal on the table. In this way, the whole ham doesn't dissapear and I am not left wondering what I can serve instead of the ham dish planned for a later day. I balance "splurge" foods with less costly foods in the same meal or make a budget meal a little later in the week.

HERE ARE SOME SHOPPING HINTS

o Shop on a full stomach. Research shows that a person who is not hungry is likely to spend less and to resist buying of impulse items or "treats".

o Try to shop without your family. Persons who are shopping with

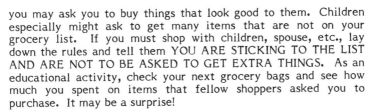

you may ask you to buy things that look good to them. Children especially might ask to get many items that are not on your grocery list. If you must shop with children, spouse, etc., lay down the rules and tell them YOU ARE STICKING TO THE LIST AND ARE NOT TO BE ASKED TO GET EXTRA THINGS. As an educational activity, check your next grocery bags and see how much you spent on items that fellow shoppers asked you to purchase. It may be a surprise!

o Impulse buying can ruin a budget. Try to buy only the things on your list unless the store has outstanding buys on items you are likely to be using (or freezing) before they spoil, etc. Don't be so rigid that you pass up good buys or fail to make substitutions.

o Plan for the use of all of the item. Food waste from not using all of a product can add up to large losses. For example, if you buy a head of cabbage and use only half for stuffed cabbage, use the remainder in stew or to make a cole slaw salad.

o Keep staples on hand so you are always prepared to fix an unexpected meal or cannot get out to get your shopping done on the day planned, etc. It is wise to have a backup day menu in case of an unexpected guest or delayed shopping. It can be something you prepared extra of and placed in the freezer for later use or a "from the pantry" recipe of items you have on hand at all times.

o Keep store and manufacturer's coupons in your purse. I also list the items that are on sale in specific stores each week and place the list in my purse. In this way, if an errand takes me near the store, I am ready to cash in on the good buys there.

o Consider cost per serving and not cost per pound, etc. Sometimes the serving portions of foods are low compared to their poundage or relative size. An example is ribs. There is a good deal of waste per pound. For one serving, you would have to buy 3/4-1 pound per serving, but for ground beef you would only have to buy 1/4 pound. So even though ground beef costs more per pound, it costs less per serving.

o Buy by weight, not size. Size can be deceptive.

o Break multiple prices down so you know how much you are actually paying per item.

o Check ads and food display prices to make sure they are reduced prices and not just a promotion.

o Store brands are usually less expensive than national brands.

o Buy according to season. Plentiful season foods will cost less and are better quality. Vegetables and fruits are seasonal as is meat.

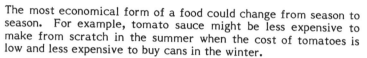

The most economical form of a food could change from season to season. For example, tomato sauce might be less expensive to make from scratch in the summer when the cost of tomatoes is low and less expensive to buy cans in the winter.

o Choose grade according to intended use. For example, apples with slight bruises or bad spots are great if you are making applesauce.

o Convenience foods cost more. Usually one-third or more of the cost is for the convenience of having someone else do the work. It is important to judge how much time is really saved compared to the cost you pay. Also, the convenience foods are highly advertised where basics aren't. This adds to the cost of convenience foods.

o Many ingredients in recipes are optional and only make the recipe more elegant. You can judge if you want to spend the extra money or not. Nuts is a good example here.

o Watch the clerk as she adds your bill. I find that I am often charged the wrong price until I draw the error to her attention. I have saved myself many hundreds of dollars over the years. Try to have all your things on the counter before the checker starts so you can pay attention as she rings up the prices. My children know they are not to talk to me at this time also.

o Watch to see that the scale is on zero before produce is weighed.

o Some great grocery buys are not at the supermarket or grocery store. Sometimes drugstores carry a few food items at a good price. Locally, larger quantities of beans are cheapest at the feed store and, of course, surplus bakeries ("day old") outlets are a wonderful bargain. Health foods are usually less at the supermarket than health food stores.

o Buying non-food items with your food purchases can destroy a budget. Keep food and non-food separate. Non-food items are usually less at variety or department stores.

o Plan snacks into the food plans for the week. Don't allow fridge raids of foods that you are planning to use for menus in the following days. Have snacks and foods that the family is allowed to eat in a specific place so there is no confusion. Also set out snacks between meals for everyone to eat.

o Candy, gum, chips, sodas and items of this type are costly and increase your food bill quickly.

o Store foods properly to avoid waste. Do not overbuy perishable items. Buy only what can be used in meals or preserved for later meals while it is still fresh.

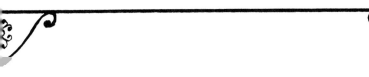

o Get more for your milk dollar by using dry milk. For drinking milk, use 1/2 whole fresh milk and 1/2 reconstituted dry milk. This is 2% milk for less then the cost of purchasing it at the store. Dry milk can be used to make sour cream, buttermilk, cream, yogurt and cottage cheese. The recipes can be found in this book. Look in the index for page numbers.

BUDGET SAVING TIPS FOR YOUR ENTERTAINING DOLLARS

Invite guests for "dessert" or hors d'oeuvres and not a full meal.

Of course, a casserole, crepes, lasagna or other type of meat extender costs less to serve than a meat dish such as ham, steak, etc. This book has a wealth of good recipes for guests and family.

Tired of cooking? Make plan-ahead meals by doubling recipes and freezing. I try to freeze one or two meals a week. When I am busy or would just enjoy the break, I use one of these meals. It sure costs a lot less than eating out.

Open an ice cream shop at home. In addition to the recipes given for frozen bars and desserts, you can use your favorite topping with a carton of ice cream to make your own sundaes.

Lunch is cheaper to buy at restaurants than dinner. Have you ever considered eating out before 3:00 p.m. to take advantage of the savings?

Proportion meat and expensive foods as mentioned earlier. Serve set amounts of ham, roast, etc. from kitchen. Have side dishes and hearty bread on table so guests will have plenty to eat and won't notice the food is being "rationed".

TRICKS TO BETTER NUTRITION

Good nutrition should be a major food goal. The more limited one's budget is, the more there is a need to plan foods wisely so that nutritional needs are met. The amount of money spent is not a factor in how well nourished the family is. Many of the low cost foods are the best nutritional values and many high cost foods provide little food value. Therefore, the amount of money you spend on your food budget doesn't determine how nutritionally sound your meals will be.

Poor nutrition is often not a factor of not enough food, but of wrong foods. A person may spend their food dollar on too many sweets, junk foods, carbohydrates or other items that are not that valuable to the body nutritionally.

The Basic Four Chart on page 13 will help you plan more nutritious meals. Make sure to include something from each of the groups in each meal if possible or at least the given amounts daily.

The costs of foods within a group will vary widely. As an example, steaks are much more costly to serve than is chicken or ground meat, lobster than turbot, chips than home prepared potatoes. Know relative costs of foods in each group. Using less expensive meats, fruits, or vegatables can make a great deal of difference to one's budget.

Labels are an important guide to buying good nutrition. The law requires that the foods contained in a can or package must be listed in order of prevalence. If you read the label, you can see what the contents really are. You will notice that some pasta dishes are only pasta and spices, but no meat. You may find "no cheese" cheese food spreads, and meat main dishes where the meat is listed so far down the list of ingredients that the amount is negligable.

SUBSTITUTION OF INGREDIENTS

The following substitution chart is very helpful if you find you do not have certain ingredients or if you want to substitute for less expensive ingredients.

When The Recipe Calls For: Use:

Milk

1 cup milk   1 cup reconstituted dry milk.

                                    1 cup reconstituted non-fat dry milk plus 2-1/2 t. butter or margarine, (whole milk) or 1/2 cup evaporated milk plus 1/2 cup water.

1 cup sour or buttermilk   1 tbsp. vinegar or lemon juice plus enough sweet milk to make 1 cup (let stand 5 minutes); or 1-3/4 t.

When The Recipe Calls For:	Use:
	cream of tartar plus 1 cup sweet milk; or 1/3 cup buttermilk mixed into 3 cups reconstituted dry milk. Let set 8 hours at room temperature. Cover and refrigerate (3-1/2 cups).
1 cup light cream (20%)	3 tbsp. butter plus about 3/4 cup milk. (Use in cooking).
1 cup heavy cream (40%)	1/3 cup butter plus about 3/4 cup milk. (Use in cooking).
Whipped cream	Undiluted evaporated whole milk can be whipped. To use in a recipe calling for whipped cream: Chill evaporated milk in a bowl in the freezing compartment of a refrigerator until ice crystals form around edges. Chill beater, too. Use 2/3 cup unwhipped evaporated milk instead of 1 cup of unwhipped whipping cream. Whip chilled milk with rotary beater or electric mixer until stiff. This makes about 2 cups of whipped milk.

To whip evaporated milk for a dessert topping: Chill 1/2 cup evaporated milk, bowl, and beater as above. Whip chilled milk until it is stiff. Add 1 tablespoon lemon juice and continue beating until milk is very stiff. Blend in 1/2 cup granulated or confectioner's sugar and 1/2 t. vanilla. This makes about 1-1/2 cups whipped topping. The foam is stable for 45 minutes to 1 hour if refrigerated.

When The Recipe Calls For:	Use:

Flour

1 cup sifted all-purpose flour	1 cup unsifted all-purpose flour minus 2 tbsp. or 1 cup plus 2 tbsp. sifted cake flour.
1 cup sifted cake flour	7/8 cup sifted all-purpose flour or 1 cup minus 2 tbsp. sifted all-purpose flour.
1 tbsp. flour (used for thickening)	1/2 tbsp. cornstarch, potato starch, rice starch, arrowroot starch, or 1 tbsp. quick tapioca.
1 cup self-rising flour	1 cup flour, 2 t. baking power, 1/2 t. salt and 1/2 t. sugar (optional).

Shortening

1 cup butter	1 cup margarine or 7/8 cup lard plus 1/2 t. salt, or 7/8 to 1 cup hydrogranated fat plus 1/2 t. salt.
1 cup lard	1-1/4 cup butter minus 1/2 t. salt from recipe.

Sweetening

1 cup corn syrup	1 cup sugar plus 1/4 cup liquid (same liquid as recipe calls for).
1 cup honey	1-1/4 cup sugar plus 1/4 cup liquid (same liquid as called for in recipe).
1/2 cup molasses	1/2 cup dark corn syrup.
1 cup sugar	3/4 cup plus 1 scant tbsp. honey minus 2-1/2 tbsp. liquid from the recipe.

Chocolate

1 square unsweetened chocolate	3 tbsp. cocoa plus 1/2 to 1 tbsp. fat, oil, butter or margarine.

When The Recipe Calls For:	Use:

Baking Powder and Yeast

1 teaspoon baking powder	1/4 t. baking soda plus 5/8 t. cream of tartar; or 1/4 t. baking soda plus 1/2 cup fully soured milk or buttermilk; or 1/4t. baking soda plus 1/2 tbsp. vinegar or lemon juice used with sweet milk to make 1/2 cup; or 1/4 t. baking soda plus 1/4 to 1/2 cup molasses.
1 tbsp. (scant) active dry yeast	1 pkg. active dry yeast or 1 compressed yeast cake.

Fruit

1 pkg. (10 oz.) frozen sliced strawberries	1 cup sliced fresh strawberries plus 1 cup sugar.
1 pkg. (12 oz.) frozen sliced peaches	1-1/3 cup sliced peeled fresh peaches plus 1/3 cup sugar.
1/2 cup seedless raisins	1/2 cup cut-up dried prunes.

Herbs and Spices

1 t. Italian seasoning	1/4 t. each oregano, basil, thyme, and rosemary.
1 t. pumpkin pie spice	1/2 t. cinnamon, 1/4 t. ginger, and 1/8 t. each nutmeg and ground cloves.
1/4 cup cinnamon sugar	1/2 t. cinnamon plus 1/4 cup granulated sugar.
1 t. allspice	1/2 t. cinnamon and 1/8 t. ground cloves.
1 t. oregano	1 t. marjoram

When The Recipe Calls For:	Use:

Eggs

1 whole egg	2 egg yolks or 3 tbsp. plus 1 t. thawed frozen egg, or 2 tbsp. and 2 t. dry whole egg powder plus an equal amount of water.
1 egg yolk	3-1/2 t. thawed frozen egg yolk or 2 tbsp. dry egg yolk plus 2 t. water.
1 egg white	2 tbsp. thawed frozen egg white or 2 t. of dry egg white plus 2 tbsp. water.

Condiment-style Seasoners

1/2 cup catsup or 1/2 cup chili sauce	1/2 cup tomato sauce, 2 tbsp. sugar, 1 tbsp. vinegar, 1/8 t. ground cloves.
Few drops red pepper seasoning	Dash of cayenne
1 t. Worcestershire sauce	1 t. steak sauce.
1/2 cup tartar sauce	6 tbsp. mayonnaise or salad dressing plus 2 tbsp. pickle relish, plus a dash of mustard if desired.

General

1 cup tomato juice	1/2 cup tomato sauce plus 1/2 cup water.
1 cup canned beef bouillon	1 beef bouillon cube, or 1 envelope instant beef broth or 1 t. beef extract dissolved in 1 cup boiling water.
1 cup chicken broth	Same as beef, using chicken bouillon cube, etc.
1/2 pound fresh mushrooms	1 can (3 or 4 oz) mushrooms.

When The Recipe Calls For:	Use:
Canned Creamed Soup	White sauce plus flavoring:
Diluted - use thin white sauce	Cheese - 1 cup grated cheese
Undiluted - use thick white sauce	Mushroom - 1/2 can (4 oz.) mushrooms plus juice for liquid if desired.
	Chicken - 1/4 cup chopped chicken and 1 tsp. chicken bouillon plus dash of poultry seasoning and parsley if desired.

MEASURING TABLE OF EQUIVALENTS

This Is Equivalent To	This
dash	less than 1/8 teaspoon
1 teaspoon	32 drops
1 tablespoon	3 teaspoons
2 tablespoons	1 fluid ounce
1/4 cup	4 tablespoons
1/3 cup	5-1/3 tablespoons
1 cup	16 tablespoons or 8 ounces
1 pint	2 cups
2 pints	1 quart
1 gallon	4 quarts
1 peck	8 quarts
1 bushel	4 pecks
1 pound	16 ounces
1 pound of butter or fat	2 cups
1 pound of all-purpose flour	4 cups (approximately)
1 pound cake flour	4-3/4 cups
1 pound whole-wheat flour	3-3/4 cups

1 pound of corn meal	3 cups
1 pound of sugar	2-1/4 cups
1 pound of confectioners' sugar	3-1/2 cups
1 pound of brown sugar	3 cups
1 pound of rice	2 cups
1 pound of macaroni	4 cups
1 pound of walnuts in the shell	1-1/2 to 2 cups nutmeats
1 pound of walnut meats	4 cups
1 pound of pitted dates	2 cups
1 pound of raisins	3 cups
1 pound of rhubarb	3-1/2 to 4 cups sliced
1 pound of potatoes	2 cups diced = 2 good sized whole
1 pound of cheese	4 cups grated
1 pound of meat	2 cups chopped
1/4 pound of marshmallows	15 to 16 large, 1-1/8 cups small
1 package of cream cheese	3 ounces
juice of 1 lemon	about 3 tablespoons
juice of 1 orange	about 1/2 cup
grated peel of 1 lemon	about 1-1/2 teaspoons
grated peel of 1 orange	about 1 tablespoon
1 ounce of chocolate	1 square
1 6-ounce package chocolate morsels	1/2 cup melted chocolate
1 can (14-1/2 oz.) evaporated milk	1-2/3 cup
9 finely crumbled saltine crackers	1 cup crumbs
11 finely crumbled graham crackers	1 cup crumbs

VEGETABLE FRUIT ·Group·

4 SERVINGS

[SE]RVING IS:
[ ]CUP   AN ORANGE
[S]MALL SALAD   ½ CANTALOUPE
[M]EDIUM-SIZED POTATO   ½ GRAPEFRUIT

[Eat] citrus fruit, melon, berries, or
[tom]atoes daily and a dark-green or
[dar]k-yellow vegetable frequently. For a
[goo]d source of fiber, eat unpeeled fruits
[and] vegetables and fruits with edible
[seed]s — berries or grapes.

BREAD CEREAL Group

4 SERVINGS

1 SERVING IS:
1 SLICE BREAD
½ to ¾ CUP COOKED CEREAL OR PASTA
1 OUNCE READY-TO-EAT CEREAL
Choose whole-grain products often.

MILK CHEESE Group

[SE]RVINGS:
[Adu]lts   2
[Chil]dren under 9 years old   2-3
[Chil]dren 9 to 12 years old
[and] Pregnant Women   3
[Tee]ns and Nursing Mothers   4
[SE]RVING IS:
[CU]P MILK OR YOGURT
[ ]OUNCES CHEDDAR OR SWISS CHEESE
[OU]NCES PROCESSED CHEESE FOOD
[ ]CUPS ICE CREAM OR ICE MILK
[CU]PS COTTAGE CHEESE

[Ski]m, nonfat, and lowfat milk and milk
[prod]ucts provide calcium and keep fat
[inta]ke down.

MEAT and Poultry Fish BEANS Group

2 SERVINGS

½ SERVING IS:
1 to 1½ OUNCES LEAN, BONELESS,
     COOKED MEAT, POULTRY, OR FISH
1 EGG
½ to ¾ CUP COOKED DRY BEANS, PEAS,
     LENTILS, OR SOYBEANS
2 TABLESPOONS PEANUT BUTTER
¼ to ½ CUP NUTS, SESAME OR SUNFLOWER
     SEEDS
Poultry and fish have less fat content
than red meats.

CAN SIZE EQUIVALENTS
(Fruits, Vegetables, Meats, Soups and Specialities)

Net Weight	Volume (approximate)	Container
8oz	1 C.	Buffet
10-1/2 to 12oz	1-1/4 C.	Picnic
14 to 16oz	1-3/4 C.	No. 300
16 to 17oz	2 C.	No. 303
1lb, 4oz	2-1/2 C.	No. 2
1lb, 13oz	3-1/2 C.	No. 2-1/2
6lb, 2oz to 7lb, 5oz	12 to 13 C.	No. 10
	(Juices)	
6 to 8oz	3/4 C.	
12oz	1 C.	
18 fluid oz.	2-1/2 C.	No. 2
32 fluid oz.	4 C.	Quart
46 fluid oz.	5-3/4 C.	No.3 cylinder

MEATY TIPS

The meat group is the most expensive of all the food groups. For this reason, it is wise to plan meat purchases wisely and avoid any waste. Get more for your money by following these three ideas:

1. Limit serving portions. Many people do not realize that the serving sizes of meat can be small. The daily recommended allowance is two 3-ounce servings. This is about the size of two hamburger patties. Cut costs by giving each person small servings and not putting seconds of meat on the table. Provide side dishes and bread to make meal more filling.

2. Make meat extender dishes like pasta and casseroles where the meat is combined with other foods to make it go further.

3. Use meat alternates, or foods with a high protein content, in place of meat. Examples of meat alternates are dry beans, cheese, eggs, peanuts, soybean products, and lentils.

When you buy a large cut of meat, plan three or four uses for it. Your plan may include dishes the same week or for the meat to be frozen for future meals. Freeze the meat in the form you would like it prepared for the future meals. In addition to the recipes given in this chapter, the "planover" ideas will help you plan uses for these meats.

I buy four or more chickens at a time and cut them up into the parts I want. I package them in the desired parts and freeze them. This is cheaper than buying parts. Do not throw out the innards. I make stuffing with the gizzards, a dish with the livers and use the neck for soup (see recipes under chicken). Chicken and turkey are interchangeable in recipes.

MEAT PLANOVERS (BEEF, PORK OR POULTRY)

o Heat the planovers slowly and gently to retain juices.

o Use broth and drippings for soups, sauces and gravies.

o Stew bones before or after the meat is cooked to get broth for soups, sauces or gravy.

o Cube meat for appetizers, fondues or hors d'oeuvres.

o Dice or slice meats for salads - green, macaroni, rice or potato.

o Make into sandwiches. Use sliced meat or make a meat salad with the meat chopped and combined with mayonnaise or salad dressing.

o Chop the meat and put into spaghetti sauce.

o Make into hash or croquettes.

o Cut the meat into strips, dip in milk and/or egg (beaten), roll in flour or crumbs and fry in hot fat. Serve with tangy sauce or dip.

o Chop meat and use for filling in tacos or enchiladas.

o Chop with vegetables and sauce and make into meat pies or turnovers. Meat pie crusts can be made from bisquit mix, pastry, whipped potatoes or bread crumbs.

o Make meatloaves or jellied meatloaves.

o Add to omelets.

o Chop and add to fried rice.

o Slice thinly and simmer in Bar-B-Q sauce for sandwiches.

o Make meat sauce for crepes, to put over rice or potatoes, bread, bisquits or waffles (main dish); or serve over vegetables such as broccoli or asparagus.

o Quiche is excellent with bits of meat added.

o Chop meat fine for stuffed vegetables such as peppers, zuchinni, tomatoes or onions.

FISH PLANOVERS

o Make into fish stew/soup.

o Make into croquettes.

o Make into crepes or cream sauce for toast or bisquits.

o Make into salad for sandwich or to stuff vegetables.

PASTA PLANOVERS

o Make macaroni-type salad.

o All types of pasta can be used to make casseroles. Casseroles often call for pre-cooked pasta. If not, cooking time can be reduced.

o Steam or add pasta to boiling water to heat for that second meal.

o Mix with a cream sauce with meats and/or vegetable and spices/ herbs for a casserole.

o Noodles can be used to make an excellent dessert dish.

o Cooked pastas are excellent to add to soups.

RICE PLANOVERS

o Make into salad with combination of meats and vegetables.

o Pre-cooked rice is often an ingredient in a variety of casseroles.

o Steam over hot water or heat in microwave for a second meal.

o Make rice pudding.

o Fried rice is a great way to use pre-cooked rice, meats and vegetables.

o Add rice to broth or other ingredients for soups.

o Put into mold while still warm and serve with sauce.

BEAN PLANOVERS

o Make bean pie or cakes.

o Refried beans are made by mashing the beans (add liquid to get desired consistency). Mexican spices can be added. Refried beans are used in tostados, enchiladas, burritos, etc.

o Make bean salad or add to green salads.

o Add to soups.

o Mash and season for bean dip.

o Ever tried a bean sandwich? Place a layer of beans and sliced onions on bread top and with cheese. Melt cheese.

EGG PLANOVERS

o Whites: Make into meringue or fluff type desserts.

Add 1 tablespoon oil and 1 teaspoon water or other liquid to make dip for coating.

To freeze: beat slightly and put into ice cube trays until frozen.

o Yolk: Use in making custard or custard-type sauce.

Make into eggnog.

Add to sauces. Decrease flour. The yolk will add flavor to sauces. Blend yolk gradually into hot mixtures.

Use as a coating for foods that are dipped in crumbs, etc. (add a little liquid).

Substitute for whole egg in mayonnaise.

Freeze by beating in 1 teaspoon salt or 2 teaspoons sugar for 6 eggs. Label if salt or sugar was used so you will know if they should be used in main dishes or desserts. Beat slightly and put into ice cube trays. Each tray should equal 1 egg.

o Hard Cooked (Boiled):

Chop or sprinkle on sauces, casseroles or salads.

Make into deviled eggs.

Make "egg gravy" by adding sliced eggs to white sauce. Serve over bread, bisquits, or cornbread.

Make into egg salad by mashing into mayonnaise. Season to taste.

CHEESE PLANOVERS

o Cheese   Make cheese straws by adding cheese to leftover pastry and cutting into slices. Bisquits with cheese added are very good also. If cheese is hard, grate and add to casseroles, soups, salads and freeze if desired.

Teriyaki Chuck Steak

I make very good tender teriyaki steaks out of chuck steak. Cut the chuck steak into two or three steaks. Sprinkle with meat tenderizer, let sit about fifteen minutes while you mix a marinade of: 1/2 C. soy sauce, 1 small clove of garlic (crushed), 1/2 tsp. ginger and 2 tbs. sugar.

I put the steak in a zip-lock freezer bag, add the marinade and refrigerate the bag until the next evening. Shake the bag every once in a while and turn it over.

Grill the steaks and no one knows they are eating chuck.

Jean Baker, Chula Vista, California

Chile Con Steak

1/4 C. salad oil
1 large onion, sliced thin and separated into rings
1 large green pepper, finely chopped
1 clove garlic, minced or mashed
1-1/2 lbs. top round, fat removed, cut into small steaks
1-1/2 tsp. salt
1-1/2 tsp. monosodium glutamate

1 tsp. sugar
1 can (1 lb.) tomatoes
1 bay leaf
3-12 whole cloves
2-3 tbsp. chile powder
2 tsp. ground cumin
1-5 drops liquid hot pepper seasoning
1 tsp. worcestershire
2 C. cooked red kidney beans or other beans

Heat oil in a large frying pan or dutch oven and cook onion, green pepper and garlic until soft. Add steak, salt, monosodium glutamate, and sugar and cook until meat is slightly browned. Add tomatoes, bayleaf, cloves, chile powder, cumin, hot pepper seasoning, and Worcestershire; cover, and simmer for about 1-1/4 hours. When meat is tender, add beans, and cook until beans are hot. Remove bay leaf and cloves. Makes about 6 servings.

-20-

Pepper Steak

1 med. clove garlic, crushed
3 tbsp. oil
2 large green peppers, sliced thin
1 large onion, sliced thin
1 C. beef broth or bouillon
2 tbsp. soy sauce
1 tbsp. cornstarch
1-1/2 tsp. ginger
1/2 tsp. sugar
1-1/2 C. julienne-cut cooked pot roast or roast beef

In large skillet, saute garlic in oil until golden. Add green pepper and onion; cook and stir three minutes. Mix well bouillon, soy sauce, cornstarch, ginger and sugar; add with pot roast. Simmer, stirring gently, until sauce thickens and meat is hot. If desired, serve over rice with chow-mein noodles. Makes 4 servings.

Mrs. Charles Boyer, Fremont, Ohio

Easy Beef Tips in Mushroom Sauce

1 round steak cut in strips
1 can cream of mushroom soup
1 pkg. onion soup mix
1-7oz. bottle 7-Up

Place meat in a deep casserole. Mix soup and soup mix and pour over the meat. Add the 7-Up. Cover the casserole and bake at 275 degrees for 4 hours.

Mrs. Thomas Kanis, Erie, Pennsylvania

Sweet-Sour Meat

4 slices bacon, cut in 1-inch pieces
1/3 C. chopped onion
1 tbsp. flour
1 C. water
2-3 tsp. cider vinegar
1 tbsp. brown sugar
1 tbsp. corn syrup
2-3 C. cubed leftover roast beef or pork

Pan fry bacon until crisp; remove from skillet and pour off all but 2 tbsp. fat. Add onion to skillet and cook 5 minutes; stir in flour and heat until flour is browned slightly. Add water slowly, then vinegar, sugar and syrup; cook, stirring constantly until thickened. Add bacon and meat pieces; season to taste. Cover skillet and cook until heated through. Serves 4-6. This is very good served on buttered poppy seed noodles. I also put curled carrot and parsley sprig on top for garnish.

Jo Wendt, Eau Claire, Wisconsin

Leftover Roast Curry

2 tbsp. chopped green pepper
1 to 1-1/2 C. leftover roast beef

1/3 C. chopped onion
1 can tomato soup

Saute pepper and onion in 2 tbsp. margarine. Add 2 tbsp. flour, 1/2-1 tsp. curry powder; gradually add 1 can tomato soup. Add 1 to 1-1/2 C. cubed leftover roast beef. Heat thoroughly. Serve over rice.

Mrs. Joyce Arnett, Winnipeg, Manitoba, Canada

Christine's "Fantastic Steak and Sauce"

Sauce
First make sauce; cook until only half-done. Cook sauce in a large pan.

2 sprigs of fresh Hungarian parsley (chopped)
1 medium onion, chopped
2 medium green peppers (chopped)

1-1/2 C. chopped celery
3 C. tomato juice
1 C. water (or more if needed)
salt and pepper to taste

Wash and cut into serving pieces 4 lbs. (approx.) round steak (don't pound). Lay in a large iron skillet and pour sauce over and cook on medium heat until it's bubbly, then turn to low and simmer until meat is tender. Add more tomato juice if it cooks down too low. Stir now and then to keep meat from sticking. Serve over mashed potatoes.

Mrs. Christine Miller, Niles, Michigan

Joyce's Swiss Steak

3 tbsp. cooking oil or shortening
3-4 lbs. chuck roast or steak
1/4 C. flour
1/4 tsp. garlic salt

1/4 tsp. pepper
1-1/2 C. catsup
1-15 oz. can stewed tomatoes
2 medium onions, sliced and separated into rings

Put oil or shortening into a large skillet or dutch oven and heat. Cut meat into serving size pieces. Mix together the flour, garlic salt and pepper. Coat meat with flour mixture and brown on both sides in hot oil or shortening. Reduce heat to simmer. Mix catsup and stewed tomatoes and pour over meat. Cover meat with raw onion slices. Place tight fitting lid on skillet or dutch oven and cook slowly for 1-1/2 to 2 hours until meat is fork tender. This makes its own gravy to pour over mashed potatoes, noodles, rice, toast or cornbread and is delicious enough to serve to company. Makes 6-8 servings.

Joyce Hollin, Monticello, Kentucky

Sunday Swiss Steak

1-1/2 lbs. round steak, 1 to 1-1/2" thick (allow 1/4 lb. per person)
1/2 C. flour
2 tsp. salt
1 large can tomato sauce

1/4 tsp. pepper
1 can water (sauce can)
1/2 C. thinly sliced onion rings
1/4 C. shortening

Combine flour, salt and pepper. Pound into meat. Brown onions lightly in hot fat in large skillet. Remove onions and brown meat. Place onions on top. Add tomato sauce and water. Set in oven for 2 hours or until tender. Watch as it may need more water. Serves six.

Esther Blatter, McClusky, North Dakota

Hawaiian Beef and Rice

3 tbsp. Soy sauce
1/2 tsp. garlic salt
1/4 tsp. ground ginger
1 lb. cube steak, round or tenderized chuck
oil
1 small onion, chopped

1/4 C. coconut
1 C. crushed pineapple and juice (8 oz.)
1 small green pepper
2/3 C. uncooked rice
1-3/4 C. water
1/4 tsp. salt

Cut meat into 1" cubes. Blend soy sauce, garlic salt and ginger. Pour over meat. Let sit for 10 minutes, turning frequently to coat meat evenly. Brown half of the meat in hot oil. Set aside. Brown second half of meat with coconut and onion. Add pineapple, pepper, rice, water, salt and unused sauce to meat. Bring to a boil. Reduce heat and simmer for 30 minutes or until rice is cooked and meat is tender.

Sukiyaki

You will need an 8-inch skillet with cover. The cooking time for this dish is 35-40 minutes.

2 tbsp. cooking oil
1-1/2 lbs. chuck steak cut in thin slices, 2 inches by 1/2 inch
1/4 C. sugar
3/4 C. soy sauce
1/4 C. water or mushroom stock
2 onions, sliced thin

1 green pepper, cut in thin strips
1 C. celery cut into 1-1/2 inch pieces
1 can (10-12 oz) bamboo shoots, thinly sliced.
1 can (8 oz) mushroom stems and pieces.
1 bunch green onions, cut in 1-inch length pieces with tops.

Heat oil in skillet, add meat and brown lightly. Combine sugar, soy sauce, and water or mushroom stock. Add this to meat, cover. Bring to steaming point. Cook about 40 minutes, or until tender. Add remaining ingredients, except green onions. Cover and cook on high heat only a short time, about 2-3 minutes. Add green onions and cook 1 minute more. Serve with hot steamed rice. Sukiyaki must be served as soon as vegetables are done so they will retain their crispness.

Theresa Nuoci, Lafayette, Colorado

Tips

3-6 lbs. stew meat or cheap roast
3/4 C. flour
1 tsp. salt
1/2 tsp. pepper

12 carrots
6 potatoes
1 good sized onion
2 C. water

Cut meat into bite-size chunks. Coat with flour, salt and pepper. Brown in skillet that can be put in oven later. Add carrots, potatoes and onion; mix with meat; add water. Pop into oven at 350 degrees for 1 hour. Check in 1/2 hour so you can mix again. You can add more water for the gravy. Serve with a green vegetable. Great for several meals.

Dorothy Lightfoot, East Grand Forks, Minnesota

Sweet and Sour Swiss

Oil
1-1/2 lbs. round, swiss or tenderized chuck steak
1 C. crushed pineapple and
juice (8 oz.)

2 tbsp. molasses
1/2 C. barbeque sauce
1/4 C. water
2 tsp. wine vinegar
1 medium onion

Cut meat into serving portions (4-6). Brown meat on both sides in
hot fat. Blend remaining ingredients and add to meat. Cover and
simmer for one hour, or until meat is tender. To serve, spoon sweet
and sour sauce over meat.

To make a complete meal in one dish, add potatoes, carrots and
other vegetables. Add 1/4 C. more water and cook for 20 minutes,
or until vegetables are cooked.

Pineapple Steak-On-A-Stick
(4 servings)

13-1/4 oz. can pineapple
chucks in heavy syrup
1-1/4 lb. sirloin steak

1 medium bell pepper
3/4 lb. bacon, thinly sliced
12 mushrooms

Trim steak and cut into 1-inch cubes. Place in marinade sauce (page
26) for 2-4 hours. Cover and keep in the refrigerator until cooking
time. Toss meat occasionally to make sure all sides are coated
evenly and well marinated.

Pre-heat oven to "broil". Start by placing a slice of bacon on the
skewer or stick. Alternate the tidbits of meat, pineapple, pepper,
and mushrooms and weave bacon in and out of each tidbit. (The
bacon adds flavor and keeps the tidbits moist). Pack loosely on
skewer. Broil until desired doneness is reached, turning occasionally
so all sides are done evenly.

For medium steak, place about halfway down in the oven on broiler
pan or a cookie sheet with rim (to catch drippings) and cook for 15-
20 minutes, turning about every 5 minutes to cook each side. Serve
on steamed rice.

Marinade Sauce

Pineapple juice drained from fruit
1 tbsp. wine vinegar
1/2 tsp. black pepper
1/4 tsp. ground ginger

1/4 tsp. ground cloves
1/8 tsp. dry mustard
1 tsp. sweet basil flakes (measured and then crushed)

Stir together.

Baked Short Ribs

3 lbs. beef short ribs
1 large onion, sliced
1 envelope packet onion instant broth

1 C. hot water
1 tbsp. flour
1 Reynolds Oven Cooking Bag (regular size)

1. Trim excess fat from short ribs.
2. Prepare oven bag with flour as directed on package.
3. Place short ribs into oven bag.
4. Lay sliced onions on the ribs.
5. Mix instant broth with hot water and pour over the ribs.
6. Fasten bag as directed and place into a casserole or oven pan.
7. Bake at 325 degrees for 1-1/2 hours. Serves 6.

Serve with mashed potatoes and salad, or corn and salad.

Roseann Strazinsky, Danville, Pennsylvania

Braised Short Ribs

1/4 C. all-purpose flour
1 tsp. paprika
1 tsp. salt
1/2 tsp. dry mustard
1/8 tsp. pepper
4 lbs. beef short ribs
3 tbsp. vegetable oil
2 medium-sized onions, peeled and thinly sliced

1 clove garlic, peeled and crushed
1-12oz. can beer
salt, pepper and flour
6 tbsp. water
Chopped fresh parsley, optional

Combine the 1/4 C. flour, paprika, 1 tsp. salt, mustard and 1/8 tsp. pepper in a pie plate. Roll short ribs in flour mixture until thoroughly covered. Reserve any remaining flour mixture. Heat oil in a heavy dutch oven or large saucepan over moderately high heat (about 275 degrees). Add onion and garlic. Cook until lightly browned. Remove onion and garlic mixture with a slotted spoon and set aside. Add short ribs and cook until lightly browned on all sides. Return onion and garlic to the pot; add beer. Bring mixture to a boil. Reduce heat to low (200 degrees) and cook, covered, 2 to 2-1/2 hours, or until meat is fork-tender. Skim off as much fat as possible from the liquid. Add more salt and pepper if desired. Measure reserved seasoned flour and add enough flour to make 3 tbsp. Combine flour and the 6 tbsp. of water in a small bowl and stir until smooth. Add about 1/2 C. of the hot liquid to the flour-water mixture and blend thoroughly. Gradually add the flour mixture to the short rib mixture. Cook over moderate heat (about 225 degrees), stirring constantly until gravy is thickened and smooth. Simmer uncovered 4-5 minutes stirring occasionally. If desired, sprinkle with chopped parsley before serving. Makes 4 to 6 servings.

Mrs. James S. Allen, South Bend, Indiana

Leftover Beef Casserole

Peel 4 or 5 potatoes; cut into small diced pieces, chop medium onion and dice cold roast beef. Put in a casserole, add water (1/2 volume of potatoes), add 1 tbsp. butter, salt and pepper to taste. Bake in moderate oven covered until potatoes are done nicely. Serve with baking powder biscuits.

Mrs. Earl Kuchenbecker, Prairie du Chien, Wisconsisn

Scalloped Leftover Meat

2 tbsp. butter or margarine	1/2 tsp. pepper
2 tbsp. all-purpose flour	2 C. diced cooked meat
2 C. tomato juice	1/2 C. fine buttered bread
2 tsp. salt	crumbs

Melt butter or margarine. Add flour and blend well. Add tomato juice slowly, then salt and pepper, stirring frequently until mixture has thickened. Place a layer of meat in greased casserole, then pour half the sauce over meat, repeat with a layer of meat, ending with the sauce on top. Sprinkle with buttered crumbs. Bake at 350 degrees until heated through. Serve from casserole. Serves 4-5.

Theresa Nuoci, Lafayette, Colorado

Muffin-Pan Hash

1 C. cold roast meat (any kind), chopped
4 cold boiled potatoes, chopped
2 small onions, chopped

3 drops tabasco sauce
Salt and pepper to taste
1 green pepper, chopped
1 egg, well beaten
1 C. canned tomatoes

Mix together the chopped potatoes, onions, and green peppers. Add the meat and tomatoes. Season with salt, pepper and tabasco sauce; add the egg. Drop by spoonfuls into muffin pans. Bake in a hot oven (400 degrees) 20 to 25 minutes. Serve with chili sauce, or the following tomato sauce.

Tomato Sauce

1 tbsp. olive oil
1 medium onion
2 cloves garlic
1 tbsp. chili powder

1/2 tsp. salt
1/2 tsp. thyme
2 C. rich meat stock
1 C. tomato puree

Brown the onion and garlic in the olive oil. Blend in all the other ingredients and simmer until slightly thickened.

Amelia M. Brown, Pittsburgh, Pennsylvania

Smiling Dutch Boy Stew

1 lb. boneless beef stew meat, cut in bite-size pieces
2 tbsp. flour
1 tsp. paprika
Pepper to taste
2 tbsp. salad oil

1/2 can beef bouillon (2/3 C.)
1 can (1 lb.) sauerkraut, drained
1 can (4 oz.) mushroom caps
1/2 tbsp. caraway seeds
4 tbsp. sour cream

Toss beef cubes in mixture of flour, paprika, and pepper; brown in oil in heavy skillet. Add bouillon, cover, simmer one hour, or until meat is tender, adding a little more bouillon or water if necessary. Add sauerkraut, mushrooms and liquid, and caraway seeds. Cook for 15 minutes, uncovered. Stir in sour cream, reheat, and serve immediately. Serves 4 adequately; 3 generously (kraut and bouillon will supply enough salt for most tastes).

Mrs. Amelia M. Brown, Pittsburgh, Pennsylvania

New England Beef Stew
(served on buttered noodles)

1 lb. cut up beef
1 large onion, chopped
2 large potatoes, diced
4 carrots, cut in circles
1 pkg. frozen tiny peas
1 can whole kernel corn, drained

1 large can tomato sauce
3 C. of water
1/4 C. oil
Salt and pepper to taste
1 tbsp. worcestershire sauce
1/4 tsp. garlic powder
1/2 pkg. medium-sized noodles

In a 5-quart saucepan, put oil, cut-up beef and onions, saute until meat is browned. Add tomato sauce and water, stir and simmer 1 hour. Stir occasionally, then add carrots, worcestershire sauce, garlic and salt to taste. Cover. Simmer, stirring occasionally 1/2 hour. Add potatoes, stir. Simmer, covered, 1 hour until most of the sauce has cooked down and becomes thick. Add peas and corn. Simmer covered 1 hour; less if sauce is thick. When sauce is cooked down and thick and meat and vegetables are tender, stew is done. In meantime, cook noodles in salted water; drain; pour melted butter over noodles. Mix well. Put noodles on plate. Laddle stew on top to serve.

Eleanor Shelley, Youngstown, Ohio

Leftover Supper Stew

Roast beef sliced or cubed
2 C. diced cooked carrots, peas, beans and corn Or 1 can mixed vegetables

3/4 C. diced celery
2 C. diced cooked potatoes and onions

Place in a casserole and pour over leftover gravy or a can of cream of tomato soup diluted with a little water. Bake 20-30 minutes at 350 degrees. Serve with a green salad and light dessert.

Lil Adams, Gettysburg, South Dakota

Hearty Beef and Barley Soup

1/2 C. uncooked pearl barley
2 C. water
1 lb. stew meat (or cubed leftover meat)
4 C. meat broth (or 4 C. water plus 4 beef bouillon cubes)
1 tbsp. worchestershire sauce
2 tsp. fine herbs
1-1/2 tsp. salt

1 large onion, cut into bite-size wedges
2-3 medium potatoes
3 medium carrots, sliced
2 medium celery sticks, sliced
1/2 C. jalapino bean dip or 1/2 C. mashed cooked beans plus dash of tabasco plus 1 tbsp. finely chopped green pepper

Soak barley in water overnight. About 2 hours before soup is to be served, bring water to a boil. Reduce heat and simmer for 30 minutes. Brown meat on all sides in hot fat (omit for cooked meat. Add after 1-1/2 hours to barley) Add meat, broth, worchestershire, fine herbs and salt to barley. Cook for 1 hour, or until meat is tender. Skim off residue from top. Prepare vegetables and add to soup. Cook until vegetables are tender (20 to 30 minutes). Blend in bean dip. 4-6 servings.

Meat Loaf Milano

1-1/2 tsp. Italian herb seasoning
2 beaten eggs
1/4 C. creamy Italian salad
dressing
1-1/2 C. soft bread crumbs
2 tsp. instant minced onions
1/4 tsp. pepper
1-1/2 tsp. salt
2 lbs. ground beef

4 oz. shredded mozzarella
cheese
3 hard boiled eggs (peeled)
1/4 C. snipped parsley
1-1/2 tsp. prepared mustard
3 tbsp. creamy Italian salad
dressing
1/2 tsp. sugar

In large bowl, combine the first 7 ingredients. Add ground beef; mix well. In a 12x7x2 inch baking dish, pat half of the meat mixture to a 9x4 inch rectangle. Sprinkle half of the cheese and all of the parsley to within 1 inch of all sides. Place boiled eggs end to end down center.

On waxed paper, pat remaining meat to a 9x4 inch rectangle. Sprinkle remaining cheese to within 1 inch of all sides, pressing well into meat.

Invert atop eggs, remove paper. Shape meat mixture into loaf, about 10 inches long, sealing ends and sides well. Make 4-5 cuts on top. Bake uncovered in 350 degree oven for 1 hour. Combine remaining salad dressing, mustard and sugar; drizzle over loaf. Bake 15 minutes more. Let stand 10 minutes before slicing.

Mrs. Judy M. Sax, San Antonio, Texas

How To Make Hamburger Taste Like Salisbury Steak

3 lbs. hamburger
1 C. cracker crumbs
1/4 C. chopped onions
1 tsp. salt and pinch of pepper

1/4-1/2 C. margarine
1/2-2/3 C. flour
1 tsp. salt
1 to 1-1/2 quarts water

Mix first 5 ingredients well. Press on cookie sheet, chill overnight to set.

Cut into squares, roll in flour and brown both sides in margarine in frying pan or electric skillet. Place in baking dish. Add remaining flour to butter in pan. Brown flour. Add 1 tsp. salt and stir enough until smooth. Pour over meat in baking dish and bake 1-1/2 hours at 350 degrees.

Zenana Warren, Wauseon, Ohio

Salisbury Steak Supreme

2 lbs. of ground beef	1 pkg. dry onion soup
1-1/2 C. of cheese flavored crackers	1 tsp. salt, pepper and celery seeds
1 C. of milk	8-10 thick slices of raw onion
3 eggs	

Mix cracker crumbs with the milk and eggs. Add the salt, pepper, celery seeds and onion soup. Mix well. Then thoroughly mix with the ground beef. Form into serving size patties and brown in bacon drippings. They brown better if rolled in flour. Place patties in a large baking dish. Use the drippings to make a thin gravy. Place a thick slice of onion on each pattie. Cover with the gravy. Cover dish with foil, and bake 45 minutes at 350 degrees. Makes 8-10 servings depending on the size of the patties.

Joy Parrish, Stamping Ground, Kentucky

Poor Man's Steak

1-1/2 lbs. hamburger	1/2 C. water
1-1/4 tsp. salt	1 can Cream of Mushroom soup
1/2 C. fine soda cracker crumbs	1 C. water

Mix all except last 2 ingredients and shaped into patties of desired size. Dip and coat with flour and fry until light brown. Put in roaster. Mix mushroom soup and water and pour over meat. Set in 350 degree oven for 1-1/4 to 1-1/2 hours. Cover while baking.

Esther Blatter, McClusky, North Dakota

Hamburger Steak with Yorkshire Pudding

2 lbs. ground beef   Yorkshire pudding
salt and pepper

Shape meat into large steak about 1-1/2 inches thick. Put in center of large heavy roasting pan. Brown in extremely hot oven (500 degrees) for 8 minutes for rare, 10 minutes for medium. Remove from oven and season with salt and pepper. Add some beef drippings or margarine to make about 1/3 C. in bottom of pan. Return to oven. When drippings are hot, pour Yorkshire pudding around meat. Reduce heat to 475 degrees and bake 20 minutes longer, or until pudding is puffy and browned. Serve at once. Makes 6 servings.

Yorkshire Pudding

Beat 2 eggs and 1 C. milk well. Add 1 C. flour and 1/4 tsp. salt. Beat well.

Marie Paule Turmel, Quebec, Canada

Western Hamburger

Sauce: Make this first

1 chopped onion   1/2 C. water
1/2 chopped pepper   1/2 C. vinegar
1 C. ketchup   1 tsp. dry mustard
                    Brown sugar to taste

Simmer 45 minutes, covered.

Beat:
9-10 eggs   1 tsp. salt

Add 1 lb. lean ground beef, 2 tablespoons at a time. Beat. Spoon out in frying pan. Fry on both sides. Make them the size of a bun. As the burgers are fried, place in a small roaster or a large pot. After all are fried, pour sauce over the meat. Bake or cook for 1/2 hour. Eat cold or hot on a bun.

Mary E. Jordan, Charleroi, Pennsylvania

Meat Rolls

2 lbs. ground beef, lean
1 C. water
1 tsp. pepper
1/4 tsp. onion salt

1/2 tsp. garlic salt
4 tbsp. morton-tender quick salt
1/2 tsp. mustard seed

Mix all ingredients well and refrigerate overnight. Form into two 1-inch rolls. Wrap in foil and bake 1 hour at 350 degrees. Slice and serve cold with assorted crackers. (10-12 servings)

Mary Biller, Willard, Ohio

Meat Loaf

2 lbs. ground round meat
2 eggs
1-1/2 C. bread crumbs
1 tsp. Accent

3/4 C. ketchup
1 pkg. Lipton onion soup
1/2 C. water (warm)

Mix all together. Cover with bacon and tomato sauce. Bake 1 hour or until done at 350 degrees.

Loretta Natale, Madison, New Jersey

Pot Roast Meat Loaf

1 lb. ground beef
1/3 C. fine dry bread crumbs
2/3 C. evaporated milk
1/4 C. catsup or chili sauce
2 eggs
1 onion minced

1 tsp. salt
2 tsp. worcestershire sauce
1/4 tsp. pepper
3 medium potatoes
3 medium carrots

Mix the ground beef, milk, bread crumbs, catsup, salt, worcestershire suace and pepper in a 1-1/2 quart bowl. Shape into a loaf in center of a 13x9x2 inch pan. Peel and slice potatoes 1/4 inch thick. Peel carrots and quarter lengthwise. Mix 2 tsp. parsley flakes, 1 tsp. salt and a few grains of pepper. Place vegetables in layers around meat. Sprinkle each layer with part of salt mixture. Cover lightly with foil. Bake at 375 degrees for 1 hour or until vegetables are done. Uncover and bake 10 minutes more to brown meat. Serves 4.

Mrs. Glenn Westphal, Gettysburg, South Dakota

Superb Meat Loaf

1 lb. ground chuck	1 C. seasoned bread crumbs
1 C. creamed cottage cheese	1/4 tsp. garlic powder
1 pkg. Lipton onion soup	1 can tomato soup
1 egg	Salt to taste
2 tbsp. ketchup	

Put all ingredients, except tomato soup, in a bowl. Mix well. Shape into a loaf and put in pan or dish to bake. Pour tomato soup over meat loaf plus 1/2 can of water. Cover and bake at 350 degrees for 1-1/2 hours; test for doneness.

Eleanor Shelley, Youngstown, Ohio

Burger 'n Vegetable Roast

2 C. each of peas, carrots and potatoes, diced or fresh	1 lb. ground beef
1 C. bread crumbs (regular or whole wheat	2 eggs, beaten
	1/2 C. cream
	1 diced small onion, optional

Beat eggs. Mix in the meat and vegetables. Put crumbs and cream in last. Mix everything, shape into loaf. Use either greased or ungreased pan. Bake at 375-400 degrees for 35-45 minutes, or until done.

Terry Timotea Rendzak, Seminole, Florida

Meat Loaf

1 egg, slightly beaten	2 tbsp. chopped onion
1/4 C. milk	1 tsp. salt
1/4 C. catsup	1/4 tsp. pepper
2 tsp. prepared mustard	1/2 C. oatmeal
1 lb. lean ground meat	

Blend egg, milk, catsup, mustard and oatmeal. Mix meat, onion, salt and pepper in bowl; add egg mixture and blend. Shape in loaf in a pan. Spread the loaf with a mixture of: 2 tbsp. brown sugar, 2 tbsp. catsup and 1 tsp. prepared mustard. Bake 1 hour at 350 degrees. Serves 4.

Mrs. Aldela Conejo, Seguin, Texas

Super Meatloaf

2 lbs. ground beef
2 medium onions, chopped fine
3/4-1 C. catsup
1/4 C worcestershire sauce
2 eggs, slightly beaten
1 C. grated sharp cheddar cheese

1/4 C. wheat germ (mix with 2 tbsp. water to each lb. of meat)
1/2 C. plain bread crumbs
1 tbsp. parsley
1/4 tsp. garlic powder-opt.
1/4 tsp. ground black pepper
1/4 tsp. celery salt

In a large bowl, combine all ingredients. Pack in 8x10 square casserole - lightly greased. Cover with a generous layer of catsup. Bake uncovered in a 400 degree oven 50 minutes or until firm. Serves 6.

NOTE: Do not cut down on amount of catsup or worcestershire sauce. These ingredients are what makes it a super meatloaf.

Margaret A. Verkon, Corning, New York

Inexpensive Meat Loaf

1-1/2 lbs. hamburger
1 medium chopped onion (add green pepper and celery chopped if you like)
1 egg
1 tbsp. flour

1 C. canned tomatoes
3 slices of dry bread soaked and squeezed out
1/2 tsp. sage
1 tsp. salt
1/4 tsp. pepper

Mix all together well and shape in long loaf with floured hands. Put some tomatoes or catsup on top. Place in center of roasting pan so juices can form around loaf. Bake in medium oven until nice and brown. Before serving, add 1 tbsp. (additional) of flour to juice with water to thicken for gravy.

Mrs. Earl Kuchenbecker, Prairie du Chien, Wisconsin

Meaty Stuffed Zucchini

4 medium zucchini
3/4 lb. ground beef
1-8 oz. can tomato sauce
1/4 tsp. oregano
1/4 tsp. chili powder

1/4 tsp. garlic powder
1/4 tsp. salt
4 slices American or Cheddar cheese

In a large pan, bring about 2 quarts of water to a boil. Wash zucchini well and slice in half. Place in boiling water. Cook for 5 minutes, or until it starts to soften. Remove from the water and scoop out the inside seed portion. Fill with meat sauce.

Meat Sauce

Break meat into small chunks and cook ground beef until done. Add tomato sauce and herbs. Simmer for 5 minutes. Place inside of Zucchini "boats". Top each stuffed zucchini with a cheese slice. Bake in oven at 350 degrees for 25 minutes.

Beef and Rice Amandine

1 lb. ground beef*
1 can condensed cream of chicken soup
1 beef bouillon cube
1 C. water
1/2-1 C. sliced celery

1 small onion, chopped
1/2 C. uncooked rice
1 tsp. soy sauce
1/8 tsp. oregano
1/2 C. toasted slivered almonds

Brown ground beef and drain. Add all remaining ingredients (except almonds). Heat to boiling, crushing bouillon cube as you stir. After bouillon is stirred in, remove skillet from heat and pour into a greased casserole dish and cover. Bake in moderate oven (350 degrees) for 30 minutes. Uncover; sprinkle almons on top and bake uncovered for an additional 15 minutes.

* For variety, 2 C. cooked chicken may be substituted for ground beef if desired.

Nancy Marshall, Jay, Florida

Ron's Slum Gullion

1 lb. ground beef	1/4 C. barbeque sauce
1 medium onion, chopped fine	1 tbsp. chili powder
1 can (16 oz.) whole kernel	1/2 tsp. garlic salt
corn - <u>do not drain off liquid</u>	salt and pepper to taste
1 can (16 oz.) pork and beans	

In a large skillet, brown ground beef and onion in a small amount of oil (if needed). Add remaining ingredients. Simmer, covered, 1/2 hour, stirring occasionally. Serves 4.

Margaret A. Verkon, Corning, New York

Hamburger-Rice Casserole

1 lb. hamburger	3 tbsp. soy sauce
1/2 C. raw rice	1 tsp. salt
1 can Cream of Mushroom	1 tsp. minced onion
soup	2 soup cans water
1 can Cream of Celery soup	Chow Mein noodles

Combine everything except noodles and bake 1 hour and 15 minutes at 350 degrees. When done, top with chow mein noodles.

Mrs. Clifford Heller, Mt. Morris, Illinois

Amelia's Special

1 large green pepper	1 egg
1 lb. ground chuck	4 level tsp. uncooked rice
1 tsp. salt	1 can (16 oz.) stewed tomatoes
Pepper to taste	

Cut off top of green pepper, remove all seeds, then cut into 4 crosswise slices. Place slices on bottom of buttered baking dish. Mix the ground beef with the salt, pepper, and slightly beaten egg. Place 1/4 of the meat mixture on top of each green pepper slice. Sprinkle 1 tsp. rice over meat. Cover with stewed tomatoes. Bake in a moderate oven (350 degrees) for 45 minutes or until peppers are tender. If desired, put a slice of cheese on top for the last 5 minutes of baking. Serves 4.

Mrs. Amelia M. Brown, Pittsburgh, Pennsylvania

Cabbage and Hamburger Casserole

1 medium onion (chopped)	1/8 tsp. pepper
3 tbsp. butter	6 C. coarsely shredded cabbage
1/2 lb. ground beef	1 can tomato soup
3/4 tsp. salt	

Brown onions in butter. Add the ground beef, heating through, but not browning. Add salt and pepper. Spread in 2 quart baking dish 3 C. of the cabbage. Cover with meat mixture. Top with rest of cabbage. Pour tomato soup over top. Bake covered for one hour at 350 degrees. 6 servings

Esther Blatter, McClusky, North Dakota

Sweet and Sour Stuffed Cabbage Rolls

1-1/2 lbs. ground beef	1 tsp. sugar
1/2 chopped onion	Salt and pepper
2 tbsp. lemon juice	

Mix all above ingredients and set aside. Clean a 1-1/2 lb. head of cabbage. Bring water to boil in large kettle. Place head of cabbage in water and cook for 5 minutes. Drain and let cool.

In large casserole dish, put 1 can tomato sauce plus 1 can water and 1/2 C. catsup. Take cabbage leaf, adding hamburger mixture and roll up and lay into sauce mixture. Continue until all leaves and meat are used. Cook on very low heat until meat is done (1 to 2 hours depending on how many cabbage rolls you have). Cool, put in refrigerator. Next day, remove fat that is settled on top. Reheat and serve.

Mrs. Ruth M. Hrubes, Wesley, Iowa

Porcupine Beef Balls

1-1/2 lbs. ground beef	1 small onion (chopped)
1/2 C. rice (washed)	1 can tomato soup or
Dash pepper	2-8 oz. cans tomato sauce
1-1/2 tsp. salt	Approx. 3/4-1 C. water

Mix all ingredients, except tomato soup and water. Shape into balls. Put in baking dish one layer deep. Pour the tomato soup and water over beef balls. Bake 1 hour and 15 minutes in 350 degree oven.

Esther Blatter, McClusky, North Dakota

He-Man Meat Balls

Sauce:

1/4 C. chopped onion	1 tsp. salt
2 cloves garlic, chopped	1 tsp. paprika
1 tbsp. butter	1/2 tsp. pepper
2 tbsp. vinegar	1-14 oz. bottle catsup
1/4 C. sugar	1/2 C. water
4 tsp. worcestershire sauce	

Saute onion and garlic in butter until tender. Add other ingredients, cook over low heat.

Meat Balls:

1-1/2 lbs. ground beef	2 tbsp. chopped onion
3/4 C. rolled oats	1 egg
1-1/2 tsp. salt	1/2 C. milk
1/4 tsp. pepper	

Mix all ingredients together well. Shape into desired size balls. Brown well on all sides in large skillet. Drain off fat. Pour sauce over meatballs and simmer covered for 30 minutes. Serves 6.

Glenna Mitchell, Merritt Island, Florida

Meatballs

1/2 lb. ground beef	1/4 tsp. pepper
1 tsp. onion	1/4 tsp garlic salt
1 tsp. molasses	1/4 tsp. worcestershire
1 tsp. prepared mustard	1 tsp. catsup
1/2 tsp. salt	

Mix all ingredients lightly. Shape into 16 balls. Saute slowly in skillet until browned and done. Serve warm.

Hamburger Shish Kebobs

On toothpicks, alternate meatballs (above) with any or all of these: pickled onions, olives, cheese, green pepper, pimento, apples. Serve as hors d'oeuvres or as a main dish for two with rice.

Marie Paule Turmel, Vallee Junction, Quebec, Canada

Company Meatballs

2 lbs. hamburger
1 C. sour cream or plain yogurt

1 pkg. dry onion soup mix
1 egg
1-1/2 C. dry bread crumbs

Mix well. Form into meatballs. Roll in mixture of 1/2 C. flour and 1-1/2 tsp. paprika. Brown in 1/4 C. margarine in skillet. Transfer to 13x9 baking dish. Mix 1 can cream of chicken soup with 3/4 C. water. Pour over meatballs. Bake at 350 degrees for 40 minutes. Serves 6-8. Freeze leftovers in meal-sized portions.

Margaret E. Edgecomb, Bar Mills, Maine

Meat in Cabbage Rolls

1 large head cabbage
1 lb. ground beef
1 lb. ground pork
1 No. 2 can tomatoes
1 tsp. salt
1 tsp. black pepper

1 tsp. paprika
1 onion, chopped fine
1 egg
1 C. cracker meal
1 green pepper (chopped fine)

Place cabbage in large pan. Salt and let boil until leaves wilt. Part leaves without tearing. Mix meat, onion, salt, pepper, paprika, green pepper, egg and cracker meal. Roll small amount of mixed ingredients in each cabbage leaf. Place in pan. Add tomatoes and enough water to cover. Sprinkle with 1 tsp. more salt and 1 tsp. paprika. Cover and simmer over low heat for about 45 minutes.

Louise Hicks, Chicago, Illinois

Hamburger Cabbage Casserole

1 medium head of cabbage
1 lb. hamburger
1/4 C. Minute Rice
1 C. sliced onion

1 pkg. spaghetti sauce mix
1 tsp. salt (to taste)
1 level tsp. of oregano

Cut cabbage into 2-inch pieces, place in a casserole (oiled). Sprinkle hamburger and rice over cabbage. Layer onions over top. Prepare spaghetti sauce as directed and pour over casserole. Cover with foil and bake at 350 degrees for 1-1/2 hours. During the last 15 minutes of baking, remove foil and sprinkle with grated cheddar cheese. Cook until cheese bubbles, serve hot.

Christine Miller, Niles, Michigan

Cabbage Stroganoff

1/2 lb. ground beef
1-3 oz. pkg. cream cheese
1 can Cream of Mushroom soup

1/4 C. milk
4 C. thinly sliced cabbage

Brown the beef with onion to taste. Add salt and pepper. Drain if needed. Add cream cheese, soup and milk. Stir and heat until cheese is melted. Add cabbage, cover and cook just to heat through. Do not let cabbage overcook.

Mrs. Gerald Hesse, Sioux City, Iowa

Cabbage Rolls

Bread Dough:

3 pkg. yeast
2 tbsp. sugar
1/3 C warm water

Mix ingredients.
Set for thirty minutes

2 C. lukewarm water
1 tsp. salt
1/2 tsp. soda
1/2 C. shortening

2 eggs beaten
7-8 C. flour
1/2 tsp. baking powder
1/2 C. sugar

Add remaining ingredients to yeast mixture. Cover and let rise for 2 hours.

Hamburger Mixture:

3 lbs. hamburger
1 or 2 onions
1-2 heads of cabbage depending on your taste.

Salt and pepper
Garlic salt

Brown hamburger, onions, garlic salt, salt and pepper until tender. Drain off fat. Add shredded cabbage and cook until 3/4 done.

Roll bread dough out as thin as you can without it breaking up and cut good sized squares. Fill these squares with hamburger mixture. Pinch sides up and put upside down (or seam side down) on greased cookie sheet. Bake at 350 degrees until bread is golden brown, 20-30 minutes.

These are great for lunch boxes. The recipe can be doubled or even tripled and these can be frozen until ready to use.

Dena Park, Alcova, Wyoming

Onion-Meatza Pie
(One 9" pie, 4-6 servings)

Onion-Meatza Crust:

1 lb. ground beef
1/2 C. evaporated milk
1/2 C. crushed canned french fried onion rings (about 1/2 can)

1/4 tsp. garlic salt
1/2 tsp. oregano (measure then crush)
1/4 tsp. salt

Mix together and pat into 9-inch pie pan. Cover sides and bottom of pan as evenly as is possible.

3-4 medium mushrooms

Wash, slice and place on top of meatza "crust".

Potato Filling:

2 C. mashed potatoes
1/4 C. sour cream

1 tbsp. chives or green onion ends
1/2 tsp. salt

Cream together. Pour into crust.

Topping:

Remainder of onions
3-4 pimento stuffed olives (opt.)

1/4 C. parmesan cheese

Arrange onions on top of potato mixture. Sprinkle with parmesan cheese. Bake at 375 degrees for 30 minutes. Top with olives, if desired.

Meat-Za-Pie

1 lb. ground beef
2/3 C. (sm. can) evaporated milk
1/2 C. fine cracker crumbs
1 tsp. garlic salt

1/2 C. catsup
1 C. shredded sharp cheddar cheese
1 tsp. oregano, finely crumbled

Mix first four ingredients in a pie plate with a fork. Pat evenly onto bottom and sides of pie plate, allowing about 1/2 inch from top of dish, otherwise it will cook over in oven. Press firmly in place. Spread catsup on meat, top with oregano and then cheddar cheese. Bake at 375 degrees for 30 minutes.

Mrs. Charles Boyer, Fremont, Ohio

Cheeseburger Pie

1 lb. ground beef
1/2 C. chopped onion
1-8oz. can tomato sauce
1/4 C snipped parsley
1-2oz. can chopped mushrooms, drained
1/4 tsp. dried oregano leaves, crushed
1/4 tsp. salt
1/8 tsp. pepper
2 pkg. refrigerated crescent rolls (8 rolls in each)
3 eggs
6 slices sharp process American cheese

In skillet, brown beef and onion; drain. Stir in tomato sauce, parsley, mushrooms, oregano, salt, and pepper; set aside. Unroll one package of rolls. Place the four sections of dough together, forming a 12x6 inch rectangle. Seal edges and perforations together. Roll to 12-inch square. Fit into 9-inch pie plate and trim. Separate one of the eggs; set yolk aside; beat egg white and remaining two eggs. Spread half over dough. Spoon meat into shell. Arrange cheese slices on top; spread remaining egg mixture over cheese. Mix reserve yolk and 1 tbsp. water; brush lightly on edges of pastry. Reserve remaining. Roll second package of rolls to 12-inch square, as before. Place atop filling. Trim, seal and flute edge; cut slits for escape of steam. Brush top with remaining egg yolk mixture. Bake in 350 degree oven for 50-55 minutes. If pastry gets too brown, cover with foil. Let stand 10 minutes. Serves 6.

LaVola Walter, Belvidere, Illinois

Pizza Meatballs

1 lb. ground beef
1 C. dried bread crumbs
1/2 C. milk
2 tbsp. instant minced onion
1 tsp. garlic salt
1/2 tsp. pepper
4 oz. pkg. mozzarella cheese cut into 12 bitesize cubes
3 tbsp. flour
2 tbsp. salad oil
1 12-15-1/2 oz. jar pizza sauce
4 C. hot cooked rice
parsley for garnish

About 45 minutes before serving: In medium bowl with fork, mix well first 6 ingredients; shape mixture into 12 large meatballs with 1 cube of cheese in center of each, making sure that cheese is completely covered with meat mixture. On waxed paper, coat each meatball lightly with flour. In 12-inch skillet over medium heat, in hot salad oil, cook meatballs until browned on all sides. Spoon off fat. Add pizza sauce to meatballs in skillet; heat to boiling. Reduce heat to low; cover and simmer 10 minutes. Serve on rice.

Mrs. Judy M. Sax, San Antonio, Texas

Friccadillies

1-1/2 lbs. ground beef
2 eggs, beaten
2 slices bread (or more)
1 C. milk
1 tsp. salt

1 can mushroom soup
1/2 soup can water
3/4 C. flour, approx.
Dash of pepper

Combine ground beef, beaten eggs, bread, milk and salt. Spoon meat mixture, about the size of a large egg, into small bowl containing the flour. Shape meat into patties and roll in flour. Place patties into lightly greased skillet. Brown on one side, then turn and brown other side. Place meatballs in 8x12 inch baking dish. When all patties are browned, pour off excess grease left in skillet and add mushroom soup diluted with 1/2 can water and stir to make a gravy. Add a dash of pepper. Pour gravy around and over meatballs and bake in 350 degree oven for about 25 mintues. Serves 8-10.

Mrs. Roy Gruenwald, Frohna, Missouri

Cornbread Pie

1 lb. ground beef
1 large onion, chopped
1 can tomato soup
2 C. water
1 tsp. salt

3/4 tsp. pepper
1 tbsp. chili powder
1/2 C. green peppers
1 C. whole kernel corn
(drained)

Brown the beef and onion in a skillet. Add the soup, water, seasonings, corn and green pepper. Mix well and allow to simmer for 15 minutes. Then fill a greased pie dish or casserole 3/4 full, leaving room for the cornbread topping. To make the cornbread top, sift together the following:

3/4 C. cornmeal
1 tbsp. sugar
1-1/2 tsp. baking powder

1 tbsp. flour
1/2 tsp. salt

After they are sifted together, add one beaten egg and 1/2 C. milk. Stir lightly and fold in 1 tbsp. of melted fat. Cover the meat mixture with this topping and bake in a medium oven at 350 degrees for 18-20 minutes. Don't be surprised when the topping disappears into the meat mixture. It will rise during the baking and form a good layer of cornbread.

Fritz Miller, Dayton, Ohio

"Andy's Sauerbraten with Noodles"

2 lbs. ground beef
1/2 C. pkg. bread crumbs
3 tbsp. instant minced onion
2 tsp. salt

1/4 tsp. ground cloves
1/4 C. milk
2 eggs

Combine all above and turn out onto wax paper surface and form into an oval. Heat 2 tbsp. butter in a large deep skillet with a lid. Brown loaf 5 minutes on each side turning with 2 large spatulas. Blend: 1/2 C. water, 1/2 C. red wine and 1/2 C. vinegar. Add to skillet. Heat to boiling, reduce heat to a slow simmer and cook covered for 45 minutes. Remove meat when done and add 5-6 (small size) ginger snap cookies to liquid in pan. Stir until smooth and serve over egg noodles.

Mrs. Bruce Anderson, Pleasant Valley, New York

Squaw Corn Casserole

1 lb. ground beef
2 tbsp. fat
1-1/2 tsp. salt
1/2 tsp. dried thyme
1/4 tsp. marjoram
1/4 C. chopped onion
2 eggs, beaten
1/4 C. milk

1 C. soft bread crumbs
1 (1 lb.) can cream style corn
2 tsp. prepared mustard
1/2 C. bread or cracker crumbs or crushed potato chips
2 tbsp. butter (omit if using potato chips

Brown beef in fat. Add seasonings, onions, eggs, milk, 1 C. crumbs, corn and mustard. Mix well and put in greased 2 quart casserole. Mix remaining crumbs and butter and sprinkle over casserole. Bake in moderate oven (350 degrees) 30-40 minutes. Note: You can get this dish ready to bake, then refrigerate; cook just before you want to serve it.

Mrs. Eileen Odle, Vero Beach, Florida

One Pot Dinner

1/2-1 lb. ground beef
3/4 lb. bacon (cut in small pieces)
1 C. chopped onion
2 cans (1 lb., 15 oz.) pork and beans
1 can (1 lb.) kidney beans (drained)

1 can (1 lb.) butter beans (drained)
1 C. catsup
1/4 C. brown sugar
1 tbsp. liquid smoke
3 tbsp. white vinegar
1 tsp. salt - pinch of pepper

Brown beef in skillet; drain off fat. Brown bacon and onions; drain off fat. Put all ingredients in crockpot. Stir together well. Cover and cook on low 4-6 hours.

Mrs. Eileen Odle, Vero Beach, Florida

Budget Saver Guess Whats

1 egg
6 tbsp. dry bread crumbs
2 tbsp. catsup
1 tsp. salt
1/8-1/4 tsp. poultry seasoning

1 lb. hamburger or 3/4 lb. ground beef combined with 1/4 lb. ground pork
Leftovers

Beat egg. Add bread crumbs, catsup, salt, poultry seasoning and the ground meat. Mix very thoroughly and form into chicken egg size balls. Flatten balls (use small breadboard) between squares of wax paper to make patties about the size of the palm of the hand. Mold meat patties (one at a time) carefully in right hand. Place 1 tbsp. of a leftover vegetable in center of patty. Mold carefully, pinching together to enclose filling and form a meat ball. Use any leftovers you have, a tbsp. in each meatball, even mashed potatoes and cheese. Dust meatballs with flour. Brown quickly on all sides in frying pan in 4 tbsp. of drippings, oil, or margarine. Lift carefully into glass pie plate or shallow casserole. Add 1 tbsp. drippings from frying pan and 2 tbsp. water. Cover. Bake in a moderate oven 350 degrees 20-25 minutes. Serve with gravy made by adding 6 tbsp. flour to drippings left in frying pan, 1 tsp. salt and browning lightly. Add 2 C. of water or beef broth stirring. Cook until thickened. Pour gravy over meatballs and serve. If you have leftover gravy use it and eliminate making the pan gravy. Save all leftovers even if there is only a spoonful. Wrap in foil and keep in one container in the freezer until you have enough for a meal.

Mrs. D. C. Brown, Pittsburgh, Pennsylvania

-47-

Mock Dressing

1 lb. ground beef
1 beaten egg
2 C. dry bread crumbs
1 small chopped onion

1/2 C. milk (more or less as required)
1 can chicken noodle soup
A little sage, salt and pepper to taste.

Mix. Place in buttered casserole. Bake at 350 degrees for 1 hour.

Mrs. Frank Douvier, Freeport, Minnesota

Best Oven Hash

1-1/2 C. coarsely ground cook-ed beef
1 C. coarsely ground cooked potatoes
1/2 C. coarsely ground onion
1/4 C. chopped parsley
1 tsp. salt

Dash pepper
2 tsp. worcestershire sauce
1 small can evaporated milk
1/3 C. slightly crushed corn flakes
1 tbsp. butter or margarine, melted

Lightly mix beef, potatoes, onion, parsley, salt, pepper, worcester-shire sauce, and milk. Turn into greased 1-quart casserole. Mix cornflakes and butter; sprinkle over top. Bake in moderate oven (350 degrees) 30 minutes or until heated through. Serves 4.

Anna Mae Pritchyk, Clarks Summit, Pennsylvania

Elegant Hash

1 lb. ground beef
2 onions diced
2 C. raw carrots, diced
6 C. raw potatoes, diced

Salt and pepper to taste
3 C. milk
Butter and bread crumbs

Brown onions and celery in a little fat. Remove the onions and celery and brown the ground beef. Season with salt and pepper. Mix onions, celery and hamburger. Put in alternate layers with carrots and potatoes. Pour over the milk. Sprinkle with bread crumbs and dot with butter. Bake in moderate oven for 2 hours.

Mrs. Lil Adams, Gettysburg, South Dakota

Hamburger Stroganoff

1-1/2 lbs. ground beef
1 envelope dry onion soup mix
1 can beer (12oz.)

1 C. sour cream
1/4 tsp. garlic powder
1/4 tsp. paprika

Brown beef, add soup and beer. Stir well and simmer 1/2 hour. Add sour cream and heat until warm throughout. Stir in garlic and paprika. Salt and pepper to taste. Serve with rice or noodles.

Mary Hicks, Hickory, North Carolina

Lumpias

1 pkg. wonton (oriental) wrappers
1 lb. ground beef

salt and pepper to taste
1 envelope dry onion soup mix

Brown ground beef, drain, add salt and pepper and onion soup mix. Stir well. Put 1 tsp. on each wonton wrapper, moisten with water and seal edges. Deep fry until golden brown. Serve hot, dip in soy sauce. Serve with salad and dessert.

Mary Hicks, Hickory, North Carolina

Yuccamondas

1 can refrigerated biscuits (8oz.)
1 lb. ground beef
Salt and pepper to taste

1 C. cooked rice
1 med. onion, chopped
1 med. green pepper, chopped
1/4 tsp. garlic powder

Brown beef, drain, add onion, green pepper, rice and seasonings. Stir well. Heat throughout. Roll out each biscuit separately. Place about 1 tbsp. (or a little more) on each biscuit. Fold over and seal (turnover) style. Place on greased baking sheet, brush with melted butter or margarine. Bake at 350 degrees until golden brown.

Mary Hicks, Hickory, North Carolina

Runsa

1 lb. hamburger
1 can or jar of kraut, drained
1 onion

Salt and pepper
1-2 loaves of frozen bread

Brown hamburger and onion; drain grease. Add kraut. Refrigerate overnight. Thaw bread; cut loaf into 8 pieces. Pat or roll out each piece. Add as much mixture as dough will hold and bring dough up around and pinch tight. Lay sealed side down in greased baking dish. No need to let rise. Bake at 350 degrees until nicely browned.

With the second loaf, roll out, spoon mixture across and roll like a jelly roll. Pinch ends tight. Bake at 350 degrees. This can be sliced and warmed in microwave.

Bonita Simmons, Albia, Iowa

Norwegian Meat Pie

5 eggs
2-1/2 C. bread crumbs
1 tbsp. chopped onion
5 strips bacon
1/2 C. chopped celery
1/4 tsp. garlic salt
1½ tsp. worcestershire sauce

3/4-1 lb. ground beef
2-1/2 C. milk
1/2 tsp. lemon juice
1 tsp. salt
1/4 lb. cheese, grated
1/2 tsp. celery salt

Beat 1 egg with 1/2 C. milk; add bread crumbs; let stand 5 minutes and add to ground beef and 1/2 tsp. worcestershire sauce, lemon juice, salt and chopped onions and mix well. Line bottom and sides of casserole dish, oblong (about 11½x8) with meat mixture. Fry bacon until crisp; crumble and sprinkle over meat in pan. Add shredded cheese over this and then add chopped celery over this. Beat remaining eggs and 2 C. milk together and add 1/2 tsp. celery salt and 1/4 tsp. garlic salt. Pour over mixture in pan. Bake at 400 degrees for 15 minutes; then at 350 degrees for 30 minutes or until mixture is firm.

Note: If hamburger is used instead of ground beef, it may take more eggs for mixture to set. If it doesn't set, I beat an extra egg or two and mix with mixture and put back in oven until set.

Mary M. West, Columbia, Tennessee

Mexican Super Salad
(Main Dish)

1 lrg head of lettuce, shredded
1 lb. ground beef, browned and drained
1 lb. cheddar cheese, grated
1 med. onion, diced
1 envelope taco seasoning
1 large bag Dorito chips, crushed
1-8oz. bottle Thousand Island dressing
2 cans (1 lb.) each of kidney beans, drained
2 medium tomatoes, diced

In a large bowl, shred lettuce; add diced onions and tomatoes. In large skillet, cook ground beef until done; drain and return to skillet. Add kidney beans, taco seasoning, and half of crushed chips. Cook over medium heat until the kidney beans are warm. Add hambruger and bean mixture to bowl of lettuce, tomatoes, and onions; mix well. Add grated cheese and remainder of crushed chips. Pour in bottle of dressing and mix well. Top with chips (optional). Serve with picante or taco sauce. Serves 6-8.

Jimmy D. O'Dell, MSgt. USAF, APO New York

Main-Dish Meat Salad

2 C. ground beef, cooked
3 hardboiled eggs, chopped fine
2 green onions, chopped
1/2 tsp. salt
1/4 tsp. pepper
Dash of cayenne
1 dill pickle, chopped
1 sweet pickle, chopped
3 tbsp. mayonnaise

Combine ingredients and toss lightly. For main dish, serve on lettuce with hot rolls and dessert. As an appetizer, spread on rye bread, garnished with slices of onion.

Rosemary Kodunc, Gilbert, Minnesota

Grandma's Hamburger Soup

2 lbs. ground chuck
2 small onions, diced
2 C. whole canned tomatoes
3 stalks celery, diced
5 carrots, cleaned and diced
3 bouillon cubes
Salt and pepper to taste
1/4 C. cooked rice
1 tsp. chopped parsley
Grated Parmesan cheese

Place meat in chunks in a large kettle; cover with water and simmer until meat is cooked. Drain the liquid and save. Let it cool and remove grease from top. Add the remaining ingredients, simmer about thirty minutes. Add the meat liquid. Sprinkle with parmesan cheese. Serves 6. Delicious if chilled overnight and served the next day.

Mary Nicita, Bayside, New York

Hamburger Stew

2 lbs. hamburger
2 tbsp. chopped onion
2 C. tomato juice
1 can peas

1 can pork and beans
4 med. sized potatoes, cubed and cooked
Salt and pepper to taste

Cook hamburger and onion until meat looses its pink color and onion is transparent. Add tomato juice and cook until meat is tender and juice is slightly thickened. Add 1 can of peas, 1 can of pork and beans, 4 medium sized cooked potatoes. Cook together a few minutes with salt and pepper to taste. Serves 8-10.

Theresa Nuoci, Lafayette, Colorado

Quick Vegetable Soup

Brown:

1 lb. ground beef
1 onion, diced

3 cabbage leaves, chopped

Cook until meat is no longer red. Add 2 cans mixed vegetables. Cook to the consistency of soup or as thick as you like the soup.

Mrs. Russell Hymes, Arenzville, Illinois

My Stuffed Onions

6 large onions, peeled, par-boiled
1 lb. hamburger

Salt and pepper to taste
1 can cheddar cheese soup
1 soup can water

Cool parboiled onions; cut in half; remove center of onion to form cups (leave 2-3 layers intact). Brown and crumble hamburger. Chop 1/2 C. of scooped out onion very fine. Add to hamburger; cook until tender. Fill onion cavities with seasoned hamburger. Dilute soup with water; stir until smooth; pour over onions in casserole. Add any browned beef to sauce around onion cups. Bake at 350 degrees for 1 hour. These are attractive in a casserole and very tasty. Serves 6.

Margaret Marvin, East Sparta, Ohio

Tator-Tot-Hot Dish

2 lbs. hamburger
1/2 tsp. salt
Dash onion salt

1 can drained green beans,
corn or mixed vegetables
1 can cream soup, any kind
1 pkg. tator tots

Pat hamburger in the bottom of a 9x3 pan, sprinkle with salt, and onion salt. Add can of vegetables, spread on the soup and then add the tator tots. Cover with foil and bake 1 hour and 15 minutes at 350 degrees. Uncover and bake thirty minutes more.

Betty Brennan, Faribault, Minnesota

Poor Boy Chow Mein

1-1/2 lbs. hamburger
1 onion, diced
1 small bunch celery, diced
1 can bean sprouts, drained

1 C. rice
5 C. water
1 can cream of mushroom soup
2-3 tbsp. soy sauce

Brown hamburger and onion, put in a large baking dish and add all of the other ingredients, mix good. Bake covered for 1-1/2 hours at 325 degrees. Uncover the last 20 minutes and sprinkle with chow mein noodles. Serve over more chow mein noodles and pass the soy sauce.

Betty Brennan, Faribault, Minnesota

Cream of Hamburger-Chicken Soup

Leftover chicken parts, neck,
back, wing tips, fat, skin,
whatever you have
3/4 lb. 1/2" noodles

1 lb. hamburger
1/2 chopped green pepper
1-10oz. pkg. frozen green peas
1/2 can evaporated milk
1 rounded tbsp. flour

Put the chicken parts in a very large pot, like a dutch oven. Add enough water to fill about 3/4 full. Add chopped onion and salt, and simmer 1/2 hour to make a nice broth. Strain. Cook noodles in the broth and, at the same time, fry hamburger with green pepper. When the meat has lost all pink color, add to broth along with the peas and continue to simmer until the noodles and peas are done. Make a thin paste of the milk and flour, and add to soup, stirring until slightly thickened. Taste and adjust seasoning, with fresh ground black pepper, and possibly more salt. The soup should be very thick with noodles.

Mrs. Linda Taylor, New Lenox, Illinois

German Meatball Stew Supreme

2 C. water	5 whole cloves
1 C. lemon-lime soda pop	1/2 tsp. black pepper
2 bay (laurel) leaves	1/2 tsp. salt

Combine all ingredients in a 3 quart saucepan and bring to a boil. Simmer while the meatballs are being prepared. Remove the bay leaves and cloves before the vegetables and meatballs are added.

1/2 C. dry bread crumbs   2 T. powdered coffee cream
1/3 C. water

Stir powdered coffee cream into cool water until blended. Soak breadcrumbs in the mixture.

1 T. margarine   2 T. chopped bell pepper
1/2 medium onion, chopped

Saute onion and pepper in hot margarine until tender, but not brown.

1 lb. ground beef   2 eggs, beaten
1/2 lb. ground pork or sausage   1 tsp. salt

Combine ground meats, onion, pepper, eggs, salt and bread mixture. Mix thoroughly and form into meatballs about the size of walnuts.

3 medium potatoes   1/2 small cabbage
4 carrots

Pare carrots and potatoes. Cut potatoes into small pieces (about 1/2 inch pieces). Slice carrots. Wash cabbage and slice.

Place carrots and potatoes into water mixture. Gently place the meatballs on top. Cover and simmer for 25-30 minutes. Add the cabbage about 12 minutes before the stew is to be done. Serves 6-8.

Maggie's Greek Pork Chops

6-8 pork chops with excess fat trimmed off
Rub well, both sides with lemon juice (I use concentrated juice)

1. Sprinkle both sides with salt and pepper. Let stand in pan for at least 1/2 hour before proceeding with recipe.

2. In a large skillet, brown chops quickly in butter on both sides. Remove from fire.

3. Add 2 medium sized onions (chopped), 1/4 C. parsley, 3 stalks celery with leaves (chopped) and 1 clove garlic (cut in half). You can prepare vegetables during waiting time.

4. Add 2/3 C. burgundy wine and just enough water to cover chops.

5. Simmer gently, covered for 1-1/2 to 2 hours or until tender.

NOTE: Delicious with venison chops too.

Margaret A. Verkon, Corning, New York

Pork Chops "Supreme"

4-6 pork chops
2 tbsp. cooking oil
2 tbsp. catsup

1 tbsp. lemon juice
1 tbsp. worchestershire sauce
1 tbsp. soy sauce

Preheat oven to 350 degrees. Arrange chops in a single layer in a baking dish or shallow roasting pan. Mix remaining ingredients together and spread half of mixture on chops. Place uncovered in oven for 30 minutes. Remove from oven and turn chops over. Spread remainder of mixture on chops and bake for 30 minutes or a bit longer until done. For variation, use garlic, onion or other spices to taste.

Margie Pulick, Yonkers, New York

Pork Chops Baked in Sour Cream

4 pork loin chops (2 inches thick)
Salt and pepper to taste

4 tbsp. butter
4 cloves

Melt butter in frying pan. Season chops and dredge with flour. Insert clove in each chop and arrange in baking dish. Add the following to drippings in frying pan: 1 tbsp. sugar, 1/2 C. water, 1/2 C. sour cream, 1 bay leaf and 2 tbsp. vinegar. Bring to boil and pour over meat. Cover and bake in 350 degree oven for 1-1/2 hours.

Clara M. Davis, Salem, Oregon

Pineapple Pork and Rice Casserole

4 pork chops, about 1 inch thick
2 tbsp. vegetable oil
1 onion, chopped
1/2 green pepper, chopped
1 C. chopped celery
1 C. long grain rice
2 chicken bouillon cubes

2 C. boiling water
14-oz. can pineapple slices
1/4 tsp. thyme
1/2 tsp. salt
12 whole cloves
1 tbsp. brown sugar
1 tbsp. butter

Preheat oven to 350 degrees. Trim fat from chops and slash sides.

Heat oil in a large frying pan. Brown chops on both sides, then set aside. Add onion, pepper and celery to fat in pan and cook until onions are soft, about 5 minutes. Stir in rice and cook until the grains are a golden color.

Dissolve bouillon cubes in water. Drain 1/2 C. of syrup from the pineapple and add to the rice mixture along with chicken bouillon, thyme and salt. Stick two cloves in each pineapple slice and set aside.

Turn rice mixture into a two-quart casserole that is wide enough to hold the chops in a single layer. Place the chops on top. Cover tightly and bake in preheated oven for one hour or until rice is puffed and most of the liquid has been absorbed.

Uncover and place pineapple slices studded with cloves on top of the chops. Sprinkle with brown sugar. Dot with butter and drizzle with remaining pineapple syrup.

Return dish to 350 degree oven and cook, uncovered, until fruit is heated through and slightly glazed. Makes 4 servings.

Mrs. Elvira Gibbons, North Sydney, Nova Scotia, Canada

Lori's Simple-But-Super Pork Chops

4 pork chops, 1 to 1-1/4 inches thick
1 C. uncooked rice (not instant)
1 medium carrot, grated
1 large celery rib, diced

1 10-3/4 oz. can condensed cream of mushroom soup
1-1/2 C. water
1/4 tsp. pepper
3/4 tsp. salt

Combine all ingredients, except pork chops, in 9x9 inch baking dish. Lay chops on top. Bake, covered, at 350 degrees for 40 minutes. Uncover, turn chops over and continue baking for 20 more minutes, until chops are brown.

Lori Prange (age 13), Lincoln, Nebraska

Szekelygulyas (Pork Sauerkraut Dish)

1 lb. lean pork (beef may be substituted)
1/4 C. oil
1 large onion
1 tbsp paprika

2 tbsp. flour (level)
1/2 C. sour cream
1-1/2 to 2 C. water
2 lbs. sauerkraut
Salt and pepper to taste

Finely chop onion and lightly brown in the oil. Cut meat into dices approximately 3/4 inch. Add meat to onions, mix in paprika and flour. Rinse out sauerkraut and add to the meat. Pour on the water, salt and pepper to taste and slow cook about one hour (beef may require longer cooking). Mix in sour cream when serving.

Margaret Heil, Winters, California

Pork Patties

1 can chicken mushroom soup
1-1/2 C. finely chopped cooked chicken or pork
1/3 C. fine bread crumbs
1 egg, beaten

2 tbsp. butter
1/4 C. water
Dash of pepper
1/4 tsp. crushed rosemary
1 tsp. lemon juice

Thoroughly mix 2 tbsp. soup, pork, bread crumbs, egg and pepper. Shape into firm patties. Brown in skillet in butter. Blend soup, water, lemon juice and rosemary. Pour over patties. Heat, stirring occasionally.

Mrs. Clyde Marvin, East Sparta, Ohio

water, lemon juice and rosemary. Pour over patties. Heat, stirring occasionally.

Mrs. Clyde Marvin, East Sparta, Ohio

Spanish Pork (or Beef) with Spaghetti

1/2 C. finely chopped onion
1 clove garlic, minced
2 tbsp. salad oil
1 20oz. can tomatoes, cut up
1 8oz. can tomato sauce
1/3 C. water

1 bay leaf
2 C. diced cooked pork or beef
1/4 C. sliced pimento-stuffed green olives
12 oz. spaghetti
Grated parmesan cheese

In medium saucepan, cook onion and garlic in hot oil until tender, but not brown. Stir in tomatoes, tomato sauce, water and bay leaf. Simmer, covered for 1 hour; stirring occasionally. Stir in pork or beef and olives; simmer 30 minutes more. Remove bay leaf. Cook spaghetti according to package directions; drain. Pour sauce over spaghetti; sprinkle with parmesan cheese. Makes 4 servings.

LaVola Walter, Belvidere, Illinois

Special Sauerkraut and Pork

1 lb. leftover ground roast pork
Pepper, salt, thyme or sage to taste
1 C. cooked rice
1 qt. sauerkraut, reserving liquid

2 medium firm apples, peeled, cored and sliced
2 onions, sliced
1 tsp. caraway seeds or several dashes of paprika
1 tsp. sugar

Season ground pork and mix in rice. Shape the mixture into 1-1/2 inch balls. Wrap the balls with drained sauerkraut. In a lightly greased baking dish, alternate layers of meatballs wraped in sauerkraut, apples, onion slices, caraway seeds or paprika. Sprinkle sugar over the top layer and add the rest of the sauerkraut if any is leftover and sauerkraut liquid. Cover and bake at 350 degrees for 45 minutes. Serves 4.

Mrs. Adeline Mazerolas, New York, New York

"Bohemian Spareribs"

2 lbs. spareribs
1 tsp. salt
1/4 tsp. pepper
1 tbsp. caraway seeds

1 No. 2 can sauerkraut
1 medium onion, sliced
1 No. 2 can tomatoes

Cut spareribs into individual servings. Season. Mix caraway seeds with sauerkraut and place in 8x12 inch baking dish. Arrange onion slices on top of sauerkraut and pour tomatoes over mixture. Place spareribs on top. Bake in a moderate oven (350 degrees) for 2 hours. Four servings.

Mrs. William Zemcik, Windber, Pennsylvania

Pork Chops and Hominy

4 thin pork chops
1 tbsp. oil
2 med. onions, sliced
1 clove garlic, minced
1 can (16oz) golden hominy, drained

1/2 C. chicken bouillon
1 tbsp. chili powder
1 tsp. salt
1 bay leaf
1 tsp. thyme

In large skillet, brown chops well in oil; remove and set aside. Add onions and garlic to dripping. Saute until onions are lightly browned. Stir in remaining ingredients, mixing well and scraping up browned bits on bottom of skillet. Place chops in single layer on top. Cover and simmer 35-40 minutes or until tender. Remove bay leaf. To serve, spoon hominy, onions and drippings over chops.

Marge Camenisch, Joliet, Illinois

Italian Sausage Skillet

1 lb. pork sausage
1 large onion, diced
1 C. uncooked rice
1 C. tomato juice

1 C. diced celery
3 tbsp. green pepper
1 tsp. worchestershire sauce
Salt and pepper

Crumble sausage and fry with onion until brown. Pour off drippings. Mix remaining ingredients thoroughly with sausage and onions. Cover tightly and cook slowly about 45 minutes. Do not raise cover. Serves 4.

Sausage-Rice Cutlets Croquettes

1/2 lb. sausage
2-1/2 tbsp. flour
1/2 C. milk
1 tsp. salt
2 tbsp. worchestershire sauce

1-1/3 C. finely sifted bread crumbs
1 C. cooked rice
1 egg

Crumble sausage and partially panfry. Make a thick white sauce of drippings, flour and milk. Add sausage, white sauce, salt, worcestershire and 1/3 C. bread crumbs to rice, mixing well. Cool. Shape into cutlets. Dip into beaten egg and crumbs. Panfry in drippings until golden brown. Makes 8 cutlets, using 1/4 C. mixture for each. Serve with tomato or cheese sauce.

Sausage Casserole

1 lb. pork sausage
1-1/2 C. sliced raw potatoes
1 C. sliced raw carrots
1 C. sliced raw onions
1/2 C. uncooked rice

1-1/2 C. canned tomatoes
1 tsp. salt
1/8 tsp. pepper
2 tbsp. sugar

Partially cook sausage and drain. In a 2 qt. casserole put layers of vegetables with tomatoes on top. Sprinkle with salt, pepper and sugar. Cover casserole and bake at 350 degrees for 1-1/2 to 2 hours. Serves 6.

Sausage Cheese Pie

2 lbs. or more bulk sausage or ground beef, browned
1 egg, beaten

Chopped onion
Shredded cheese
1 pkg. hot roll mix

Brown meat with onion; drain well. Mix together first four ingredients. Prepare hot roll mix according to directions on package. When it has risen to double, roll half out on floured surface. Place in 13x9x2 inch pan. Top with meat, cheese, onion, and egg mixture. Roll out second half of dough, top on filling. Bake in 350 degree oven until brown, about 20-30 minutes.

Maxine Davis, Centralia, Illinois

Sausage Casserole with Rice

2 lbs. sausage
1 green pepper, chopped
1 onion, chopped
6 stalks celery, chopped

1 C. uncooked rice
1 C. water
1 pkg. Lipton noodle soup

Brown sausage, onion and pepper. Drain. Add other ingredients and place in casserole dish. Bake at 350 degrees for 1 to 1-1/2 hours.

Winifred L. Kerwin, Rossville, Kansas

Sausage and Corn Casserole

1 lb. sausage
1/4 C. bell pepper, chopped
1 can whole kernel corn (drained)

1 large can evaporated milk
2 tbsp. flour
1/2 tsp. salt
1/2 to 1 C. grated cheese

Brown sausage and pepper until sausage is cooked (drain). Add to corn in casserole dish. Blend 2-3 tbsp. sausage drippings with flour and salt over medium heat in skillet. Add milk and simmer 2-3 minutes (stirring continuously) or until thickened. Pour over sausage and corn mixture and mix. Top with grated cheese. Bake 25-30 minutes or until bubbly at 350 degrees.

Mary M. West, Columbia, Tennessee

Pork Roll-Ups

Biscuit pastry
2 C. cooked ground pork
1/4 C. grated carrot
1 tbsp. shredded green pepper
(or if you prefer use 1 tbsp.
chopped parsley

1 tbsp. grated onion
1/2 tsp. salt
2 tsp. soy sauce
1/4 C. milk

Prepare pastry. Combine meat with remaining ingredients; mix well. Spread mixture on rolled out pastry and roll as for jelly roll. Cut into twelve 1 inch slices. Place rolls on greased baking sheet. Bake at 425 degrees for 25 minutes or until pastry is lightly browned. Serve with mushroom sauce (below). Serves 6.

Mushroom Sauce

2 tbsp. butter
1 can (4oz.) mushrooms, sliced
(reserve liquid)
3 tbsp. flour

1 C. evaporated milk
1/2 tsp. salt
1/4 tsp. paprika

Melt butter in a heavy saucepan; add mushrooms and heat together. Add flour and mix well. Add liquid from can of mushrooms (about 1/3) then add evaporated milk, salt and paprika. Stir until sauce is thickened. Makes 1-1/4 C.

Jo Wendt, Eau Claire, Wisconsin

Sausage Cheddar Loaf

1 lb. pork sausage
6 eggs
2 C. milk
2 C. bread cubes

1 C. grated cheese (cheddar)
1 tsp. salt
1 tsp. dry mustard

Brown sausage and drain off grease. Beat eggs. Add all ingedients. Bake at 350 degrees for 45 minutes. Put in 8x8 pan or 9 inch pie plate, lightly greased. Make sauce of 1 can of cream of mushroom soup and 1/2 C. sour cream. Heat to boiling and pour over sausage loaf.

Marge Camenisch, Joliet, Illinois

Swiss-Ham and Potato Scallop

1/2 C. chopped onion
2 tbsp. butter
3 tbsp. flour
1/2 tsp. salt
1/8 tsp. pepper
1-1/4 C. milk

1/2 C. shredded processed
swiss cheese
2 C. cubed cooked ham
3 C. cubed cooked potatoes
1-1/2 C. soft bread crumbs
2 tbsp. margarine, melted

Cook onion in the 2 tbsp. margarine until tender, but not brown. Blend in flour, salt and pepper. Add milk; cook and stir until thickened and bubbly. Stir in cheese until melted. Add ham and potatoes. Turn into 1-1/2 qt. casserole. Combine crumbs and 2 tbsp. butter; sprinkle on top. Bake in 400 degree oven for 25-30 minutes. Makes 5-6 servings.

LaVola Walter, Belvidere, Illinois

Ham-Potato Casserole

1 C. leftover ham
1 can sliced potatoes or 2 C.
leftover sliced potatoes
1 tbsp. onion

1 C. mayonnaise
1 C. cubed Velveeta cheese
1 tbsp. catsup

Mix together and put in buttered baking dish. Top with sliced green olives if desired. Heat at 350 degrees for 30 minutes.

Joan Rieck, Whitefish Bay, Wisconsin

Working Man's Feast

2 lbs. leftover boiled or baked
ham cut in slices
1 bunch of carrots, cut up
1 stalk of celery, cut up
1 onion, peeled and cut in
rings

1-1/2 lbs. Irish potatoes, peeled
and sliced in thick slices
1 can cream of chicken soup
1 can cream of mushroom soup
1 soup can of water
1 tsp. pepper

Place ham over the bottom of a medium size baking dish or pan. After ham is placed, take carrots, celery and onions and place on top of the ham. Place potato slices over these ingredients and sprinkle pepper on top. After all of the above ingredients are placed in dish, take the chicken and mushroom soup and pour over the top of the ingredients. Take the one can of water and pour around the edge of the dish. Cover with tin foil and cook for 1 hour and 45 minutes at 350 degrees. Serves 10-12.

Mrs. Marie Brown, Wilson, North Carolina

Ham and Rice Casserole

1 can cream of celery soup	1 tsp. lemon rind, grated
1 can cream of mushroom soup	1/4 tsp. rosemary
1 C. light cream	1/8 tsp. black pepper
1 C. sharp cheddar cheese	4 C. cooked rice
1/2 C. parmesan cheese, grated	4 C. leftover ham or tuna
1-1/2 tbsp. minced onion	1 can cut green beans
1 tbsp. prepared mustard	1 can french fried onion rings

Combine soups and cream in saucepan; stir until smooth. Heat gently, but do not boil. Stir in the cheeses, then onion, mustard, lemon rind, rosemary and pepper. Add rice and ham. Combine thoroughly. In a 3 quart casserole, alternate layers of ham and rice and sauce. Sprinkle onion rings on top. Bake uncovered at 350 degrees for 15-20 minutes. Serves 10.

Louise Hicks, Chicago, Illinois

Leftover Ham Casserole

1 lb. ham (or more if desired)	1 tsp. salt
1-1/2 C. rice, washed	Dash of pepper
Sauerkraut (1 lb. can or 2 C.)	About 3 C. water

Mix all ingredients together and set in oven at 350 degrees until rice is soft. Cover while baking. NOTE: watch. Sometimes one may have to add a bit more water if it gets too dry before rice is done.

Esther Blatter, McClusky, North Dakota

Gourmet Ham Patties

2 C. ground cooked ham
1/4 C. grated raw potatoes
2 tbsp. finely chopped onions
1-1/2 tsp. brown sugar
1/4 tsp. dry mustard

Dash cinnamon
1 tbsp. shortening
1/2 C. pineapple juice
1 C. sour cream

Combine first six ingredients and shape into 4 patties about 1/4 inch thick. Heat shortening in heavy skillet. Add patties and brown on both sides. Cover and cook over low heat for about 5 minutes. Combine pineapple juice and sour cream and pour over patties. Simmer 5 minutes.

Jo Wendt, Eau Claire, Wisconsin

Hash-Brown Ham Dinger

2 lbs. frozen hash-brown potatoes (cubes, not shredded,
thawed for 1/2 hour)
1 can cream of chicken soup
1/2 C. sour cream with minced
green onions (chives) (com-
mercial)

1-1/2 C. diced baked or boiled
ham
1-1/2 C. sharp, cheddar
cheese, diced small
1 C. breadcrumbs, combined
with 1/3 C. melted margarine

Mix potatoes, soup, sour cream and onions. Layer in a greased 9x12 inch pyrex baking dish with ham and cheese cubes. Combine breadcrumbs and margarine; put on top of casserole. Dust with paprika if desired. Cover with aluminum foil and bake for 1 hour at 350 degrees. Uncover the last 10 minutes to brown. Serves 4-6.

Mrs. Lorry L. Mudge, Detroit, Michigan

Pressed Meat

Leftover ham, chicken or turkey. Grind the meat coarsely and add salt and pepper to chicken or turkey, but not to ham. Put broth in pan and bring the broth to a boil. Mix meat and broth until soupy, place in dish. Put plate on top of the meat and weight it down and set to cool until firm.

Zenana Warren, Wauseon, Ohio

Easter Sausage

2 lbs. ham (cut into small pieces)
1 large loaf of white sandwich bread, day old
18 eggs, beaten

4 slices bacon, cut up and pan fried to golden brown
3 large bunches of green onions (green part only)
1/4 C. corn meal
Salt and pepper to taste

Cut up ham, bread and onions. Add bacon chips, corn meal, salt and pepper. Mix well. Beat eggs and add to bread mixture and mix. Grease 2 loaf dishes (glass). Put strips of bacon on each loaf. Put glass dish in metal pan and fill 1/2 full of water. Cover entire pan with foil. Bake at 350 degrees for 1-1/2 hours.

Marge Camenisch, Joliet, Illinois

Cheese n' Ham Muffinettes

4 English muffins, halved and toasted
8 slices leftover boiled or baked ham
8 slices firm, red fresh tomatoes, 1/2" thick

2 cans cheddar cheese soup, heated with 1/2 can milk or cream (cheese sauce)
Cherry tomatoes & parsley for garnish

Place two muffin halves on each warmed plate. Top each with a ham slice, either doubled over or cut to fit muffin. Place tomato slices on and pour on cheese sauce. Garnish plate with tomatoes and parsley. Serve with a fruit jello or lettuce salad.

Mrs. Lorry L. Mudge, Detroit, Michigan

Curried Ham in Popovers

2 tbsp. chopped green pepper
1 tbsp. chopped onion
1 tbsp. margarine or butter
1 10-1/2 oz. cream of celery soup
1/3 C. salad dressing or mayonnaise

1/3 C. reconstituted nonfat dry milk
1/4 tsp. curry powder
2 C. cubed, fully cooked leftover ham
Popovers

Cook vegetables in butter until tender. Stir in next 5 ingredients; cook and stir until heated through. Serve in hot popovers (page 67). Split lengthwise. Serves 6.

Popovers: Place 2 eggs in mixer bowl; add 1 C. reconstituted nonfat dry milk, 1 C. sifted all-purpose flour and 1/2 tsp. salt. Beat 1-1/2 minutes with rotary beater or electric mixer. Add 1 tbsp. cooking oil; beat 30 seconds more. Fill 6 well greased 5oz. custard cups half full. Bake at 475 degrees for 15 minutes. Reduce heat to 350 degrees; bake until browned and firm; 25-30 minutes. A few minutes before removing from oven, prick with fork.

Jo Wendt, Eau Claire, Wisconsin

Skillet Ham Salad

1/4 C. chopped green onions	1/4 tsp. salt
1/4 C. green pepper	Dash pepper
2 C. diced cooked ham	1/4 C. mayonnaise or salad
1 tbsp. fat	dressing
3-4 medium potatoes, cooked	1/2 lb. sharp process American
and diced (3 C.)	cheese, diced (1-1/2 C.)

Cook onions, peppers and meat in hot fat, stirring occasionally until meat is lightly browned. Add potatoes, salt, pepper and mayonnaise. Heat, mixing lightly. Stir in cheese; heat just until it begins to melt. Garnish with green onions, if desired. Makes 4 servings.

Anna Mae Pritchyk, Clarks Summit, Pennsylvania

Summertime

1 C. ham, cubed	1 tbsp. chopped parsley
1/2 C. chopped celery	1/2 tsp. dry mustard
1/4 C. chopped dill pickle	1 C. mayonnaise
1 tbsp. chopped onion	1 C. rice

Cook rice by package directions; add celery, pickle, onion, parsley and mustard. Mix well, cover and chill for an hour. Add ham and mayonnaise and garnish with hard-cooked egg slices and stuffed olives. Serves 4.

Rosemary Kodunc, Gilbert, Minnesota

Creamy New England Soup

1 C. or more cut-up ham
3 large potatoes
1/2 medium cabbage
2 carrots

2 small onions
Salt and pepper to taste
Water
Ham bone

In large pan, boil ham bone with vegetables until vegetables are done (in just enough water to cover). Remove bone. Cool; the rest enough to put in blender. Blend vegetables with broth, but don't use all the liquid at once. After vegetables are smooth, add the liquid to thickness or thinness desired. Add ham to mixture.

Joan Rieck, Whitefish Bay, Wisconsin

Ham and Cabbage Soup

1-1/2 qts. water or leftover broth from cooking ham
1 C. tomato juice
2 C. diced leftover ham

1 small head of cabbage, chopped
1 small onion, diced
1 large potato, diced
Salt and pepper to taste

Put all ingredients in pan and cook until potatoes and cabbage are tender.

Mrs. Eleanor Shelley, Youngstown, Ohio

Savory Roulades

4 boned chicken "scalopine"	1/2 C. chopped fresh parsley
6 tbsp. butter or oil	1/2 tsp. grated lemon rind
1 med. onion, diced (1/2 C.)	1 egg, beaten
2 tbsp. chopped celery	Salt, pepper, and paprika
1-3/4 C. coarse bread crumbs	1/4 C. apple juice
1/8 tsp. nutmeg	

Prepare chicken as directed below. Heat 2 tbsp. butter or oil; cook onion until transparent. Add celery and crumbs; cook, stirring until celery is glazed; crumbs golden. Add nutmeg, parsley, lemon rind; remove from heat. Add egg. Place 2 tbsp. filling mixture on each chicken piece; spreading to within 3/4 inch of edges. Starting from wide end roll up chicken, folding sides in to encase filling. Roll to narrow point. Place point down on greased baking pan. Season with salt, pepper, paprika. Dribble remaining butter or oil over chicken; sprinkle with apple juice. Bake at 350 degrees uncovered for 45-60 minutes, basting often. Serve with tomato sauce (below).

Tomato Sauce

2 C. canned Italian tomatoes	1/2 tsp. chopped parsley
1/2 tsp. dried basil	Salt and pepper
1/4 tsp. dried thyme	1 tbsp. sweet cream

Remove chicken from baking pan. Into pan stir all ingredients except cream. Cook on top of burner, stirring often, for 15 minutes. Blend sauce in processor or puree. Return to pan; bring to boil. Remove from heat; stir in cream. Spoon on plate with chicken. Makes 4 servings.

Boning Leg and Thigh

1. Buy large leg and thigh parts in one piece. Starting at the top, peel skin from thigh like a sock. At base of leg, pull hard to strip.

2. Place leg and thigh on cutting board, thin side up. Slit leg meat down to the bone. Cut meat all around with small, sharp knife until 1" from joint, then slit meat down to thigh bone; cut from bone. Meat should be one piece. If a hole occurs, salt edges lightly. Overlap before pounding.

3. Place meat flat on sheet of waxed paper, cover with second sheet and pound flat. Use as you would veal. If you buy whole chickens, breast meat can also be used.

Mrs. Clyde Prange, Lincoln, Nebraska

Oven Fried Chicken Parmesan

1/2 C. (2oz.) grated parmesan
cheese
1/4 C. flour
1 tsp. paprika
1/2 tsp. salt and pepper

2-1/2 lbs. broiler-fryer, cut up
1 egg, slightly beaten
1 tbsp. milk
1/4 C. margarine

Combine cheese, flour and seasonings. Dip chicken in combined egg
and milk. Coat with cheese mixture. Place in baking dish. Pour
margarine over chicken. Bake at 350 degrees for 1 hour or until
tender. 3-4 servings.

Marilyn Tatro, Ashkun, Illinois

Moist Baked Chicken

2-3 chicken breasts, spit (4-6
pieces) skin removed
4 tbsp. butter or margarine
1 4-6oz. can mushrooms,
drained
1/2 tsp. dried basil or rose-

mary
3/4 tsp. salt
1/8 tsp. pepper
1 can cream of mushroom,
chicken or celery soup
1/2 can milk

Lightly brown chicken in butter or margarine in skillet. Remove to
a 9x13 pan lined with heavy-duty aluminum foil. Saute mushrooms
lightly. Add can of soup and milk to mushrooms. Stir until blended.
Sprinkle chicken with herbs, salt and pepper. Pour soup mixture
over chicken in pan. Cover tightly with more aluminum foil. Bake
in 350 degree oven for 1 hour.

Dorothy L. Denitto, Sykesville, Missouri

Oven Fried Chicken with Almonds

1 chicken cut into serving
pieces
1/2 C. sour cream
1 tbsp. lemon juice
1 tsp. celery salt
1 tsp. worcestershire sauce

1/2 tsp paprika
1 clove garlic, crushed
1 tsp. salt
Ground pepper
1 C. finely ground almonds or
bread crumbs

Mix all except chicken and nuts or crumbs. Dip chicken in mixture
and coat with nuts or crumbs. Place in buttered baking dish and
bake at 350 degrees without a cover for 45-60 minutes or until done.

Sesame Chicken

1-3 lb. frying chicken, cut up
1 C. Kraft Catalina salad
dressing
1-1/2 to 2 C. flour

1/4 C. sesame seeds
1 tsp. salt
Cooking oil or shortening

Marinate chicken pieces in salad dressing for several hours or
overnight. Mix flour, sesame seeds and salt in a paper or plastic
bag. Drop pieces of chicken, one at a time, in the bag and shake to
coat well. Heat cooking oil (1-1/2 to 2 inches deep) in large skillet
or dutch oven. Brown chicken on all sides. Reduce heat to low and
cook 30 minutes, or until done.

Joyce Hollin, Monticello, Kentucky

Chicken Paprika

1 medium chicken
1/4 C. oil
2 large onions
1-4oz can sliced mushrooms
1-10oz can condensed tomato
soup diluted with same amount
of water
1 C. sour cream

1/2 green pepper, diced
1 bay leaf
1 tbsp. paprika
1 tsp. black pepper
1/2 tsp. garlic salt
1/2 C. flour
Salt and pepper to taste

Cut up chicken into serving size pieces. Roll pieces in flour and fry
to a golden color on all sides. Remove chicken and lightly brown the
sliced onions. When onions are done, add back the pieces of chicken
and pour the diluted tomato soup, into which you mixed the sliced
mushrooms, diced the green pepper, bay leaf, paprika, black pepper
and garlic salt. Slowly cook 45 minutes. When done, remove from
heat and stir in sour cream. Serve on top of rice or egg noodles and
sprinkle with finely chopped parsley.

J. R. Heil, Winters, California

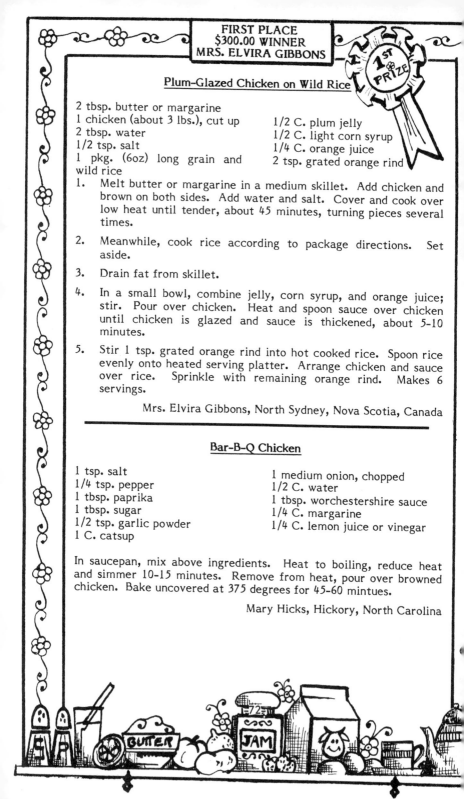

1ST PRIZE

Plum–Glazed Chicken on Wild Rice

2 tbsp. butter or margarine
1 chicken (about 3 lbs.), cut up
2 tbsp. water
1/2 tsp. salt
1 pkg. (6oz) long grain and wild rice

1/2 C. plum jelly
1/2 C. light corn syrup
1/4 C. orange juice
2 tsp. grated orange rind

1. Melt butter or margarine in a medium skillet. Add chicken and brown on both sides. Add water and salt. Cover and cook over low heat until tender, about 45 minutes, turning pieces several times.

2. Meanwhile, cook rice according to package directions. Set aside.

3. Drain fat from skillet.

4. In a small bowl, combine jelly, corn syrup, and orange juice; stir. Pour over chicken. Heat and spoon sauce over chicken until chicken is glazed and sauce is thickened, about 5-10 minutes.

5. Stir 1 tsp. grated orange rind into hot cooked rice. Spoon rice evenly onto heated serving platter. Arrange chicken and sauce over rice. Sprinkle with remaining orange rind. Makes 6 servings.

Mrs. Elvira Gibbons, North Sydney, Nova Scotia, Canada

Bar-B-Q Chicken

1 tsp. salt
1/4 tsp. pepper
1 tbsp. paprika
1 tbsp. sugar
1/2 tsp. garlic powder
1 C. catsup

1 medium onion, chopped
1/2 C. water
1 tbsp. worchestershire sauce
1/4 C. margarine
1/4 C. lemon juice or vinegar

In saucepan, mix above ingredients. Heat to boiling, reduce heat and simmer 10-15 minutes. Remove from heat, pour over browned chicken. Bake uncovered at 375 degrees for 45-60 mintues.

Mary Hicks, Hickory, North Carolina

Easy Teriyaki Chicken

Remove skin from 3 lbs. of cut-up chicken (except for wings). Lay on cookie sheet with fleshy side down. Douse with soy sauce. Sprinkle lightly with onion salt, garlic salt and ginger. Cover lightly with foil. Bake at 250 degrees for 2 hours. Serve with rice.

Joan Rieck, Whitefish Bay, Wisconsin

Drumsticks Parmesan

1 C. crushed packaged herb stuffing
2/3 C. grated parmesan cheese
1/4 C. chopped parsley

1 clove garlic, minced
8 frying chicken drumsticks
1/3 C. melted butter or margarine

Combine herb stuffing, parmesan cheese, parsley and garlic. Dip drumsticks in melted butter; roll in crumb mixture. Place pieces, skin side up and not touching, in greased jelly roll pan. Sprinkle with remaining butter and crumbs. Bake in moderate oven (350-375 degrees) about 1 hour or until done--don't turn.

Anna Mae Pritchyk, Clark Summit, Pennsylvania

Black Dragon Chicken

1 frying chicken, cut up
2 tbsp. worchestershire sauce
2 tbsp. butter or margarine
2 tsp. oil
4 medium green onions, or 1/4 C. chopped onion
1/2 C. water

1/4 tsp. ginger
1/4 tsp. salt
4 medium mushrooms
2 tbsp. water
3 tsp. cornstarch
1/4 C. water

Marinate chicken in worchestershire sauce for 20 minutes, tossing occasionally to coat evenly and thoroughly. Heat butter and oil in a frying pan with a tight fitting lid. Chop onions and set aside. Place chicken in hot fat on medium heat and brown on all sides. Add onions just before browning is complete. Reduce heat and continue cooking chicken for about 5 minutes. Add 1/2 C. water, salt, ginger, mushrooms and leftover worchestershire sauce. Cover with a tight lid. Simmer for 20 minutes or until chicken is done. Remove chicken from pan and set aside. Leave drippings and liquid in pan for sauce. Blend cornstarch with 1/4 C. cool water. Add to pan liquids and bring to a boil. Cook until thickened. Pour sauce over chicken before serving. 3-4 servings.

Risotto–Chicken Polynesian

2 double chicken breasts, boned (or 1 fryer cut into pieces)
1 pkg. Rice-a-Roni Risotto rice mix
Oil
2-3/4 C. water (2-1/2 C. if pineapple juice is used)
1 chicken bouillon cube
8-1/4 oz. can crushed pineapple in heavy syrup
1/4 tsp. ground cloves
1 tsp. sweet basil (measured then crushed)
1/8 tsp. garlic salt
1/8 tsp. chili powder
1/8 tsp. ground ginger
1/2 C. bell pepper, diced (1 small)
1/3 C. raisins

Bring water, bouillon cube, pineapple juice, spices and risotto sauce envelope (inside rice mix) to a boil in a 1-1/2 qt. or 2 qt. saucepan with a tight lid. Meanwhile, bone chicken and heat 2 tbsp. oil in frying pan. Brown chicken. Remove from frypan and place in water mixture in saucepan. Add more oil if necessary, to the frypan and brown rice-vermicelli mixture, stirring until well coated, but not browned. Bring water to boiling; add rice. Turn heat down and simmer for 5 minutes. Add raisins, pepper and crushed pineapple and continue cooking for 15 minutes or until chicken is done and rice is tender.

Chicken Breasts

Bone chicken breasts and coat with sour cream. Roll in crushed cheese crackers and bake in oiled pan at 350 degrees for 30 minutes. Turn over and bake for another 30 minutes.

Adela Conejo, Seguin, Texas

Beany Chicken Bake

1 broiler-fryer chicken, cut in parts
1/2 tsp. each: garlic salt and Durkees Italian Salad seasoning
1/2 C. melted margarine
1-1/2 C. cheese cracker crumbs

Mix first 3 ingredients. Dip each chicken piece in margarine, then coat with cheese crumbs (press down on skin top). Place skin side up on shallow pan. Bake at 350 degrees for 35 minutes. Top with

Baco-Bean Sauce (below). Bake 30-40 minutes until fork can be inserted with ease, sprinkle with parsley.

Baco-Bean Sauce

1 each: 8 oz. pkg. cream cheese (softened) and 10-3/4 oz. can of bean and bacon soup. Stir together until blended.

Mrs. Angeline Martis, Merrillville, Indiana

Chicken Peperonata

2 tbsp. each of oil and butter
3 lb. fryer chicken, cut up and dried
6 sweet bell peppers, green or mixed with red and green when in season
2 medium sized sweet onions, sliced thin

1 garlic clove, minced
1 lb. tomatoes, peeled and chopped, or use canned and cut up
3 tbsp. olive oil
Salt and pepper to taste
1/4 C. chopped fresh basil or 2 tsp. dried

Cut cores from peppers, seed and cut in strips. Season chicken pieces with salt and pepper. Saute in heated oil and butter until browned. In separate skillet, heat the 3 tbsp. olive oil over low heat. Saute onions, do not brown, just soften. Add garlic; heat slowly then add peppers and tomatoes. Add salt and pepper to taste. Add basil. Add to chicken; cover and simmer 25-30 minutes.

Mrs. Libia Foglesong, San Bruno, California

Fried Chicken and Dumplings

After frying chicken golden brown, put in 6 qt. heavy kettle with lid so no steam can escape. Put chicken in oven for 1 hour or until it is done. Just before serving, remove chicken, put in pan and keep warm in oven. Add water to the brownings in the pan until about 1/2 full. Make thickening for gravy from cornstarch adding slowly to chicken juices. Add salt to taste. In mixing bowl mix 2 C. white flour, 3 tsp. baking powder and 1 tsp. salt. Add enough milk to mix together. Bring chicken gravy to boiling and add dumplings by tablespoons until all are added. Put lid on and turn heat down just so it will continue boiling for 12 minutes. Do not open up kettle until time is up. Dumplings will be light and tasty.

Mrs. Ruth M. Hrubes, Wesley, Indiana

Chicken and Dumplings Delight

Boil 1 lb. or so of chicken parts in enough water to cover. Remove chicken from broth. To broth add: 1 can of cream of chicken soup, 1/2 tsp. salt, dash pepper, 1 C. frozen peas (or canned) and 1 small can of mushroom stems and pieces. Stir well, bring to a boil, add dumplings made from biscuit mix. Simmer uncovered 10 minutes. Cover and simmer 10 more minutes. Serve the dumplings and broth over the boned and sliced chicken.

Jean Baker, Chula Vista, California

Chicken Chipper Pie

1-1/2 C. finely crushed potato chips
1/3 C. butter, melted
2 C. cooked, cubed chicken
1 C. finely chopped celery
2oz. can chopped mushroom pieces, drained
2oz. jar chopped pimento
1/2 C. whole kernel corn, drained

10-3/4oz. can condensed cream of chicken soup
1/4 tsp. seasoned salt
1/4 tsp. poultry seasoning
1/4 tsp. curry powder
1 C. crushed potato chips
1/2 C. grated sharp cheddar cheese

Combine 1-1/2 C. potato chips and butter. Press into an ungreased 9" pie pan. Bake at 375 degrees for 5 minutes. Cool. Combine the next 9 ingredients. Pour into the crust. Sprinkle with a mixture of the remaining 2 ingredients. Bake at 375 degrees for 20-25 minutes. Serves 6-8.

Cynthia Kannenberg, Milwaukee, Wisconsin

Chicken (Divan) and Broccoli

1 C. cooked chicken or turkey
1 pkg. frozen chopped broccoli or 1-1/2 C. fresh cooked
1/2 can cream of mushroom soup
1 tsp. chicken bouillon

1/3 C. milk
1/2 C. American or cheddar cheese
1/2 tsp. lemon juice
1/4 tsp. curry powder
3/4 C. buttered bread crumbs

Place broccoli on bottom of baking dish. Then chicken, sauce and buttered crumbs. Bake at 350 degrees for 30 minutes.

Chicken Croquettes

1-1/2 C. leftover turkey or chicken
3 potatoes (medium)
Parsley

Garlic to taste, finely chopped
Salt and pepper to taste
1 egg
Grated peel of one lemon

Grind the leftover meat. Cook the potatoes in boiling water; peel, mash and put through a sieve or a food mill. Add the chopped parsley, garlic, grated lemon peel, salt and pepper. Mix the whole thing with the egg. Form into flat, neat patties that you can hold in your palm. Saute them in a little butter. Makes 3-4 servings.

Arlene Krug, Cedar Rapids, Iowa

Delicious Chicken Casserole

1/2 C. onion, chopped
1/2 C. celery, chopped
1/2 C. green pepper, chopped
2 C. cooked diced chicken
2 slightly beaten eggs
1-1/2 C. milk or 1 C. milk and
1/2 C. broth

1 can condensed cream of mushroom soup
1/2 C. shredded cheese
8 slices bread
3/4 tsp. salt
Dash of pepper
1/2 C. mayonnaise
Butter

Butter 2 slices of bread and cut into cubes; set aside. Place 6 slices of bread in bottom of casserole or pan. Combine onion, celery, green pepper, chicken, salt, pepper and mayonnaise. Combine with bread cubes. Pour over bread in baking dish. Combine eggs, milk and soup. Pour over chicken mixture. Chill about 1 hour. Sprinkle cheese over the top. Bake 1 hour at 325 degrees.

Mrs. Pauline Pepera, Lansing, Michigan

Chinese Chicken

4 slices canned pineapple
3 tbsp. butter
4 tbsp. flour
1-1/2 C. chicken stock
2 C. cooked chicken, diced

1/2 C. celery, sliced
1/2 C. green pepper, minced
1/4 C. almonds
1/4 C. olives
3 C. cooked rice

Chop the pineapple fine. Melt the butter and saute pineapple. Add flour and blend, slowly stir in the chicken broth, and cook until the mixture is thick. Add the chicken, celery, green pepper, and salt (to taste). Cook slowly for 10 minutes. Stir in the almonds. Arrange in the center of a large plate or platter and border with the cooked rice. Garnish with olives.

Amelia M. Brown, Pittsburgh, Pennsylvania

Chicken Jambalaya

1/4 C. margarine	1-1/2 C. cooked, diced chicken
1/2 C. chopped celery	1 tsp. salt
1/2 C. chopped onion	1/4 tsp. pepper
1/2 C. chopped green pepper	1 C. cooked rice
1-1/2 C. chopped tomatoes	1/2 C. soft bread crumbs

Melt 2 tbsp. margarine in skillet. Add celery, onion and green peppers and cook until tender. Add tomatoes, chicken, salt, pepper and rice. Turn into 1 quart baking dish. Melt remaining margarine, mix with crumbs and spread on top. Bake at 350 degrees about 20 minutes.

Grace F. Cantrell, McKenney, Virginia

Chicken Augratin

2 C. leftover chicken or turkey
2 C. thin noodles, cook and drain
4oz. grated (shredded) swiss cheese

Layer ingredients in buttered baking dish.
Sauce: Melt 1/2 C. margarine in pan and add 2 tbsp. onion and heat until soft. Blend in 1/4 C. flour, 2 C. milk, 1/4 tsp. poultry seasoning and 1/4 tsp. curry (if desired). Cook and stir until thick. Beat 1 egg with 1/4 C. milk. Add to rest and heat through. Pour over layers in pan. Top with buttered bread crumbs if desired. Bake at 350 degrees for 25 minutes.

Joan Rieck, Whitefish Bay, Wisconsin

Stuffed Peppers

6 green peppers
1-1/4 C. minced cooked meat
(veal, chicken or ham)
1-1/4 C. moistened bread
crumbs

Salt and pepper
1 tbsp. fat
1/2 onion, grated
1 C. water or stock

Cut a slice from stem end of each pepper. Remove seeds and parboil pepper for 10 minutes. Mix minced meat with bread crumbs. Add salt and pepper, melted fat and onions. Stuff peppers with mixture and place in baking dish. Add water or stock. Bake at 375 degrees for 30 minutes, basting frequently. Serves 6.

Lorena Hockert, Alexandria, Minnesota

Lovely Leftovers

3 C. seasoned mashed potatoes
2 eggs
1/4 C. milk
3 C. leftover sage dressing*

1 C. leftover cooked peas (or
peas and cubed carrots)
3 C. baked chicken or turkey
meat, cut into small pieces

Combine first 3 ingredients and set aside.

* If you do not have dressing leftover, use these ingredients: saute 1 C. chopped onion and 1/2 C. chopped celery in small amount of drippings; add 3 C. soft bread cubes, 1 tsp. sage, 1 tsp. poultry seasoning, 1 tsp. salt and 1/4 tsp. pepper; mix all together well.

Combine other ingredients and mix well; put into buttered baking dish, sprinkle with your favorite grated cheese and a little paprika. Bake at 350 degrees for about 45 minutes or until golden brown and all heated through. Cut in squares and serve with leftover gravy from either the chicken or turkey, or use a can of cream of mushroom (or celery) soup diluted with 1 can milk.

Serve with a crisp vegetable, tossed salad, rolls and butter, and beverage.

Mrs. Henry S. Kubat, Owatonna, Minnesota

Chicken Casserole

2 cans cream of chicken soup
4 chicken breasts (or 4 C.
cooked chicken or turkey)
2 soup cans of broth from
chicken

1 pkg. Stove Top Cornbread
Stuffing
1 stick margarine

Stew chicken, do not salt. Remove from the bones. Melt the margarine and stir in the stuffing mix. Grease a 13x9 dish. Put a layer of dressing crumbs, then chicken, then 1 can soup diluted with one can of broth (reserve some stuffing crumbs for top of casserole). Add another layer of crumbs, then chicken, then the other can of soup diluted with can of broth. Top with reserved stuffing crumbs and bake at 350 degrees until brown (about 45-60 minutes).

Mrs. Jacquita Newberry, Mackinaw, Illinois

Chicken Supreme

4-5 chicken backs
4-5 chicken necks
1/4 C. chopped celery
1/4 C. chopped tomatoes
1/4 C. chopped bellpeppers

1/2 C. chopped lettuce
1/4C. chopped onions
1-1/2 C. Bar-b-que sauce
1 tsp. Heinz 57 sauce

Bring chicken to boil, adding a dash of salt and pepper. Prepare the next 5 ingredients in about 15-20 minutes. Skin chicken and strip the meat from the bone. Cut meat into strips. Add next 5 ingredients; mix well, then add sauce. Heat at 450 degrees for 5-10 minutes. Serve as sandwiches or as you wish.

Mrs. Tarlisa Palmer, Littlerock, Arkansas

Chicken a la King Toastwich

8 slices day old bread, crusts
removed
2 eggs beaten
2-2/3 C. milk
1/3 C. butter
1/3 C. flour

2 C. chopped cooked chicken
3/4 C. cooked mushrooms
1/2 C. chopped celery
2 tbsp. chopped pimento
1 tsp. salt

Cut each slice of bread in half diagonally. Combine beaten eggs and 2/3 C. milk. Dip 8 half slices into egg-milk mixture and arrange into bottom of a 2 qt. shallow baking dish. Melt butter in a heavy saucepan; blend in flour. Add 2 C. milk and bring mixture to boil over medium heat; stirring constantly. Remove from heat; add chicken, mushrooms, celery, pimento and salt. Spoon over bread in bottom of baking dish. Dip remaining bread in egg-milk mixture and arrange over top of the chicken. Bake at 350 degrees for 30 minutes. Serves 8.

Lorena Hockert, Alexandria, Minnesota

Chicken Loaf

1 (5 lb. approx) stewing hen
1 C. cooked white rice
2 C. toasted breadcrumbs
1 C. milk
1/2 C. chopped onion

1 small jar chopped and drained pimentos
4 beaten eggs
1-8oz. can peas (drained)

Cook hen in salted boiling water; take from broth and remove from bones and grind. Reserve 2 C. broth. Combine ground chicken, 2 C. broth, and rest of ingredients. Spoon gently into a lightly greased 9x5 loaf pan. Bake at 375 degrees about one hour or longer until loaf is firm. Serves 8-10.

Jodie McCoy, Tulsa, Oklahoma

Chicken Loaf

1/4 C. butter or margarine
1/2 C. all-purpose flour
1/2 C. milk
1 C. chicken broth
4 C. chopped cooked chicken

2 C. fine dry bread crumbs
2 tbsp. chopped green pepper, cooked
1 tbsp. chopped onion
1 tsp. salt

Preheat oven to 350 degrees. Melt butter or margarine in large heavy saucepan. Blend in flour. Gradually add broth and milk. Cook, stirring constantly until thickened. Stir in remaining ingredients. Spoon into a greased 9x5x5 inch loaf pan and bake 1-1/2 hours or until done.

Arlene Krug, Cedar Rapids, Iowa

Chicken Casserole

4-5 chicken breasts
2 cans cream of chicken soup

Dressing or stuffing

Boil chicken until almost done; then pull all the meat off the bones. Line the bottom of a 9x13" pan with the chicken; put the cream of chicken soup (diluted with water, about 1-1/2 cans) on top of that. Cover with the dressing or stuffing. Cook at 350-400 degrees until dressing or stuffing is brown.

Eva Gail Edmonds, Wellford, South Carolina

Chicken Livers Aloha

1/4 C. margarine
1/2 C. chopped onions
1-1/2 lbs. chicken livers
1 15-1/2oz. can pineapple
chunks, drained
1-1/2 tsp. salt
2 tbsp. cider vinegar

1 C. chopped celery
1 medium green pepper, sliced
2 tbsp. brown sugar
1 tbsp. cornstarch
3/4 C. water
3 C. hot cooked rice

About 30 minutes before serving: In 12-inch skillet over medium heat, in hot margarine, cook celery, onion and green pepper until tender crisp, about 5 minutes. Add chicken livers; cook about 10 minutes longer, stirring, frequently, add pineapple. In small bowl, mix brown sugar, cornstarch and salt; gradually stir in water and vinegar until smooth. Gradually stir into chicken livers and cook, stirring, until thickened. Serve with hot rice.

Mrs. Judy M. Sax, San Antonio, Texas

Fried Chicken Livers

2 lbs. chicken livers
1 large onion, chopped
1 tsp. chopped parsley
1 tsp. oregano

1/2 C. wine
2 tbsp. oil
Salt to taste

Saute onion; add balance of ingredients. Cover and simmer 15 minutes. Serve over spaghetti or rice.

Faye Amendola, New Haven, Connecticut

Oven Fried Chicken and Coating

Mix: 1 C. pancake mix, 2 tsp. salt, 1 tsp. paprika, 1/4 tsp. garlic powder, and 1/4 tsp. pepper. Shake chicken pieces in sack to coat. Lay in pan with 1/2 C. melted margarine; skin side down. Bake 30 minutes at 400 degrees. Turn chicken pieces and bake 30 mintues more.

Jean Baker, Chula Vista, California

Chicken Coating Mix
(Enough for 4 chickens)

2 C. dry bread crumbs (very fine)	4 tsp. paprika
	2 tsp. poultry seasoning
1/2 C. flour	1 tsp. pepper
4 tsp. salt	1/2 C. shortening

Mix bread crumbs, flour, salt, paprika, poultry seasoning and pepper thoroughly. Cut in shortening until mixture resembles coarse crumbs. Place in covered container and store in a cool place. Dip chicken (cut up) in water or milk; then in 1 C. mix until well coated. Place in single layer in ungreased baking dish; uncovered. Bake at 400 degrees for 40-50 minutes. 1 chicken serves 4.

Barbecued Wings

Mix: 1/2 C. catsup, 1/4 C. brown sugar, 1 tbsp. vinegar and 1/2 tsp. ginger. Cut 12 chicken wings in half to make 24 pieces, lay in greased pan and pour sauce over. Bake at 350 degrees for 45-60 minutes.

Jean Baker, Chula Vista, California

Chicken Spread

My daughter bought a very small can of chicken sandwich spread for which she paid $1.09. I bought some turkey wings for 39¢ a lb. and cooked them overnight in the slow cooker. The next day I cooled and boned the meat, cut it into small chunks, added diced pickles, diced celery, a dash of white pepper and onion juice, mixed in enough mayonnaise to moisten and made a 2 lb. margarine bowl of sandwich spread. Spread that was not only cheaper, but better than the bought. You can add chopped boiled eggs if you like or olives, just anything you like in a sandwich spread. Spread. This way you also have that good broth to use. I use it to make stuffing or dressing, in soups, to cook rice in, or noodles. There are many ways to use it.

Jean Baker, Chula Vista, California

New Year's Chicken Champagne Supreme

6 tbsp. butter	2 tbsp. butter
12 whole chicken breasts,	6 tbsp. butter
skinned and boned	6 tbsp. flour
1/2 tsp. poultry seasoning	3 C. half and half
1 C. chicken broth	2 tsp. cracked black pepper
1 C. champagne	1 tsp. seasoned salt
12 mushroom caps	1 tsp. prepared mustard

Heat oven to 325 degrees. Melt 6 tbsp. butter in roasting pan. Add chicken to butter; turn to coat all of the chicken. Arrange the pieces in a single layer in the pan. Sprinkle with the poultry seasoning. Add the broth and the champagne to the pan. Cover pan tightly with foil and bake 40 minutes. Place cooked breasts in 2 oven-proof baking dishes. Reserve 1 C. of the juices. Saute mushroom caps in the 2 tbsp. butter in a skillet over low heat until light brown. Set aside the mushrooms. Add 6 tbsp. butter to the skillet. Stir in the flour. Cook and stir over medium heat for 2 minutes. Add half and half gradually. Cook, stirring constantly, until mixture thickens. Stir in reserved juices gradually. Add cracked pepper, seasoned salt and mustard. Cook until boiling; stirring. Pour over the baked chicken. Bake, covered 30 minutes. Place one mushroom cap on each breast. Bake 5 minutes more.

Cynthia Kannenberg, Milwaukee, Wisconsin

"Free" Stove Top Stuffing

"I freeze leftover cornbread and chicken necks and wing tips (parts that no one eats anyway). When I have enough of each, I make what I call free stove top stuffing." Melt 2-3 tbsp. margarine in large skillet. Saute 1/2 C. each of chopped celery and onion. Add 5-6 C. crumbled cornbread crumbs to skillet and stir to coat. Stir in 2 tbsp. poultry seasoning or sage. Cover with chicken broth (about 3 C.). Simmer until broth is absorbed.

Jean Baker, Chula Vista, California

Turkey Cutlets

Season 1-1/2 C. very thick cream sauce highly with salt, pepper, sage, cayenne, worchestershire, and a little onion juice. Fold in 2 C. chopped turkey. Chill. Shape into flattened cutlets. Dip in flour, then in beaten diluted egg (1 tbsp. water to 1 egg), then in crushed

cornflakes or bread crumbs. Chill for several hours. Fry in deep
390 degree fat. Serve with Poultry Sauce (below). Serves 6.

Poultry Sauce

Stir 1 tbsp. flour into 1-1/2 tbsp. melted butter. Add slowly, stirring
constantly, 1 C. turkey or chicken broth. Reduce heat as low as
possible. Mix together 1 egg yolk and 1/2 C. cream and stir slowly
into the sauce, stirring and cooking until thickened (do not let boil).
Season to taste with salt, sage and lemon juice. Spoon a generous
ribbon of sauce over each cutlet and garnish with paprika and
chopped chives.

Best Ever Turkey Pot Pie

1 recipe of pie crust	1/2 C. cream
2 tbsp. butter	10oz. pkg. peas and carrots
2 tbsp. flour	1 can small onions
2 C. cooked turkey, cut in	1/8 tsp. thyme
pieces	1/2 C. broth (turkey)
1 tsp. salt	

Make crust and put in pie pan; set aside. Melt margarine, blend in
flour, salt, thyme; add broth and cream; cook until thick. Cook and
drain peas and carrots; add to thickened broth. Add turkey pieces
and onions; pour into unbaked shell. Top with crust. Slit to vent.
Bake at 400 degrees for 45 minutes.

Margaret Marvin, East Sparta, Ohio

Stuffed Breast of Turkey

1 small turkey breast (raw or	2 medium apples
leftover, approximately 1-1/2	2 medium size onions
to 2-1/2 lbs)	Salt and pepper to taste
8 thin slices of bacon	

Thinly slice turkey breast and lightly brown if you start with the raw
meat. Line a baking dish or pan with aluminum foil. The size of
dish will depend on the amount of meat available. Place four slices
of bacon in the bottom of lined dish. Place half the amount of
turkey breast over bacon. Thinly slice one onion and layer on top of
meat. Thinly slice one cored apple and lay over onion. Salt and
pepper to taste. Repeat layers; bacon, meat, onion slices, apple
slices, salt and pepper to taste. Cover loosely with foil and bake
one hour at 350 degrees. Serve with brown rice or mashed potatoes.

Margaret Heil, Winters, California

Turkey Squares with Mushroom Sauce

3 C. coarsely chopped cooked turkey
2 C. soft bread crumbs
1 C. water with 1 bouillon cube (chicken)
2/3 C. minced celery

2 tbsp. minced parsley
1 tsp. Accent
3 eggs, slightly beaten
1 tbsp. lemon juice
2 tbsp. instant minced onion
1 tbsp. pimento, chopped

Mix all ingredients together. Season with salt and pepper to taste. Put in baking dish or loaf pan and put in pan of hot water. Bake 50-60 minutes at 350 degrees. Cut into squares and serve with following: 1 can cream of mushroom soup and 2/3 C. milk. Combine soup and milk and cook to boiling point. Simmer 2 minutes, stirring occasionally.

Mrs. William R. Long, Willow Grove, Pennsylvania

Turkey Casserole

3 C. turkey, cubed
1 pkg. noodles (10oz.)
1 can cream of celery soup
1 can cream of chicken soup

1/4 C. margarine or butter
2 C. crushed potato chips (if desired)

Cook the noodles in salted water as directed. In casserole, mix celery soup, mushroom soup, noodles and turkey pieces. Dot margarine over top. Sprinkle crushed chips on top. Bake in 350 degree oven for 30 minutes.

Esther Blatter, McClusky, North Dakota

Turkey Pizza

1/2 pkg. active dry yeast
6 tbsp. warm water
1-1/4 C. biscuit mix
Olive oil
2 C. chopped cooked turkey
1 C. well drained canned tomato pulp
1 can (6oz) tomato paste

1/4 C. finely chopped onion
1 tsp. salt
1/2 tsp. oregano
1/2 tsp. thyme
1/4 tsp. pepper
1/2 lb. mozzarella cheese, sliced

Dissolve yeast in the water. Beat in the biscuit mix. Knead on lightly floured board until smooth. Roll into a round slightly larger than a 12" pizza pan. Place in the pan. Turn extra dough under and scallop or flute the edge. Brush dough with olive oil. Spread turkey over dough. If necessary, season with salt and pepper. Blend tomato pulp with next 6 ingredients. Spread over turkey. Top with cheese. Bake at 450 degrees for 15 minutes or until crust is golden and cheese is bubbly. Serve hot. Cut in wedges. Serves 6-8.

Lorena Hockert, Alexandria, Minnesota

Turkey Goodie

1-1/2 lbs. leftover turkey, diced
1/4 C. flour
1 egg, slightly beaten
1/2 C. bread crumbs
1/4 C. grated parmesan cheese
2-1/2 tbsp. butter or margarine
1/2 tsp. dry mustard

1/4 tsp. salt
1/8 tsp. pepper
1-1/2 tsp. worcestershire sauce
1/2 C. beef broth, canned or bouillon or homemade stock
1 tbsp. chopped parsley, fresh or dried

Cut turkey, coat in flour and then in beaten egg. Coat with mixture of crumbs and cheese. Let stand a few minutes to dry. Brown all quickly, about 2 minutes; keep stirring until all nice and brown. Remove turkey and keep warm. Add butter or margarine to pan and heat. Add mustard, salt, pepper, worcestershire sauce and broth to skillet. Stir to loosen brown bits on bottom of pan. Heat to a boil. Serve this sauce over hot turkey; sprinkle with parsley. Serve with buttered noodles. Serves 4.

Adeline Mazerolas, New York, New York

Hot Turkey

6 slices white bread
1/2 C. chopped onion
1/2 C. chopped celery
3/4 tsp. salt
2 beaten eggs
1 can mushroom soup

2 C. leftover turkey, diced
1/2 C. green pepper, diced
1/2 C. mayonnaise
1-1/2 C. milk
1/2 C. grated cheese

Cube 2 slices of the bread and place in 8x8x2 baking pan. Combine turkey, vegetables, mayonnaise and seasonings and spoon over bread cubes. Trim crusts from remaining bread and arrange slices on top of turkey mixture. Combine eggs and milk and pour over all. Cover and chill for 1 hour, or leave overnight in refrigerator. Spoon soup over top and bake at 325 degrees for about 1 hour or until set. Sprinkle cheese and bake 5 minutes more.

Rosemary Kodunc, Gilbert, Minnesota

Turkey Stroganoff

2 C. leftover turkey pieces (or chicken)
2 C. cooked wide noodles
1 can Golden Cream of Mushroom soup

3/4 soup can of milk
Sliced onions (optional)
1 chicken bouillon cube
1 C. water

Cook water and bouillon until cube is dissolved. Add cut-up turkey pieces and heat slowly. Add onions, if desired. Into a medium size bowl, mix the soup and measure about 3/4 can of milk; blend well. Pour over turkey, blend well. Heat until soup is warm. Add cooked noodles. Serves four.

Roseann Stazinsky, Danville, Pennsylvania

Turkey Stroganoff

1 large onion, chopped (1 C.)
2 tbsp. butter or margarine
2-3 C. julienne strips of cooked turkey

1-1/2 C. turkey gravy or one can (about 11oz) chicken gravy
2 tbsp. catsup (optional)
1 C. dairy sour cream
Parsley noodles

Saute onion in butter or margarine, just until soft, in large frying pan. Stir in turkey or chicken gravy, and catsup; simmer 5 minutes. Stir in sour cream. HEAT JUST TO BOILING. Serve over hot noodles tossed with chopped parsley. Serves 4-6.

Mrs. Teresa Doria, Butler, Pennsylvania

Turkey Loaf

Dissolve 3 pkg. Knox gelatine
in 1 C. cold water and add
8 C. cubed leftover turkey
2 C. water
3 tsp. poultry seasoning

2 tsp. onion salt
2 tsp. celery salt
1/2 tsp. pepper
Salt
3 chicken bouillon cubes

Simmer for a few minutes. Pack into loaf pans. Chill. May be stored frozen.

Mrs. Stanley Ellingson, Wolverton, Minnesota

Turkey Salad

4 C. cooked turkey,
cut in chunks
1 C. coarsely diced celery
1 C. finely diced green pepper
2 tsp. grated onion

1/4 C. light cream
2/3 C. mayonnaise
1 tsp. salt
2 tbsp. vinegar

Combine turkey, celery, green pepper and onion. Blend together cream, mayonnaise, salt and pepper and toss with turkey and chill. Serve on crisp greens. Good for leftover turkey.

Arlene M. Krug, Cedar Rapids, Iowa

Fish Fillets with Cucumber Sauce

32oz. fresh or frozen flounder
or ocean perch fillets
1/2 tsp. salt
1/3 C. butter or margarine
1 tsp. dill weed, or your favorite herb

2 med. cucumbers, scored and
thinly sliced
2 bunches scallions, thinly
sliced
2 tbsp. white wine
1/4 tsp. white pepper

Brush 13x9 inch baking dish with salad oil. Cut fillets into serving
size pieces; place fillets in baking dish; sprinkle with salt. Bake in
450 degree oven for 20-25 minutes until fish flakes easily when
tested with fork. About 10 minutes before fish is done, in 2 quart
saucepan over medium heat, in hot butter or margarine, cook
cucumbers, onion, wine, pepper and dill weed for about 5 minutes,
stirring occasionally. To serve, spoon sauce over and around fish,
we like this dish with mashed potatoes.

Mrs. Judy M. Sax, San Antonio, Texas

Baked Fillets of Fish in Savory Sauce

1 small onion
2 lbs. fillets
3 tbsp. butter
3 tbsp. flour
1 tbsp. prepared mustard

1 tsp. salt
1/8 tsp. pepper
1/2 C. diced cheddar cheese
1-1/2 C. milk

Make white sauce. Add mustard and cheese; stir until cheese melts.
Pour over sliced onions and fillets in baking dish. Bake at 400
degrees for 20 minutes. Slide under broiler to brown top.

Baked Fish with Sour Cream

6 fish fillets
1/2 C. sifted flour
2 tsp. salt
1/4 tsp. pepper

1 tbsp. butter
1-1/2 C. sour milk
3/4 C. sour cream
1 C. buttered bread crumbs

Roll each fillet in mixture of flour, salt and pepper. Arrange in one layer in shallow, buttered baking dish. Pour sour milk over fish. Bake at 350 degrees for 40 minutes until fish is tender and nearly all of milk has been absorbed. Cover with sour cream, top with crumbs and bake at 450 degrees for 10 minutes longer until crumbs are nicely browned.

Stuffed Fillets

Dressing:
2 tbsp. onion, finely chopped
1/4 C. celery, finely chopped

2 tbsp. butter
1/2 C. seasoned bread crumbs
1/4 C. water

Saute celery in butter for a few minutes. Add water and steam for about 3 minutes. Add onion and bread crumbs; toss lightly to mix.

Fillets:
1 lb. fillets
1 tbsp. worchestershire sauce

1-1/2 tsp. lemon juice
Butter
Fresh parsley, finely chopped

Stir worchestershire and lemon juice together in a small bowl. With pastry brush, coat each side of the fillets with the sauce. Lay fillets out flat. Divide stuffing according the size of fillets and place stuffing on the largest end of fillet. Roll fish around stuffing. Place end down on bottom of buttered baking dish. Top each fillet with chopped parsley and dot with butter. Bake at 400 degrees for 20 minutes.

Fish Fillets, Spanish-Style

1-1/2 lbs. fish fillets
1 medium onion, sliced
3 tbsp. oil or shortening
2 tbsp. all-purpose flour
1-1/4 C. canned tomato juice
or canned tomatoes

1/2 green pepper, minced
1 tsp. salt
Dash black pepper
1/2 tsp. sugar
1 bay leaf

Cook onion in oil or shortening until tender; stir in flour. Add all remaining ingredients except fish, and simmer, stirring constantly, until thickened. Remove bay leaf. Arrange fish fillets in a shallow baking dish and cover with sauce. Bake uncovered at 350 degrees for 30 minutes, or until fish flakes readily when tested with a fork. 6 servings.

Fillets Elegante

1 lb. pkg. frozen fish fillets
1 tbsp. butter or margarine
Dash pepper
1 can condensed cream of
shrimp soup

1/4 C. shredded parmesan
cheese
Paprika

Thaw fish fillets (sole, haddock, halibut or cod) enough to separate. Arrange in buttered 9-inch pie plate. Dash with pepper and dot with butter. Spread soup over fillets and sprinkle with cheese and paprika. Bake at 400 degrees for 25 minutes. Serve with lemon wedges. Serves 4.

Anna Mae Pritchyk, Clarks Summit, Pennsylvania

Budget Scallop Creole

1 tbsp. cooking oil
1 tbsp. butter
1/2 C. onion, chopped
1/2 C. green pepper, chopped
1/4 tsp. garlic salt
1 can tomato soup
1/2 can water

1/2 tsp. paprika
1/2 tsp. salt
1/4 C. basil, crushed
1 large bay leaf
1/2 lb. fresh or frozen
(thawed) scallops, not breaded
4 servings of rice

Prepare rice. Heat oil and butter in skillet. Add onion and pepper and brown lightly. Add tomato soup, garlic salt, paprika, salt, basil and bay leaf. Cover and simmer for 15 minutes. Cut scallops into 3/4 inch pieces. Add scallops to tomato sauce after the 15 minute cooking period. Simmer 7 minutes more. Remove bay leaf. Serve over rice.

Cheap Chowder

In a large kettle, fry out the *pork fat (a good sized piece, diced). Add 2 coarsely minced onions, 6 diced potatoes, salt and pepper, a cup or more of flaked leftover fish. Cover with boiling water, thicken slightly with a tbsp. each of flour and butter melted together. Simmer until the potatoes are tender, stir in a quart of warm milk, 2 tbsp. butter or margarine, heat and serve. For variation, try canned tomato soup diluted with water to cook the potatoes and onions in. Add thickened milk and heat. *I use fatback which is a lot less expensive in recipes calling for salt pork. It works as well and you don't get the added salt. You can make a very good fish chowder with leftover fish and one good slice of fatback.

Jean Baker, Chula Vista, California

Seafood Casserole with Corn Chips

3 C. of corn chips (1 C. for topping)
1-1/2 lb. of flaked fish (catfish is especially good)
3 tbsp. oil
1/2 C. chopped onion

2 tbsp. flour
1 tsp. salt
1 can cream of shrimp soup
1/2 C. milk
1 pkg. frozen peas (may be partially cooked)

Cook the flaked fish and the onion in the oil until fish is crumbly. Add the salt, flour and stir well. Then add the soup, milk and peas. Put 2 C. of chips in the bottom of a 12x15 inch baking dish. Pour in the fish mixture and after crushing the remaining cup of chips, spread them over the casserole. Bake for 1 hour at 350 degrees.

Mrs. Joy Parrish, Stamping Ground, Kentucky

Tuna Rounds with Sauce

1 6-1/2oz can tuna
1 can celery soup
2-1/2 C. soft bread crumbs
1/2 C. milk
2 tbsp. minced parsley flakes
1/2 tsp. lemon juice
1/2 tsp. onion powder
1/8 tsp. pepper
1/4 tsp. basil
1/2 tsp. paprika
1 tsp. Beau Monde Seasoning
2 eggs

Flake tuna. Add remaining ingredients as listed. Place in a covered container in refrigerator for approximately 2 hours. Pour tuna mixture in a larger container and hand mix again. Bake in greased muffin pan (be sure to grease bottom and sides) and bake at 350 degrees for 20-25 minutes.

Sauce:
2 tbsp. butter
2 tbsp. onion powder
2 tbsp. flour
1-1/2 C. strained cooked tomatoes
1/8 tsp. salt
1/8 tsp. pepper

Melt butter, add onion powder, blend in flour and brown, slightly. add strained cooked tomatoes gradually and heat to boiling, stirring constantly 3-4 minutes. Add salt and pepper and serve hot over tuna rounds. This makes 1-1/4 cups.

Mrs. John Eudy, Des Moines, Iowa

Tuna Noodle Crisp

4oz. uncooked noodles (cooked)
1/4 C. shortening
1/3 C. chopped onion
2 tbsp. chopped green pepper
1 10-1/2oz. can cheese soup
1 can (6-1/2 or 7oz) tuna
1/2 C. milk
1 tbsp. pimento
1 tsp. salt
1/2 tsp. pepper
1/2 C. bread crumbs

Add onion and green pepper to melted shortening and cook until tender. Stir in soup, milk, pimento, salt and pepper and bring to boil. Add cooked noodels and tuna. Place in quart casserole dish, sprinkle with bread crumbs. Bake at 350 degrees for 25-30 minutes.

Mary M. West, Columbia, Tennessee

Tuna Luncheon Salad

1 envelope plus 1/4 tsp.
unflavored gelatin
1/4 C. water
2 C. mayonnaise
2 can water-packed tuna
drained

2 hard boiled eggs (chopped)
1/2 C. celery (cut very fine)
3/4 C. tiny peas (drained)
1/2 C. stuffed olives (chopped)

Mix gelatin with cold water, then set in a bowl of hot water to dissolve. Blend warm gelatin into mayonnaise, then add remaining ingredients and mix well. Pour into mold rinsed with cold water and chill until set.

Mrs. Carol Bradley, Fort Dodge, Iowa

Tuna Patties in Sauce

2 C. biscuit mix
1/2 tsp. celery salt
1 egg
2/3 C. canned milk
1 tbsp. lemon juice

1 can tuna (7oz)
1 tbsp. minced onion
1 tbsp. minced bell pepper
1 tbsp. minced parsley

Mix all ingredients together. Heat a small amount of oil in skillet and drop mixture by tbsp. into oil and brown both sides. Add 2 C. of medium white sauce and heat. Serve warm with mashed potatoes or rice.

Jean Baker, Chula Vista, California

Tuna Loaf

2 (7oz) cans tuna drained and
flaked
1 can cream of celery soup
3/4 C. cracker crumbs

1/2 C. bread crumbs
1/4 C. evaporated milk
4 eggs
1/4 tsp. salt and pepper

Preheat oven to 350 degrees. Combine all ingredients in a bowl; mix until well blended. Spoon into a greased loaf pan (9x4x3). Bake 45-50 minutes or until done. Cool and slice for main dish or sandwiches.

Arlene Krug, Cedar Rapids, Iowa

Tuna Pie

2 (7oz) cans tuna, drained
3 tbsp. salad dressing
3 tbsp. dairy sour cream
1 tbsp. chopped pimento
1 small onion, sliced very thin
and separated into individual
rings

3-4 potatoes cooked and
mashed
1 C. grated cheddar cheese
packed lightly

Flake tuna and stir into it the salad dressing, sour cream, chopped pimento and onion. Spread mixture over bottom of ungreased 9-inch pie pan. Gently top with mashed potatoes. Sprinkle generously with grated cheese. Put into pre-heated 375 degree oven for about 15 mintues or until cheese has melted. Let stand at room temperature about 5 mintues, then cut into wedges and serve. Serves 5 generously.

Jodie McCoy, Tulsa, Oklahoma

Frozen Tuna Sandwiches

1 can tuna
1 7-1/2oz can cream of mushroom soup
Chopped onion

12 slices bread
Crushed potato chips
Egg, slightly beaten

Mix drained tuna, soup and chopped onion together. Divide between 6 slices of bread. Top with remaining bread slices. Wrap individually in foil and freeze. When wanted, take out desired number of sandwiches and cut in half. Dip frozen sandwiches in egg and then in crushed potato chips. Place on buttered cookie sheet. Bake at 350 degrees for 25-30 minutes, turning once.

Other meats may be used in place of tuna. Also a slice of cheese may be put on filling before top bread slice.

Mrs. Gerald Hesse, Sioux City, Iowa

Tuna (or Chicken) Pie

1 C. tuna (or cooked chicken)
2 C. diced potatoes
2 C. diced carrots
1 onion, chopped
1 C. peas

2 C. milk
4 tbsp. flour
4 tbsp. fat
Salt and pepper

Cook vegetables in water. Make white sauce of flour, fat and milk. Add vegetables and tuna to white sauce. Place in baking dish and cover with biscuit dough. Bake at 400 degrees until crust is done (or serve as a sauce over bisquits, rice or toast).

Fish Shortcake

Thicken mushroom soup to the consistency of medium white sauce. Add a pimento cut in strips and canned tuna fish or salmon. Heat until piping hot. Serve over hot biscuits.

Herb Salmon Bake

2 C. herb-seasoned croutons
1 tall can (16oz) salmon, re-move skins and bones
2 C. grated (1/2 lb.) cheddar cheese

4 eggs
2 C. milk
1/2 tsp. worcestershire sauce
1/2 tsp. dry mustard
1 tsp. salt

Alternate layers of croutons, salmon, and cheese in a 1-1/2 quart casserole or 8-inch baking dish. Beat eggs slightly, add milk, worcestershire sauce, mustard and salt, and mix well. Pour over ingredients in baking dish. Bake in a moderate oven (350 degrees) for 1 hour or until knife inserted near center comes out clean. Serves 4 generously.

Mrs. D. C. Brown, Pittsburgh, Pennsylvania

Salmon on the Half Shell

8 shells cleaned and oiled
1 can (16oz) salmon, remove
skin and bone
Juice of 1 lemon
1 C. mashed potato

1/2 C. cracker crumbs
2 eggs, beaten
1/2 tsp. black pepper
1 small onion, minced fine
1 tbsp. melted butter

Mix lightly salmon, lemon juice, potato, cracker crumbs, eggs, pepper, onion and butter. Pile in shells. Wet fingers with water. Smooth tops of salmon mixture. Bake in moderate oven (350 degrees) 35-50 minutes, or until well puffed up and golden brown.

Mrs. D. C. Brown, Pittsburgh, Pennsylvania

Lamb Casserole

1 pkg. (8oz) shell macaroni
2 C. diced cooked lamb
1 can condensed cream of
celery soup
1 (4oz) can sliced mushrooms

1/2 C. milk
1/2 tsp. rosemary
Salt and pepper to taste
1/2 C. grated parmesan cheese

Cook macaroni in boiling salted water; drain. Meanwhile combine the next 7 ingredients and mix well. Mix with macaroni. Turn into 2-qt. casserole. Sprinkle with cheese. Bake at 350 degrees about 35 minutes. Serves 6.

Lorena Hockert, Alexandria, Minnesota

Corned Beef and Cabbage

5 medium size potatoes, thinly
sliced
1 small onion, chopped
1 tsp. salt
1/2 tsp. pepper

4 C. shredded cabbage
1 can corned beef
1 can cream of celery soup
1-1/2 C. milk

Place potatoes in baking dish. Cover with onion, salt and pepper. Add shredded cabbage. Crumble corned beef and spread over cabbage. Cover with celery soup diluted with milk. Cover and bake at 375 degrees for 1-1/2 hours. Makes 5 servings.

Mrs. Teresa Doria, Butler, Pennsylvania

Rueben Casserole

12oz. corned beef (shredded)
canned or leftover
16oz. can sauerkraut
1/4 C. catsup
1/4 C. thousand island dressing

1-1/2 C. seasoned croutons
6oz. pkg. swiss cheese
(shredded)
1/4 tsp. salt
1/4 tsp. pepper

Line corned beef on bottom of baking dish. Mix sauerkraut, catsup, dressing, salt and pepper together. Lay on top of beef. Sprinkle cheese on top, then add croutons. Bake in 400 degree oven for 25-30 minutes. Serves 7-8.

Barbara Moore, Rock Island, Illinois

-99-

Tasty Liver and Onions

1 lb. liver (or 1/4 lb. per person)
1 large onion

1/4 C. flour
1 tsp. salt
Pepper
Oil

Cover bottom of frying pan with oil. Heat oil in frying pan. Fry onions for a few minutes. Mix flour, salt and pepper. Coat liver with flour mixture. Push onions to side of pan. Fry liver on each side until well browned. Turn down heat. Cover liver and cook ten minutes or until completely done.

Liver and Onion Gravy

Coat 6-8 slices of liver with flour (I also fix round steak this way). Melt 3 tbsp. shortening in skillet and brown meat. Add one envelope of dry onion soup mix and 3-4 C. warm water. Cover skillet and simmer for 1 hour. Serve with rice or mashed potatoes.

Jean Baker, Chula Vista, California

Savory Liver Kabobs

3/4 lb. liver
1/2 tsp. worchestershire sauce
1/4 tsp. Lawrey's seasoned salt
8 slices bacon

1 small onion, cut in wedges
8 mushrooms
1 small green pepper, cut in wedges

Remove outside membranes and veins from liver. Cut into 1-inch pieces. Sprinkle and toss with worcestershire sauce and seasoned salt to coat evenly. Let stand while vegetables are prepared. Starting with bacon, thread liver, mushrooms, onion and pepper on skewers, bending bacon accordion fashion around each. Broil in mid-oven position until bacon is crisp, about 5 minutes. Turn to brown other side and evenly cook thoroughly. Serve with rice or buttered noodles. Makes 4 large or 8 small kabobs. Serves 4.

Corn Fritter Dogs

1-1/4 C. unsifted flour
3 tsp. baking powder
1 tbsp. sugar
1/2 tsp. salt
3 eggs beaten

1 pkg. instant potatoes (2oz)
2 tbsp. oil
4 hot dogs, diced
1 C. corn, drained
1 C. milk, approx.

Combine all ingredients and drop in hot oil, frying until golden brown, turning to brown evenly, drain on paper towels.

Mary P. Bossen, Davenport, Iowa

Corn Dogs

Mix:
1 C. biscuit mix
1/2 C. yellow corn meal

1 egg, beaten
3/4 C. milk

Dip hot dogs into batter and deep fry in oil until brown. Serve hot with dip. Makes 6-8 corn dogs.

Dip:
3/4 C. catsup
2 tsp. mustard
1/4 tsp. garlic powder

Jean Baker, Chula Vista, California

Franks and Potato Bake

1 pkg. (16oz.) franks
1 can cream of onion soup
(undiluted)

1/2 C. milk
1/2 tsp. salt
4 C. sliced potatoes

In bowl, combine soup, milk and salt. Cut hot dogs lengthwise and then in half. Alternate with hot dogs, soup mixture and potatoes. Cover and bake at 350 degrees for 1-1/2 hours. During the last 1/2 hour, take cover off and let brown.

Loretta Natale, Madison, New Jersey

Mexican Franks

6-8 frankfurters, sliced into
1/2-inch slices
1 onion, chopped
1 pkg. French's Sloppy Hot
Dog Seasoning Mix
1/2 C. water
1-15oz. can tomato sauce

1-8oz. can kidney beans
1-10oz. pkg. frozen corn
(canned can be used)
2 C. uncooked noodles
2 tsp. green bell pepper flakes
1/8 tsp. majoram
1-2 tsp. chili powder (optional)

Combine tomato sauce, water, seasoning mix and bell pepper flakes in a bowl and set aside. Cook frankfurters and onion in 1 tbsp. oil in a large skillet until onion is tender and meat is brown. Stir in liquid; then add corn, beans, and noodles. Bring to a boil; reduce heat and cover and simmer for 20-25 minutes or until noodles are tender. Serves 4-6. NOTE: Use 1-1/2 to 2 C. cubed pork, beef or chicken leftovers in place of franks. 1 C. rice in place of noodles.

Joyce Cunningham, Alliance, Ohio

Hash Brown Dogs

1 hot dog per person
1/4 to 1/2 lb. potatoes per
person

1 medium onion
1/2 C. flour for 2 lbs. potatoes

Chop hot dogs. Peel potatoes and place in salad shredder. Shred onion. Place potatoes, onion and hot dog in bowl and add flour. Mix together and fry on each side until light brown and desired doneness. Do not cover pan and do not salt until after cooking or potatoes will be sticky. Note: Jerusalem artichokes may be prepared same way as potatoes. Do not peel. Artichoke hash brown will be darker brown but much like potato hash browns in flavor.

Jim Cherry, age 11 when recipe developed, Pittsburgh, Illinois

Bologna Stretcher

Run a pound of bologna through the food grinder, add a couple of diced hard boiled eggs and pickles, onions and bell pepper (whatever you like in a sandwich). Mix with enough mayonnaise or salad dressing to moisten.

Jean Baker, Chula Vista, California

California Salsaghetti

2 tbsp. corn oil
i lb. lean ground beef
4-5 onions, sliced
1/4 green pepper, chopped coarsely
3-4 cloves garlic, minced
1-8oz. can tomato sauce

1-6oz. can tomato paste
1 small can green chili salsa
1 tbsp. chili powder
1 tsp. salt
Pepper (to taste)
2 C. water
1/4 lb. sliced fresh mushrooms

In a 4-quart pressure cooker, place <u>all</u> ingredients. Mix lightly to combine. Place cover on and cover securely. Bring mixture to point where boiling occurs. Place pressure regulator on vent and, when rocking begins, cook for 30 minutes. Uncover and cook slowly for 30 minutes to thicken. Delicious served over whole wheat or regular spaghetti. Fresh grated parmesan is an added touch.

Fran Golomb, Tujunga, California

Florentine Macaroni Bake

1 7-1/4oz. pkg. macaroni and cheese dinner
1-8oz. pkg. cream cheese (cubed)
1-10oz. pkg. frozen chopped spinach (cooked and drained)

6 crispy cooked bacon slices (crumbled)
2 eggs, beaten
1/4 tsp. salt
Dash of pepper

Prepare dinner as directed on package, except omit margarine. Add cream cheese and stir over low heat until smooth. Add the remaining ingredients; mix well. Pour into a 9-in pan. Bake at 350 degrees for 30 minutes. Let stand 5 minutes before serving. 6 servings.

Betty Belair, Cumberland, Rhode Island

-103-

Saucy Turkey Manicotti

6 manicotti shells
1-3oz. pkg. cream cheese, softened
1/4 C. milk
1-3oz. can chopped mushrooms, drained
1 tbsp. snipped parsley
1 envelope cheese sauce mix
1 tbsp. instant minced onion
1 envelope sour cream sauce mix
1/4 C. grated parmesan cheese
2 C. leftover diced cooked turkey or chicken

Cook manicotti shells in large amount of boiling salted water until tender, 15-20 minutes; drain. Combine onion and 2 tbsp. water; let stand 5 minutes. Stir together cream cheese, sour cream sauce mix, and milk. Stir in onion, mushrooms, parsley, 1/4 tsp. salt and 1/8 tsp. pepper; add turkey. Spoon into shells. Arrange in single layer in 10x6x2-inch baking pan. Prepare cheese sauce mix according to package directions; pour over manicotti. Sprinkle with parmesan cheese. Cover and bake in 350 degree oven for 35-40 minutes or until heated through.

Karen Colmer, Mansfield, Illinois

Pasta Casserole

Amounts will vary with family size and tastes. You can make your own tomato sauce, use the prepared sauce, or use V-8 juice slightly thickened, can also use cream of chicken or mushroom soup in place of tomato sauce. The following is how I do mine when I have fresh vegetables on hand.

Sauce: (I make enough to freeze for various uses, however, six large tomatoes will make about 4 cups of sauce.)

Peel ripe tomatoes by dipping in hot water, then in cold water, slip off skins. Cut up and put in blender. In large saucepan, melt 2-3 tbsp. of oil or margarine and saute chopped onion and garlic. Add pureed tomatoes and about 1/2 C. water, little salt, bit of sugar, bay leaf and little Italian seasoning. Simmer for an hour or so, as it will cook down a little. I add a bit of lemon juice to the finished sauce. (This sauce is milder than purchased)

Ingredients: You can use vegetables of your own selection. You can use spaghetti, macaroni or noodles. You can use ground beef or other chopped cooked meat. I do the following:

Cook Spaghetti: While cooking spaghetti, I cook ground beef in a frying pan with 2-3 tbsp. of oil or margarine, then add finely grated, chopped vegetables, such as carrots, celery, green onions

-104-

with tops, garlic, zucchini, mushrooms and green pepper and saute a few minutes.

To the drained pasta, to which was added a small piece of butter to keep from sticking, I added the sauteed vegetables and sauce to moisten.

Spoon into lightly buttered casseroles (if more than one). Top with parmesan cheese. Bake in moderate oven until heated through.

Mrs. A. Jackson, Niland, California

Egg Lasagna

Cook 1/2 C. diced onion and 2 chopped garlic cloves in 1 tbsp. oil for 3 minutes. Add 8oz. chopped tomatoes, 8oz. tomato sauce and 1 tbsp. Italian seasoning; simmer 30 minutes. Cook 5 lasagna noodles and drain. Mix 1/4 C. parmesan cheese, 1 C. cottage cheese, 1 egg and salt and pepper to taste. In 8" square pan, layer noodles with cheese and sauce adding 4 sliced cooked eggs. End with sauce. Top with 6oz. of mozzarella cheese, sliced. Bake for 30 minutes at 350 degrees. Let stand 10 minutes. Serves 4.

Joan LeViness, Winsted, Connecticut

Turkey Tertrozzine

1/4 C. butter or margarine	1-1/2 C. cooked spaghetti
1/4 C. all-purpose flour	1/2 C. mushrooms
2 C. milk	1/4 C. chopped pimento
1-1/2 tsp. salt	3/4 C. shredded cheddar
1/8 tsp. pepper	cheese
1-1/2 C. diced cooked turkey	3/4 C. dry bread crumbs
	Melted butter or margarine

Mix 1/4 C. butter in heavy pan; add flour and stir until blended. Gradually add milk and cook over low heat for 5 minutes, stirring constantly. Add seasoning. Combine this white sauce with turkey, spaghetti, mushrooms, pimento and cheese. Place in buttered 2-quart casserole. Combine bread crumbs and melted butter and sprinkle over top. Bake at 325 degrees for about 25 minutes or until well browned. 6 servings.

Arlene Krug, Cedar Rapids, Iowa

Spaghetti Supreme
(8 servings)

1-1/2 lbs. ground beef
1 tbsp. butter or margarine
3 cans (8oz each) tomato
sauce
1 tsp. salt
1/4 tsp. pepper
1 C. cottage cheese
1 pkg. (8oz.) cream cheese,
softened

1/4 C. sour cream
1/2 C. thinly sliced green
onions and tops
1 tbsp. finely chopped green
pepper
1 pkg. (7oz.) thin spaghetti,
cooked and drained
2 tbsp. butter, melted

Brown beef lightly in 1 tbsp. butter in a large skillet; add tomato sauce, salt and pepper. Remove from heat. Beat cottage cheese, cream cheese, and sour cream until blended. Stir in onions and green pepper. Spread half of spaghetti in a shallow 2-quart baking dish. Top with cheese mixture, then remaining spaghetti. Dribble butter over all. Cover with meat sauce. Bake at 350 degrees for 45 minutes.

Eleanor Allen, South Bend, Indiana

Pasta with Spicy Red Clam Sauce

1 pkg. spaghetti (1 lb. size)
3 tbsp. oil (olive oil is best)
1 clove garlic, crushed
1 tsp. each of thyme and oregano, crushed
1 can baby clams (10oz. size),
drain and hold aside liquid

1/2 C. chopped onion
1 can ground tomatoes, or use
whole and chop up more (1 lb.
size)
1 can green chile salsa (7oz.
size)
Parsley for garnish

Cook pasta as package directs, using plenty of boiling water. In skillet, heat oil and saute onion and garlic over low heat to soften onion, do not burn. Add tomatoes, green chile salsa and juice from drained clams. Simmer over brisk heat for 15 minutes to slightly thicken sauce. Add the clams, blend well and heat all for a few minutes. Have drained spaghetti ready in heated platter and pour on sauce and combine. Sprinkle top with chopped parsley and serve.

Mrs. Libia Foglesong, San Bruno, California

Pale Lasagna

1/2 lb. ground beef
Chopped onion
1 can cream of mushroom soup
1-2oz. can mushrooms

Granulated bouillon
Uncooked lasagna noodles
Grated cheese

Brown ground beef with onion until done. Meanwhile, mix soup, undrained mushrooms, 1-2 tsp. bouillon and enough water to make 3 C. Add to beef and bring to a boil. Butter a 7x11 glass baking dish. Put a thin layer of sauce in pan, then a layer of uncooked noodles. Continue layering, making 3-4 layers ending with sauce. Top with cheese. Make sure sauce covers top layer by pushing down lightly. If more liquid is needed, add a mixture of water and bouillon. Mixture will be very thin, but noodles will absorb it as it cooks. Cover with a piece of wax paper, then foil. Seal tightly. Bake at 350 degrees about 1 hour and 15 minutes. Remove from oven and leave covered. Let sit at least 15 minutes and as much as 30 minutes. The longer it sits, the firmer it becomes. 4 servings.

Mrs. Gerald Hesse, Sioux City, Iowa

Macaroni Saute

1-1/3 C. macaroni (uncooked)
1/2 tsp. oregano, measure, crush
1/4 tsp. garlic salt
5 franks, sliced

1 medium green pepper, sliced thinly
1/2 medium onion
1-16oz. tomato sauce
Salt
2 tbsp. oil

Cook macaroni until almost done. Saute onion and pepper in oil until slightly cooked. Add all ingredients to macaroni; simmer 15 minutes.

Macaroni and Cheese Plus

1-8oz. pkg. elbow macaroni
2 C. shredded cheddar cheese
1 C. bread crumbs

1 egg
2 C. milk
Salt and pepper to taste

Preheat oven to 325 degrees. Boil macaroni according to directions on package. Drain macaroni and put half of it in a casserole dish. Sprinkle over it half of the cheese, half of the bread crumbs, the salt and pepper. Add rest of macaroni and top with remaining bread crumbs and cheese. Beat egg into milk and pour over macaroni. Bake for about an hour until light brown on top. Recipe can be used as above or if desired, tuna, leftover ham, chicken. etc. can be added.

Margie Pulick, Yonkers, New York

Pasta Fazel (Italian Soup)

Serve topped with parmesan cheese and fresh hard crusted Italian bread on the side.

1 large can tomato paste	2 C. of ditalini macaroni or
1/2 C. oil	elbow macaroni
1 tsp. basil	1 large can of great northern
1 C. tomato juice	beans drained and rinsed or
3 C. of water	3 C. cooked beans
2 cloves of garlic, cut in half	Salt to taste
	Parmesan cheese

In 5-quart saucepan, put oil, tomato paste, basil, tomato juice, water, garlic and mix well. Simmer for 1 hour. In the meantime, cook macaroni in salted water until almost done, drain and rinse. Open can of great northern beans, drain and rinse in cold water. Add beans and macaroni to tomato mixture, stir; add salt to taste. Pan should be full to within 1-inch from top; if not, add water to fill. Let simmer 15 minutes. Serve hot sprinkled with parmesan cheese.

Eleanor Shelley, Youngstown, Ohio

Baked Rice

1 C. rice, raw
1/2 C. oil
1 onion, chopped
1 can consomme soup

1/3 C. water
1/2 tsp. salt
1/2 tsp. oregano

Mix well and pour into greased covered dish. Bake 1 hour at 325 degrees.

Mary Biller, Willard, Ohio

Baked Rice (Meatless)

3 C. cooked rice
1/2 C. grated cheese
1/4 C. chopped pimento
1-1/2 C. tomato juice
1-1/2 tsp. salt

Dash of black pepper
2 C. corn flakes, crushed
slightly
2 tbsp. butter, melted

Combine rice, cheese, pimento, juice and seasonings. Pour into oiled 1-1/2 quart casserole. Mix corn flakes with melted butter. Sprinkle over rice. Bake in 350 degrees oven for 30 minutes until well heated. Serve at once. 6 servings of 2/3 C. each.

Miss Adela Conejo, Seguin, Texas

Fried Rice with Egg and Bacon

Heat in skillet: 2 tbsp. salad oil and 1 C. cooked, chopped bacon or ham. Stir in 6 eggs, slightly beaten and 2 C. cold cooked rice (measure 2/3 C. uncooked). Brown over slow heat, stirring often. Serves 6.

Fried Rice

Mix 2-3 C. cooked cold rice, 2 green onions, chopped (or use regular onion) and 1 C. or more of diced leftover meat (chicken, pork, fish, ham, etc.). Heat in oiled skillet. Add about 1 tbsp. soy sauce and one fried egg chopped. Heat and serve. Add small amounts of leftover vegetables if desired.

Jean Baker, Chula Vista, California

Rice with Sausage

1 lb. sweet sausage
3 tbsp. olive oil
3 tbsp. butter
1/2 C. chopped onion
2 tbsp. grated cheese
1-1/2 C. raw rice

1-1/2 tsp. salt
2 C. Italian tomatoes
1-1/2 C. hot water
1/2 tsp. basil
1 clove garlic

Cut sausage in 1-inch pieces; brown and drain. Heat oil and one tbsp. butter; saute onion and garlic. Stir in rice until transparent. Add tomatoes, half the water, salt and basil. Cover; cook over low heat for 20 minutes. Add remaining water occasionally; stir in remaining butter, cheese and sausage. Cook 5 minutes longer. Serves 6.

Faye Amendola, New Haven, Connecticut

Pronto Spanish Rice

8-10 frankfurters, diced
2-8oz. cans tomato sauce with onions (or plain plus 1 onion chopped)
1-1/4 C. water

1/2 tsp. salt
1 tsp. chili powder
2 tbsp. chopped green pepper
1 C. raw rice
1/2 C. grated cheese

Cook franks, green pepper and onion in skillet until peppers are soft. Stir in remaining ingredients, except cheese. Bring to boil; stir. Cover and simmer 30 minutes. Stir in cheese before serving.

Mary M. West, Columbia, Tennessee

Tasty Chili Con Carne with Beans

2 tbsp. olive oil or salad oil
1-1/2 lbs. ground chuck
1 medium size onion, chopped
2 cloves garlic, minced
1 bell pepper, chopped
1 large can ground tomatoes,
or whole tomatoes, chopped
(1lb., 12oz.)
1 can tomatoes with green
chiles (10oz. size)

1 small jar or can green
chiles, drained and chopped
4 C. cooked beans, pinto or
kidney beans, drained
1/2 C. red wine
2 tbsp. oregano
3 tbsp. chili powder
1 tsp. cumin powder
Salt and pepper to taste

Use heavy pot like dutch oven. Heat the oil and add beef stirring to break up. Add onion and garlic; cook all until no pink in meat. Add chopped bell pepper; cook 1 minute more. Add all the rest of ingredients and bring to simmer on low heat; let simmer 40 minutes until nicely thickened. Test for salt and pepper. Can be served with shredded cheddar cheese on top. Serve with crackers.

Mrs. Libia Foglesong, San Bruno, California

Bargain Bean and Hamhock Soup

1 lb. small white navy beans or
great northern beans
1 lb. hamhocks
2 onions, medium size,
chopped
3 tbsp. oil

2 tbsp. chopped fresh parsley
1 can green chile salsa (7oz.)
1/2 tsp. allspice
1 bay leaf
1 tsp. hungarian paprika
Salt and pepper to taste

Soak beans overnight in water to cover; drain. In heavy pot, saute onions and parsley in oil until onions are limp. Add beans and hamhocks with plenty of water to cover; about 2-1/2 quarts. More water may be needed as soup simmers. Add seasonings and green chile. Simmer for 1-1/2 hours. Take hamhocks out and dice in small pieces and return to soup. Simmer 1/2 hour more and check for seasonings. Serve with plenty of french bread or plain croutons.

Mrs. Libia Foglesong, San Bruno, California

Baked Lima Beans

1 lb. dry lima beans
1/2 lb. bacon, cut up
3/4 C. brown sugar
1 can tomato soup

2 tbsp. prepared mustard
1 green pepper, chopped
1 medium onion, chopped

Cook beans until done; drain off most of liquid. Mix all ingredients together. Bake in 9x13 cake pan for 1-1/2 hours at 350 degrees. Serves 8-10.

Mrs. Clifford Heller, Mt. Morris, Illinois

Imitation Sausage

2 C. cooked blackeyed peas
1/2 tsp. sausage seasoning
1 raw egg
Dried red pepper to taste

1/8 C. finely grated onion (optional)
1/3-1 '2 C. flour or amount necessary to make mixture hold together and able to shape into patties

Mash peas to a consistency of coarse sausage. Add rest of ingredients and mix well. Taste mixture to obtain desired amount of spice. Make patties as you would with sausage and fry until golden brown.

Mrs. Stephanie O'Dell, New York, ew York

World's Best Chili

4-1/2 lbs. coarse ground beef
3 medium onions, ground
3 tbsp. chili powder
1 tsp. cayenne pepper
1 heaping tsp. cumin seed

1 tsp. oregano
1 tsp. salt
2 qts. slightly diluted
tomato puree

Let simmer 1 hour. Add 1 gallon chili beans and heat. 12-16 servings.

Lil Adams, Gettysburg, South Dakota

Baked Beans

1 large can pork and beans
1 small onion, chopped
1/4 C. brown sugar

1 tsp. dry mustard
1/2 C. molasses (optional)
6 strips bacon

Mix together first five ingredients. Spread in oblong baking dish. Spread bacon strips across top of mixture. Bake at 400 degrees for about 45 minutes or until bacon is well done. Serves 6.

Lucille Johnson, Connelly Springs, North Carolina

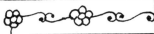 
Italian Zucchini Pie

6 fresh zucchini, about 8-inches long, washed and dried well. Cut in half, then slice 1/4-inch round. Brown in 1/4 C. oil until slightly soft. Drain and set aside.

Filling: Mix in a bowl
6 eggs, 2 well beaten
2 lbs. fresh ricotta cheese
2 C. grated romano cheese
1 C. Italian procuitti or pepper, but cut or chopped up fine
1/2 C. grated brick cheese
1/4 C. fresh parsley or dried parsley, chopped
1 tsp. black pepper

Mix all this good. Start with a layer of fried zucchini on the bottom of baking dish, then spoon filling all over to cover the zucchini. Continue to layer the zucchini and the filling. Bake in 325 degree oven for about 1 hour. Test for doneness by inserting fork; if it comes out clean, the pie is done. If it browns too fast, cover with aluminum foil.

Mrs. Henry Rise, Greensburg, Pennsylvania

Cheese and Broccoli Casserole

10oz. chopped frozen broccoli
or 1-1/2C. fresh, cooked
8oz. jar cheese whiz
1 can cream of chicken soup

1 C. chopped onions
1 C. Minute Rice
1 can milk

Cook minute rice as directed and set aside. In saucepan, put cheese, milk and chicken soup. Cook over low heat until cheese is melted. Mix rice, onion, broccoli and cheese mixture in large casserole. Bake in 325 degree oven for 40 minutes.

Vivian Behrens, Franklinville, New Jersey

Italian Stuffed Eggplant

Cut 2 small eggplant in half lengthwise and remove pulp, leaving a 3/4 inch shell. Cut pulp into 1/2-inch cubes. Heat oven to 350

degrees and toss cubes in 1 tbsp. oil. Bake for 15 minutes. Cook 4oz. (1-1/3 C.) dry spaghetti, in 2-inch pieces, in water as directed on package. Drain. Add oregano, salt, pepper and garlic powder to taste, 1/3 C. diced onion, 1 C. cottage cheese and the eggplant cubes. Stuff into shells and top with shredded mozzarella or munster cheese. Bake 10 minutes more. Serves 4.

Joan LeViness, Winsted, Connecticut

Hot Tofu Pitas

Saute 2 C. cubed peeled eggplant with 1/2 C. chopped onion in 3 tbsp. oil, adding 1/2 C. chopped mushrooms (if desired), 1/2 tsp. garlic powder and dash pepper. Cook 5 minutes. Add 2 chopped, peeled tomatoes, 1/3 C. chili sauce or spice tomato sauce. Add 8oz. cubed tofu and simmer 10 minutes. Spoon into 6 warmed pita breads with a slice of mozzarella cheese in each. Makes 6 servings.

Joan LeViness, Winsted, Connecticut

Zucchini Goulash

3 small unpeeled zucchini, sliced 1/8-inch thick
1/2 lb. hot Italian sausage
1 C. of leftover spaghetti sauce
3/4 C. of water
3 hard boiled eggs, cut in half sideways or leave whole (optional)

1. Brown and drain hot sausage in a skillet breaking sausage up in small chunks. Set aside.

2. Wash, dry and cut zucchini; put in boiling salted water about 2 minutes; drain. Set aside.

3. Hard boil eggs. Peel, cut in half or leave whole (optional).

4. In a pan, put sauce, water and sausage. Simmer 10 minutes; add zucchini. Simmer 5-10 minutes more. Stir occasionally, add eggs the last 2 mintues just to heat. Serve in vegetable dish.

Mrs. Eleanor Shelley, Youngstown, Ohio

Creamy Potato Soup

Leftover mashed potatoes
1 onion, chopped (size depends on amount of potatoes)
3-4 slices of American cheese (sharp or velveeta may be used)
1 tbsp. chopped parsley (or flakes)
2 tbsp. butter or margarine
Salt and pepper to taste

Partially cover potatoes with water, in saucepan. Simmer on low heat while you break up the potatoes. They will get creamy. Add chopped onion, parsley, salt and pepper. Simmer approximately 20 minutes until onion is cooked. Add butter and cheese and simmer until cheese melts. Serve with croutons if desired.

NOTE: If a thinner soup is desired, add more water or milk until you have desired consistency. If a thicker soup is desired, add some instant potato flakes until desired thickness is obtained. For variation, add 2 sliced franks or 1 C. drained corn.

Joanne Weinzen, Coal Center, Pennsylvania

Potato Cheese Soup
(Serve with cornbread)

2 C. leftover mashed potatoes
2 ribs celery, diced
1 large onion, diced
2 C. chicken broth
1 C. water
1/2 C. of shredded brick
or monterey jack cheese

1/4 stick margarine or butter
3 tbsp. flour
2 C. milk or 1/2 cream and 1/2 milk
Salt to taste

In saucepan, put mashed potatoes, celery, onion, chicken broth and water; stir and simmer until celery and onion are cooked; reserve. In a double boiler, put in margarine and melt; add flour and stir. Add milk and make a smooth sauce; add cheese. When sauce is thickened, add the chicken broth, celery, onion, and mashed potato mixture to the sauce. Salt to taste and serve hot with fresh bread.

Mrs. Eleanor Shelley, Youngstown, Ohio

RoseAnne's Egg Pie

1-9 inch ready made pie shell
4 large eggs, beaten well
1 small onion, chopped fine

4oz. can mushrooms or 10
large fresh
4oz. shredded cheese
Salt and pepper

Place onions and mushrooms on bottom of pie shell. Then add eggs. Sprinkle cheese all over top of pie. Place in oven at 450 degrees until golden brown. Serves 4. You can make it with any leftover meat or vegetable, just be sure to cut in small pieces.

RoseAnne Mahoney, Las Vegas, Nevada

Asparagus Impossible Pie

1 can of asparagus, drained,
reserve juice
1/2 C. green onion, chopped
1/2 C. green pepper, diced
1/2 C. shredded cheese: brick,
swiss or monterey jack

1 C. milk
3/4 C. of Bisquick
3 eggs
Salt to taste

Heat oven to 400 degrees. Grease a 9-inch pie plate. Cut or chop asparagus and put in pie plate. Put green onions on top of asparagus, then chopped green pepper, then shredded cheese. In blender mix eggs, salt, Bisquick and milk; blend 1 minute and pour over other ingredients in pie plate. Bake 35-40 minutes or until knife comes out clean. Let set 5-10 minutes before cutting. Can be served as is or with a sauce.

Sauce: 1 tbsp. margarine, 3 tbsp. flour, reserved juice from asparagus, 1/2 C. milk and salt to taste. In double boiler, put margarine in and melt. Mix in flour to make a sauce. Add asparagus juice, milk and salt. Cook until thickened like a gravy. If too thick, add more milk. Serve over cut wedges.

Eleanor Shelley, Youngstown, Ohio

Hot Deviled Eggs

6 hard-cooked eggs
1 tsp. prepared mustard
1/2 tsp. salt
1 can cream of mushroom soup
1/4 C. milk
1 tbsp. instant or 1/4 C. finely chopped raw onion
1 tsp. worchestershire sauce
Dash cayenne pepper
1/4 tsp. chili powder
1-1/2 C. soft bread crumbs
3 tbsp. melted butter or margarine
1 tbsp. grated parmesan cheese

Cut eggs in halves lengthwise. Remove yolks, mash yolks. Blend in mustard, salt and 3 tbsp. of the undiluted soup. Refill egg whites with this mixture. Arrange in a 9-inch pie plate. Heat remaining soup, stir in milk, onion, worchestershire sauce, cayenne and chili powder. Pour over eggs. Toss crumbs with butter and sprinkle over top. Sprinkle cheese over all. Bake in a hot oven (400 degrees) about 20 minutes or until heated and browned on top. Serve at once from baking dish. Yield: 4 servings.

Louise Hicks, Chicago, Illinois

Golden Rod Eggs

2 tbsp. butter
2 tbsp. flour
1 C. scalded milk
1/2 tsp. salt
1/8 tsp. pepper
3 hard-cooked eggs

Melt butter, add flour and blend. When smooth, but not browned, add seasonings and scalded milk. Cook over low heat, stirring constantly until sauce boils. Cook 5 minutes. Add 3 hard-cooked egg white slices and 2 yolks, also sliced. Pour egg and sauce mixture over slices of dry whole wheat bread toast, biscuits or cornbread. Serve the third egg yolk over the sauce and eggs. Serve hot.

Miss Adelia Conejo, Seguin, Texas

Waste Not - Want Not Quiche

Crust: 1/4 lb. margarine, softened, 1 C. flour, and 1/4 tsp. salt. Cut flour, salt and butter together until a ball forms. Pat dough into a quiche pan or a 9-inch pie tin. Prick well with fork and bake at 425 degrees for 5-7 minutes.

Sprinkle on 1/2 to 1 C. grated cheese (whatever you have on hand). Mix enough leftover meat and vegetables to make 1-1/2 C. Put over grated cheese. Combine 6 eggs, 1-1/2 C. milk and your favorite seasonings until well blended and pour over filling. Bake at 375 degrees for 30-35 minutes or until a knife inserted into center comes out clean. Let stand for 5 minutes before cutting. Serves 6.

Sally J. McCabe, Neward, Ohio

How To Make Cottage Cheese From Dry Milk

Mix 2 quarts nonfat dry milk with 1/2 C. buttermilk. Let stand overnight in warm place until it clabbers or until curd is set (a gas oven is great). Set mixture over hot water on very low heat. Do not let water boil; heat only until the whey comes to top. Stir around, test curd with finger. Curd should be soft and not tough. Heating takes about 5-10 minutes. Pour mixture into strainer over a bowl, let drain, don't mash. When drained, break up curd with a fork. Add a little salt to taste. Use as you would cottage cheese. Especially good in lasagna and casserole.

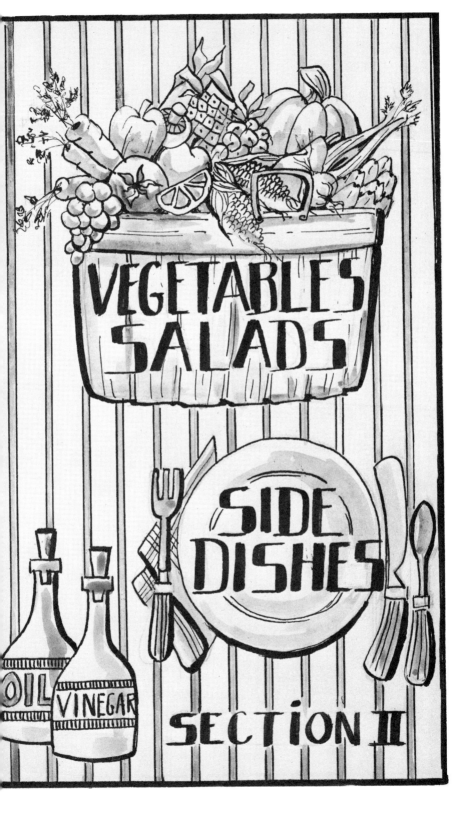

VEGETABLES
SALADS

SIDE
DISHES

OIL VINEGAR

SECTION II

TIPS FOR BUYING VEGETABLES AND FRUITS

o Select good quality by looking carefully for any blemishes or bad spots.

o Do not pay full price for damaged produce. Often however, these are discounted and are a good buy.

o Try a farmer's market. Do you have a weekend market area? Are there local farms that sell produce? How about growing your own?

o Often stores will have a specific day or time when produce and other products are inspected for freshness and placed on sale. Ask when these times are; you might find good reductions. Be sure the produce isn't in too poor of a condition.

VEGETABLE PLANOVERS

o Try to reheat vegetables for as little time as possible.

o Add all leftovers into a jar that is kept in the fridge or freezer until you have enough for a vegetable and or meat stew or soup.

o Add to omelets or souffles.

o Make into fritters.

o Mix with other vegetables to make a mixed vegetable combination. Add cooked vegetables when uncooked vegetables are cooked rather than at the beginning of cooking time.

o Use broth and juices for sauces and soup stock.

o Puree for cream soups and sauces.

o Cream vegetables by making a white sauce with spices, herbs or cheese.

o Make au gratin vegetables by layering with white sauce (with spices, herbs and/or cheese). Top with buttered crumbs and bake at 375 degrees until warmed well and browned on top.

o Add to salads.

o Leftover chunks of broccoli, carrots, etc. can be served cold with dips or vinegarette dressing.

o Add odds and ends of vegetables to bean salads.

Potatoes:

o Fry with onions to make hash browns, patties or home fries.

o Quarter or eighth baked potatoes and fry with skins on in margarine and/or oil (gourmet french fries).

o Add meats to make croquettes.

o Make into potato soup.

o Make into potato salad.

o Use as "crust" for meat pies or casseroles.

Cabbage Wedges with Nippy Sauce

1 medium head cabbage
3 tbsp. butter, melted
2 tbsp. flour
1/2 tsp. onion salt

1 C. milk
1 tbsp. prepared yellow mustard
1 egg yolk
Lemon juice (to taste)

Cut cabbage into six wedges. Cook, covered in a small amount of boiling water until crispy tender. Meanwhile, prepare nippy sauce by combining butter, flour and onion salt; blend in milk and egg yolk. Cook over moderate heat until thickened, stirring constantly; add mustard and lemon juice. Spoon sauce over thoroughly drained cabbage wedges. Yield, 6 servings.

Elizabeth Swain Lawson, Delbarton, West Virginia

Cabbage, Noodle and Onion Casserole

1 head cabbage, shredded
1 large onion, diced
1 pkg. medium sized noodles

1-2 tbsp. butter or margarine
1/4 C. oil
1/2 C. water

In a pan of salted water, cook noodles until done and drain; set aside. In a skillet with 1/4 C. oil, saute cabbage and onion; then add 1/2 C. water; cover and simmer until cabbage and onions are done and tender. Put melted margarine in a casserole; add noodles and stir until noodles are covered with butter. Add cooked cabbage and onions and whatever remaining liquid is in skillet; mix well and heat to serve.

Mrs. Eleanor Shelley, Youngstown, Ohio

Horseradish Carrots

8 medium carrots
2 tbsp. grated onion
1 tbsp. horseradish
1/2 C. mayonnaise

1 tsp. salt
1/4 tsp. black pepper
1/3 C. bread crumbs
Paprika

Pare and cut carrots crosswise. Cook in salted water until tender; drain. Place carrots in greased casserole and add about 2 tbsp. water. Mix mayonnaise and grated onion, horseradish, salt and pepper. Spoon over carrots; sprinkle with bread crumbs and paprika. Bake 15 minutes at 350 degrees, or until hot. Serves 4.

Grace Sahli, Little Rock, Arkansas

Sweet Potatoes

4 large yams
4 large bananas
2 C. Sugar Frosted Flakes

Brown sugar
Salt and cinnamon
1/4 lb. butter
Pecan halves

Pare and cook yams in salted water until tender; mash with bananas and cinnamon. Place in 8x8x2" glass baking dish and cover with 1/2-inch of brown sugar. Melt 1/4 lb. butter and coat the Sugar Frosted Flakes, crushed. Sprinkle over top of brown sugar and cover all with pecan halves. Bake at 350 degrees until hot.

Grace Sahli, Little Rock, Arkansas

Carrot and Cheese Casserole

6 C. of carrots washed, pared, sliced, and cooked in salted water and drained.
1-12oz. pkg. cream cheese, cut in cubes and softened.
2 eggs, beaten
Salt and pepper to taste

Mash carrots with the cream cheese. Season with salt and pepper to taste. Stir in beaten eggs. Butter a casserole or pie plate. Put well mixed carrots in plate. Top with bread crumbs, dot with butter. Bake at 350 degrees for 20-25 minutes. Set 10 minutes before cutting.

Mrs. Eleanor Shelley, Youngstown, Ohio

Crispy Nutty Sauced Cauliflower

1 med. sized head cauliflower,
separated into flowerets
1/2 C. butter
1/2 C. peanut butter

1/4 C. salad dressing
1 tbsp. sugar
1 tsp. lemon juice
1 tsp. catsup

Parboil the cauliflower until tender crisp; drain. Melt the butter in a skillet. Add cauliflower and saute until lightly browned; drain. Combine the peanut butter, salad dressing, sugar, lemon juice, catsup and mix well. Spoon over the hot cauliflower and serve at once. Serves 4.

Cynthia Kannenberg, Milwaukee, Wisconsin

Spicy Cream Celery

3 tbsp. butter
1 tbsp. oil
2 celery leaves, chopped finely
1/4 C. onion, chopped
3 C. celery, sliced 1/4" thick
2 tsp. worchestershire sauce

1 tbsp. flour
2/3 C. milk
1/4 tsp. salt
Toasted sesame seeds or
toasted slivered almonds
(optional)

Wash celery and remove tough strings and damaged parts. Saute celery leaves and onion in hot fat (butter or oil) on medium heat until lightly browned. Add celery, worcestershire sauce and water. Cover and reduce heat immediately. Simmer for 15 minutes (celery will be firm, but tender). Move celery to one side of pan and tilt pan so fat runs into cleared areas. Mix flour with fat until smooth. Stir in milk. Mix all ingredients together. Heat on medium heat until sauce thickens. Top with sesame seeds or almonds.

Green Beans, Cream Style

1-10oz pkg. frozen green beans
1-3oz. pkg. cream cheese, softened

1 tbsp. milk
1/4 tsp. celery seed
1/4 tsp. salt

Cook beans according to package directions; drain. Combine remaining ingredients; blend thoroughly. Add to beans and heat through. Serves 4.

Anna Mae Pritchyk, Clarks Summit, Pennsylvania

Leftover Mashed Potatoes

Form into small balls, add a little minced onion if you like, place on cookie sheet or flat pan, greased, brush with beaten egg yolk, sprinkle with paprika. Heat in 375 degree oven.

When I have quite a bit leftover, I use the next day to make mashed potato salad. Just add what you would to regular potato salad.

Jean Baker, Chula Vista, California

Potato Casserole

1-32oz. pkg. frozen hash
browns
1/2 C. melted butter
1 can cream of chicken soup
8ozs. sour cream

12oz. grated American
cheese
1 tsp. salt
1/4 C. chopped onions
2 C. crushed corn flakes
1/4 C. melted butter

Place potatoes in a 9x13 casserole. Mix next 6 ingredients and pour over potatoes. Put corn flakes on top and pour 1/4 C. butter overall. Bake at 350 degrees for 45 minutes.

Mrs. Louise Goodendorf, Rockford, Illinois

Leftover Boiled Potatoes

2 C. boiled potatoes
1 tsp. salt
1/4 tsp. pepper

4 eggs
4 slices bacon

Slice potatoes and place in a shallow greased baking dish. Sprinkle with salt and pepper. Beat eggs slightly and pour over potatoes. Place bacon strips across the top and bake at 350 degrees for 25 minutes or until eggs are set and bacon is browned.

Amelia M. Brown, Pittsburgh, Pennsylvania

Potato Casserole

5 large potatoes (boiled in
jackets and diced coarsely)
1/4 lb. cheddar cheese
1 medium onion
1/2 C. chopped parsley
1/2 small can pimentos

1/2 green pepper (chopped)
1/2 slice fresh bread (cubed)
1/4 C. melted butter or margarine
1/2 C. milk
1/2 C. corn flakes

Chop all ingredients. Mix and place in baking dish. Pour melted butter and milk over top. Sprinkle with corn flakes. Bake for 30 minutes at 400 degrees. Serves 6.

Mrs. Teresa Doria, Butler, Pennsylvania

Garlic Tomatoes

6 large fresh tomatoes
1 large clove garlic, minced

1/2 tsp. basil
1/2 C. oil

Wash and dry tomatoes in a bowl. Cut tomatoes in eights; put minced garlic on tomatoes and toss, add basil and oil; toss and let stand or marinate about 15 minutes. Salt to taste; juice will form. Put in serving dishes along with some of the juice. Very good served with hard crusted bread and butter and fresh cooked corn on the cob.

Mrs. Eleanor Shelley, Youngstown, Ohio

Scalloped Salsify

1/2 lb. cracker crumbs
1/2 C. salsify, sliced and cooked until tender

Put half of cracker crumbs in 1-quart baking dish. Put salsify in layers on top. Put rest of cracker crumbs in layers on top. Add salt and pepper to taste. Dot with butter. Bake at 350 degrees for one hour. Salsify and oyster plant are the same (similar to parsnips, but darker).

Mrs. Russell Hymes, Arenzville, Illinois

Delicious Spinach

1 pkg. frozen spinach
1/4 tsp. chicken bouillon instant granules

1/2 tsp. dehydrated minced onions
Italian salad dressing

Put frozen spinach in a double boiler; add all ingredients except Italian dressing. Cook until spinach is done; stir to mix ingredients. When ready to serve, put Italian dressing on spinach.

Eleanor Shelley, Youngstown, Ohio

Squash Casserole

2 lbs. summer squash or
zucchini
1 carrot
1 small onion
1 stick margarine, melted

1-8oz. pkg. dry herb stuffing
1 C. dairy sour cream
1 can cream of chicken soup
1/2 C. cheddar cheese

Slice squash very thin. Pare and grate carrot and onion. Melt
margarine and mix with stuffing. Add 1/2 of the buttered stuffing
to squash, carrot and onion, then add sour cream, cheese and cream
of chicken soup (undiluted). Mix all together and turn into shallow
buttered casserole, topping with remaining stuffing. Bake at 350
degrees for 20-25 minutes.

Carol Favreau, Brunswick, Maine

Sweet Potato Casserole

Slice leftover baked sweet potatoes in casserole. Cover with syrup
and bake 30 minutes at 325 degrees.

Syrup:
1/2 C. white sugar
1/2 C. brown sugar

2 tbsp. cornstarch
1/4 C. butter
1 C. water

Mix together, cook until clear and thick. Can use boiled potatoes.

Carrie Wright, Buena Vista, Colorado

Zucchini Pie

1 double pie crust
4 C. zucchini, peeled and thinly sliced
3/4 C. sugar
2 tbsp. tapioca
1 tbsp. lemon juice

1/2 tsp. salt
3/4 tsp. cinnamon
2 tbsp. cornstarch
2 tbsp. butter
2 tbsp. milk

Combine all ingredients, pour in pie shell and dot with butter. Put
the other crust on top with slits on top. Brush with milk on top.
Bake at 350 degrees for 35-40 minutes or until light brown.

Theresa Nuoci, Lafayette, Colorado

Tasty Zucchini Casserole

2 lbs. young zucchini, sliced
and cooked
1 C. grated parmesan cheese
2 eggs

1 small onion
1 C. mayonnaise
1/4 C. green pepper, chopped
Salt and pepper to taste

Drain squash, set aside. Mix all remaining ingredients and combine with squash in buttered casserole. Sprinkle with salt and pepper. Bake 30-45 minutes in 350 degree oven. Serves 8.

Audrey Gall, Hendersonville, North Carolina

Company Zucchini

3 small zucchini, washed and
cut in circles 1/8-inch thick
1 tbsp. butter

1/4 tsp. chicken bouillon instant
granules
1 tsp. parmesan cheese

Wash and cut zucchini in 1/8-inch thick circles, put in double boiler. Add butter, chicken bouillon granules; cook until tender. Stir to mix ingredients. When tender, serve topped with a generous sprinkle of parmesan cheese.

Eleanor Shelley, Youngstown, Ohio

Think Ahead Chef's Salad

What special foods do you have for those once a year occasions? Turkey for Thanksgiving? Roast beef for Christmas? Ham for New Years? When the turkey no longer draws thrilled anticipation, it is time to cube a cup of the meat, and reserve in the freezer. Serve slightly smaller portions of the roast beef and add one-half cup of the cubed beef to the freezer bag. Finally, julienne one cup of ham in one inch pieces. Anytime now, make the salad.

Add to the meat:
1-3/4 C. torn greens
1/4 C. shredded red cabbage
1 C. chopped celery
1/2 C. chopped onion
1/2 C. slivered carrots

1/4 C. slivered pimentos
1 C. flavored croutons
3 hard-cooked eggs, peeled
and quartered
Preferred or California
dressing (below)

Combine vegetables, beef and turkey cubes and croutons. Toss well with a moderate amount of dressing so that each particle is coated. Garnish, after placing in a large bowl, with ham juliennes and egg quarters, arranged in an attractive pattern.

California Dressing

2/3 C. oil, 1/3 C. lemon juice, 1/4 tsp. garlic powder. Mix and refrigerate. Shake before using.

Stella M. Wharton, Mikado, Michigan

Grandmaws Potato Salad

Dressing:
6 eggs
1/2 C. vinegar
1/2 C. sugar

1 tbsp. oleo
1/4 tsp. salt
1 tsp. mustard
2 heaping tbsp. mayonnaise

In a medium saucepan, put vinegar and sugar; heat and stir until sugar melts. Let cool. Beat the eggs and add them to the cooled vinegar and sugar in saucepan. Add salt. Cook over medium heat, stirring constantly until mixture becomes thick like lemon pudding. Do not cook until its hard, just thick. Remove from stove and add mustard and mayonnaise. Stir to mix; set aside. (continued)

Salad:
7 potatoes boiled with skin on, cool
2 ribs of celery, diced fine
1 green pepper, diced fine

1 bunch green onions, diced
Salt to taste
1 tbsp. celery seed
2 hard-boiled eggs
Dash of paprika

Peel boiled, cooled potatoes and dice in a large bowl. Add diced celery, onion, green pepper, salt, celery seed; reserve the hard-cooked eggs and paprika. Pour dressing over the potatoes in bowl; mix well. Cut reserved hard-cooked eggs on top. Sprinkle with paprika. Refrigerate for several hours.

Mrs. Eleanor Shelley, Youngstown, Ohio

Italian-Style Potato Salad

7 medium red potatoes
1 C. frozen green peas
3 tbsp. red pepper chopped (sweet pepper)
4 green onions, chopped

2 tbsp. dried parsley
3/4 C. Italian salad dressing
1 tsp. salt
1/8 tsp. pepper

Cook potatoes until tender; drain and set aside. Cook peas according to package directions and drain. Peel potatoes while warm and cut into cubes; combine in bowl with peas and remaining ingredients. Mix well. Cover; refrigerate overnight or until cool. Mix again before serving.

Betty Perkins, Arlington Heights, Illinois

Green Bean Salad

2 regular size cans green beans (or French style green beans or yellow wax beans), well drained
4 slices bacon, cut finely

1/4 C. finely chopped onion
1/2 C. ketchup
1/4 C. brown sugar
1 tsp. worcestershire sauce

You can use yellow and green beans together. Cook onion and bacon until bacon is crisp; add ketchup, sugar and sauce. Simmer for 2 minutes. Let all the bacon fat in. Put beans in casserole and pour mixture over top. Do not stir. Bake, uncovered, 45 minutes in 325 degree oven.

Mrs. Teresa Doria, Butler, Pennsylvania

Sauerkraut Salad

1 large can sauerkraut, washed
in cold water and well drained
1/2 C. green pepper, diced
1/2 C. celery, diced

1/2 C. onion, diced
1/2 C. oil
1/2 C. vinegar
1/2 C. sugar

Rinse and drain sauerkraut; meanwhile dice pepper, celery and onion. In a small saucepan, put sugar and vinegar; heat and stir until sugar melts. Remove from stove and let cool. In a bowl, put drained sauerkraut, green pepper, onion, and celery; mix with the cooled sugar and vinegar. Add the oil; pour mixture over sauerkraut mixture. Mix well. Marinate overnight. Serve with sandwiches or a buffet dish.

Eleanor Shelley, Youngstown, Ohio

Economical Macaroni Salad

3 C. cooked macaroni
1 can green peas, chilled and
drained
1 C. salad dressing
3 eggs, hard-cooked and diced
1/2 C. diced celery

Dash of tabasco sauce
1/4 C. diced green pepper
2 tbsp. chopped pimento
2 tbsp. chopped onion
4 tsp. instant chicken bouillon
granules

Combine all ingredients in large bowl and mix well. Chill for several hours. Stir before serving. Serves 6-8.

Jodie McCoy, Tulsa, Oklahoma

Cold Slaw Mold

Dissolve 1 pkg. lemon gelatin in 1 C. boiling water. Add 1/2 C. mayonnaise, 2 tbsp. vinegar, 1/4 tsp. salt and pepper. Mix well and set in refrigerator until it becomes thick. Fold in 2 C. finely chopped cabbage, 2 tbsp. finely chopped green pepper, and 2 tsp. grated onion. Pour in mold and chill. No dressing is required.

Arlene M. Krug, Cedar Rapids, Iowa

Barbeque Salad

1 (3oz) pkg. orange gelatin
1 C. boiling water
1 (8oz) can tomato sauce

1-1/2 tbsp. cider vinegar
1/2 tsp. salt
Dash of pepper

Dissolve gelatin in boiling water and add all remaining ingredients. Blend thoroughly and pour into a 3 C. mold. Chill about 4 hours or until very firm. Serve on lettuce leaves. A dollop of salad dressing may be used for garnish. Very tasty and refreshing. Excellent with casserole dishes.

Jodie McCoy, Tulsa, Oklahoma

Cracker Salad

1 stack saltine crackers
1 C. chopped onion
1 C. sweet relish
1 small green pepper, chopped

1 small jar pimento
6 boiled eggs, chopped
2 C. mayonnaise

Crush crackers, put in large mixing bowl. Add all ingredients; mix. Put in plastic container. Chill several hours.

Mrs. T. J. McCaughan, Fort Worth, Texas

Fluffy Orange Rice

1 C. chopped celery	1-1/4 C. water
1/4 C. chopped onion	1/2 tsp. salt
1/4 C. butter	1-1/3 C. packaged precooked
2 tbsp. orange juice concen-	rice
trate	

In a saucepan, cook celery and onion in butter until tender. Add orange juice concentrate, water and salt. Bring mixture to boiling. Add rice and continue cooking following package directions. Serves 4.

Anna Mae Pritchyk, Clarks Summit, Pennsylvania

Garden Patch Sandwich Spread

1/4 C. soft butter or	1 tbsp. minced green pepper
margarine	Swiss cheese slices (cut in
1 tbsp. minced zucchini	half)
1 tbsp. minced carrot	White bread slices
1 tbsp. minced celery	

Combine butter, zucchini, carrot, celery and green pepper. For each sandwich, you will spread two slices of bread with butter mixture. Put 1/2 slice of Swiss cheese between the two buttered slices and cut in half so you have two sandwiches. This mixture makes enough for 4-5 sandwiches. Very good and different.

Jo Wendt, Eau Claire, Wisconsin

Hrudka (Easter Cheese)

1 dozen eggs	1 tsp. salt
1 quart milk	1 tbsp. sugar

Beat eggs well, mix into milk, sugar and salt in big pot. If you double recipe, use low burner and keep stirring until it all curdles. Strain through cloth or cheese cloth, forming with hands to make a ball. Let excess milk (looks like water when done) drain for several hours or overnight. I double recipe or you can triple. Double recipe makes a cheese size of canteloupe.

Julia Newman, North Bradock, Pennsylvania

-135-

Spiced Prunes

1-1/2 C. sugar
1-1/2 C. hot water

12 whole cloves
2 sticks of cinnamon

Bring to a boil and add a bag of prunes that have been already cooked. Remove from heat and let cool and store in airtight container. Will keep for several weeks. These should stand several days for better flavor. They are something different for your relish tray.

Mrs. Carol Bradley, Fort Dodge, Iowa

SECTION III

DESSERTS

SUGAR

VANILLA

o Chop pieces of leftover fruit into bite-size pieces and add to coconut and sour or sweet cream for fruit salad.

o Serve odds and ends on plates with cottage cheese or ice cream for fruit salad dish.

o Make fruit cup of bits and pieces.

o Add to cereal.

o Make into sauce by pureeing or using juices.

o Make a fruit Betty.

o Place on the bottom of cake mix like pineapple upside down cake.

o Puree and dry to make fruit leather.

o Top plain cake with bits of fruit and cream. A sauce might also be added.

o Use juice from fruit for punch. Pour all juices in container until ready to use. (Freeze if it will be more than 4-5 days before the juices are used)

o Grate rinds of citrus fruits for flavorings. Freeze until ready to use.

o Add stewed fruit to make meat dishes.

o Make into jams or jellies.

o Overripe bananas can be mashed and frozen for muffins and banana breads.

o Use the juice from plumping raisins as juice drink.

-138-

COOKIE OR CAKE PLANOVERS

o If cake or cookies are slightly dry, layer with fruit or ice cream and sauce.

o Make into crumbs for fruit Betty or layered dessert. Make layered dessert by placing crumbs on bottom of greased pan, put apples or other fruits over top put another layer of crumbs. I usually add butter and sugar to the crumbs. Bake until fruit is cooked. Serve warm or cold with cream or ice cream.

o Roll ice cream or cream cheese balls in crumbs. Top with sauce and cream if desired.

o A crumb mixture is even better if butter/margarine and finely chopped nuts are added. The crumb mixture can be used for cream pies or gelatin "crusts"; just pat the mixture into the pan and pour the filling over the top.

o Cube cakes and make a fruit or chocolate fondue to dip the cake cubes into. Roll in nuts or coconut if desired.

SPICES

COOKIES

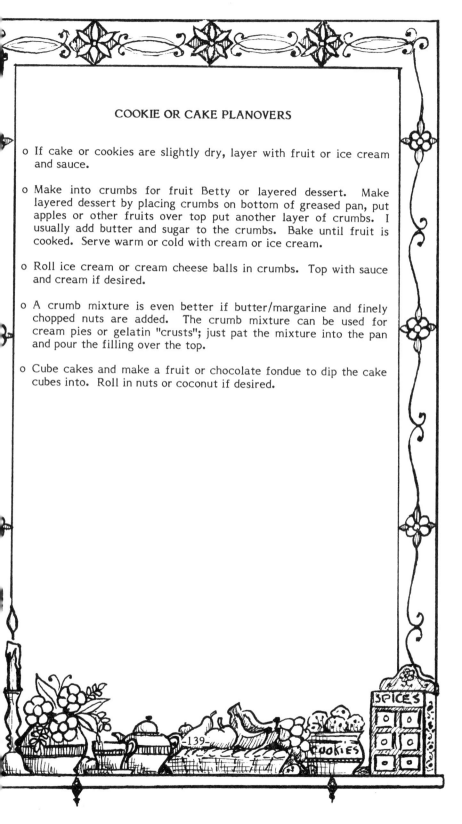

FRUIT

Fruit Pizza

Spray a cookie sheet with Pam. Slice an 18oz. tube of slice and bake sugar cookies 1/8-inch thick. Place on pan, overlapping edges slightly. Bake at 375 degrees for 10 minutes. Mix an 8oz. pkg. cream cheese, 1 C. sugar and 2 tsp. vanilla until fluffy. Spread on cooled crust. Drain a 12oz. can of crushed pineapple; spread over cream cheese mixture. Arrange slices from 1 can peaches over pineapple. Dot with pecans and maraschino cherries. Refrigerate 4-5 hours before serving.

Elsie Gingerich, Kokomo, Indiana

Fruit Pizza

1 tube sugar cookes
1-8oz. cream cheese
1/4 C. powdered sugar

1 tsp. vanilla
1/4 C. apricot preserves, melted

Slice sugar cookies on pizza pan to slightly overlap. Bake 10 minutes (you can use your own sugar cookie recipe if you prefer). Cool. Beat cream cheese, sugar, vanilla and spread over cooled crust. Put a variety of fresh fruit on top, or well drained fruit (watermelon, melon balls, and blueberries is one combination or strawberries and pineapple). Drizzle apricot preserves over top. Take out of pizza pan before adding cheese or fruit and put on a pretty plate. This is a good summer dessert and very attractive.

Mrs. Carol Bradley, Fort Dodge, Iowa

Fruit and Nut Dessert
(made the day before serving is best)

Crust:
1 C. graham cracker crumbs
1 C. flour

3/4 C. margarine, softened

Mix like a pie crust. Add 1/2 C. chopped walnuts. Spread into a 9x13" pan. Bake at 350 degrees for 10-15 minutes and let cool.

Filling:

2 (2oz.) pkgs. Dream Whip
1 C. milk
1 C. powdered sugar
1 tsp. vanilla

1 (8oz.) pkg. cream cheese, softened
1 can of fruit pie filling (cherry or blueberry)

Whip Dream Whip and milk until stiff. Add softened cream cheese, powdered sugar and vanilla. Spread on cooled crust. Spread fruit pie filling over cream. Chill.

Roseann Strazinsky, Danville, Pennsylvania

Quick Cobbler

1 stick butter
1 C. flour (self-rising)

1 C. sugar
1 C. milk
Fruit

Preheat oven to 400 degrees. Melt stick of butter in oblong pan (13x9"). Mix flour, sugar, and milk. Pour on top of butter evenly. Use your favorite fruit (peaches, cherries, apples, etc.) Pour fruit in middle of pan, do not spread. Bake 45 minutes to 1 hour.

Mrs. D. A. New, Lilbourn, Missouri

Fresh Fruit Coconut Nests

8oz. pkg. whipped cream cheese
1/2 C. sugar
1 tsp. milk
1 tsp. vanilla

2 pkg. (8 Cups) shortcake dessert cups
1-1/3 C. flaked coconut
1 qt. fresh sweetened fruit (peaches, strawberries, etc.)

Combine cream cheese, sugar, milk and vanilla; beat until smooth. With fork, remove small amount of center from each dessert cup. Frost cups with cream cheese mixture; sprinkle with coconut. At serving time, spoon fruit into centers. Enjoy.

Mrs. William R. Long, Willow Grove, Pennsylvania

Applesauce Freeze in Peach Cups

1-1/3 C. applesauce
1/2 C. orange juice
2 tbsp. lemon juice
2 egg whites

Pinch of salt
2 tbsp. sugar
1 can peach halves, drained
Chopped walnuts

Combine applesauce with orange and lemon juices. Freeze to a mush in refrigerator tray. Beat egg whites with salt until stiff. Add sugar. Combine frozen applesauce mixture with egg whites. Return to refrigerator tray and freeze. Place peach halves in lettuce cups, on salad plates. Fill hollow of each peach half with applesauce freeze. Top with chopped nuts. Serves 6.

Amelia M. Brown, Pittsburgh, Pennsylvania

Apple Mousse

Combine 1 C. applesauce with 1/2 C. cultured sour cream and a pinch of salt. Spoon into 2-3 serving dishes or sherbet glasses. Chill. Just before serving, sprinkle about 2 tbsp. brown sugar and 1-2 tbsp. chopped nutmeats over each serving. Recipe can be easily doubled.

Amelia M. Brown, Pittsburgh, Pennsylvania

Hot Apple Pudding

1 box vanilla tapioca pudding mix
1 tsp. vanilla
1 tbsp. margarine
Nutmeg

1-1/2 C. water
6 medium apples
Whipped cream or topping or ice cream

In saucepan, mix pudding mix and water. Bring to boil and remove from heat. Add vanilla and margarine. Quarter the apples and put in baking dish. Pour pudding mix over apples. Sprinkle with nutmeg. Cover and bake at 350 degrees until apples are tender (30-40 minutes). Serve warm with whipped cream or ice cream. Can be served chilled also, but is luscious warm.

Joan Rieck, Whitefish Bay, Wisconsin

Apple Pudding Delight

1 C. biscuit mix	1/3 C. melted butter
1 C. sugar	2-1/2 C. sliced all-purpose
1/2 tsp. salt	apples
2 tsp. pumpkin pie spices	1/2 C. raisins
1/2 C. milk	1/2 C. chopped nuts (optional)

Preheat oven to 375 degrees. Lightly grease a 9-1/2x5-1/2 inch baking dish. Mix first 6 ingredients together. Stir in apples and raisins, pour mixture into baking dish, sprinkle on nuts and bake for 35-40 minutes or until golden brown. Serve warm or cold and if desired, with whipped or ice cream. Serves 8.

Barbara Moore, Rock Island, Illinois

Applesauce Pudding

8 slices firm-textured white	1/2 C. brown sugar
bread	2 eggs
1-16oz. jar applesauce	2-1/2 C. milk
1/3 C. raisins	1/2 tsp. vanilla
1/2 tsp. ground cinnamon	1/4 tsp. salt

Spread one side of each slice of bread with butter or margarine. If desired, remove crusts. Arrange 4 slices of bread, buttered side up, in greased 8x8x2-inch baking dish. Mix applesauce, raisins, cinnamon and 2 tbsp. of the brown sugar. Spread over bread in dish. Cut remaining slices of bread into triangles; arrange on filling, covering entire surface. Beat together eggs, milk, vanilla, salt and remaining brown sugar. Pour over bread. Sprinkle with additional cinnamon. Bake in 350 degree oven for 50-55 minutes. Serves 6.

LaVola Walter, Belvidere, Illinois

Apple Dumplings with Ginger Sauce

1 recipe pastry	3 tbsp. hot water
4-5 large tart apples pared,	1 C. sugar
cored and sliced	3 tbsp. butter or margarine

Roll out pastry into six or seven 4-inch squares; place apples in center of each pastry square. Wet edges of pastry; bring together to form a triangle. Press edges with fork and prick top. Put water in large greased baking dish; place dumplings in water. Sprinkle with sugar and dot with butter. Bake at 400 degrees for 35-45 minutes. (Continued)

Ginger Sauce:

1 C. sugar
2 tbsp. flour
2 tbsp. butter

3 tbsp. crystallized ginger or
1 tsp. ground ginger
3/4 C. milk or water

Combine all ingredients except milk; stir in milk. Cook until thick; serve hot or cold with dumplings. 6-7 servings.

Amelia M. Brown, Pittsburgh, Pennsylvania

Apple Brown Betty

2 C. bread crumbs
1/4 C. melted butter
6 C. sliced apple (about 8)
1/2 C. sugar, gran. or brown
1/2 tsp. nutmeg

1/2 tsp. cinnamon
1-1/2 tbsp. lemon juice
1 tbsp. lemon rind (grated)
1/2 C. water

Combine bread crumbs and butter. Layer in baking dish with apples, sugar and spice mixture. Cover and bake at 350 degrees for 1/2 hour. Uncover. Bake 1/2 hour more at 350 degrees. Serve warm with hard sauce or cream. Other fruits can be used in place of apples.

Apple Fritters

1-1/3 C. sifted enriched flour
1 tbsp. sugar
2 tsp. baking powder
1/2 tsp. salt
2 beaten eggs

2/3 C. milk
1 tbsp. salad oil
3-4 apples pared, cored and
cut in small strips
Confectioners' sugar

Sift together flour, sugar, baking powder and salt. Blend eggs, milk and salad oil. Gradually stir into dry ingredients. Mix until smooth. Stir in apple strips. Fry in deep hot fat (375 degrees) until golden. Drain and sprinkle with powdered sugar.

Baked Apple Dumplings

3 tart apples, peeled and
sliced thin
2 C. flour
3 tsp. baking powder

1/2 tsp. salt
1/2 C. shortening, cut in
2/3 C. milk

Mix to a soft dough. Roll out thin and cut into six 5-inch squares. Put apples on each square and sprinkle the following mixture over: 1/4 C. sugar, 1/4 tsp. cinnamon and 1/8 tsp. nutmeg. Wet edges of dough and bring up to center pressing together. Heat 3/4 C. water, 1/2 C. sugar, 2 tbsp. butter and few grains salt. Pour all except 1/4 C. over dumplings and bake at 375 degrees for 45 minutes. Serve hot with remaining sauce.

Apfel Kuchen (Apple Cake)

1/2 C. margarine, softened
1/2 C. flaked coconut
1/2 C. sugar
1 C. dairy sour cream
1 pkg. yellow cake mix

1-20oz. can pie sliced apples
(drained)
1/2 tsp. cinnamon
1/2 tsp. cardamon
2 egg yolks or 1 egg

Heat oven to 350 degrees. Cut margarine into dry cake mix until crumbly; mix in coconut. Pat mixture lightly into ungreased oblong pan (13x9x2), building up to a slight edge, bake 10 minutes. Arrange apples slices on warm crust, mix sugar, cinnamon and cardamon; sprinkle on apples. Blend sour cream and egg yolks; drizzle over apples. Bake 25 minutes or until edges are light brown (do not overbake).

Mrs. Judy M. Sax, San Antonio, Texas

Spiced Apples or Pears

6 baking apples
1 C. water
1 stick cinnamon

1-1/2 C. sugar
1 tsp. whole cloves

Wash and core the apples, and peel a strip from the top third of each apple to prevent splitting during baking. Arrange apples in a baking dish. Make a syrup by combining the sugar, water, spices, salt and cornstarch. Boil 2 minutes. Add enough food coloring to color light pink. Pour syrup over the apples and bake uncovered in a 350 degree oven about 45 minutes, or until tender, basting frequently with the syrup. Serves 6.

Apricot Slices

4 eggs (separated)
2 sticks margarine
1/2 C. sugar
2 heaping C. flour

1 can apricot pie filling
1/2 C. finely chopped nuts
1 tsp. vanilla

Mix egg yolks, margarine and sugar until fluffy. Sift flour into creamed mixture and mix well; pat dough out on cookie sheet 11x16. Bake 15 minutes at 350 degrees. Beat 4 egg whites until stiff. Add vanilla and 1 C. sugar; beat again. Spread apricot filling on dough while hot. Put egg whites on top and sprinkle nuts on top and rebake 20 minutes.

Louise Hicks, Chicago, Illinois

Blueberry-Apple Salad

1 pint fresh or frozen
blueberries. Cook with 1-1/2
C. water; sweeten to taste.

1 package lemon jello
1-1/2 C. sweetened applesauce

Add lemon jello to hot berries; stir until jello is dissolved. Add applesauce and stir. I use frozen applesauce and stir until it is thawed; then refrigerate until firm. Top with a mixture of equal amounts of cream cheese or Dream Whip (or Cool Whip) whipped together.

Clara Davis, Salem, Oregon

Blueberry Dessert

Mix 16 graham crackers (crushed fine), 1/2 C. melted butter and 1/4 C. white sugar. Press into 8x9-inch pan. Beat 1 egg. Add 1/2 C. sugar and 1 (8oz) package cream cheese. Mix until well blended. Pour over the cracker mixture. Bake at 350 degrees for 15 minutes; cool. Heat 1 can blueberry pie mix with 1 tsp. lemon juice. Stirring constantly. Cool, then spread over cheese layer; refrigerate several hours or overnight. Can be served with whipped cream if desired.

Esther Blatter, McClusky, North Dakota

Peach Dessert

1 large can light syrup cling
peaches
3/4 C. biscuit mix
1/2 tsp. salt

1 tsp. cinnamon
1/2 tsp. nutmeg
6 tbsp. melted margarine
1/2 C. sugar

Preheat oven to 375 degrees. Lightly grease a 9-1/2x5-1/2 baking dish. Mix all ingredients and pour into dish. Bake for 40 minutes and serve warm. Serves 8.

Barbara Moore, Rock Island, Illinois

Pineapple-Coconut Surprise

1 pkg. coconut cookies (or coconut flavored)
1 (20oz.) can drained crushed pineapple
1 C. coconut
1 (8oz) carton Cool Whip

Dip cookies in milk for a few seconds. Layer them in 9x13 glass pan. Put 1/2 of the pineapple over the cookies, then half the coconut and half the Cool Whip. Repeat layers and top with more coconut. Chill and serve.

Mary Hicks, Hickory, North Carolina

Quick Rhubarb Dessert

1 C. graham cracker crumbs
1/2 C. sugar
1/4 C. butter or margarine,
melted

4 C. rhubard diced
Whipped cream or ice cream

Preheat oven to 350 degrees. Combine crumbs and sugar; stir in butter. Press about half of mixture into a small pan. Spread rhubard over crumbs and top with remaining crumbs. Bake 45 minutes or until rhubard is cooked through. Serve with whipped cream or ice cream. Makes 4-6 servings.

Arlene Krug, Cedar Rapids, Iowa

Strawberry Fruit Cup

1 pint fresh strawberries	1/2 C. water
1/2 large grapefruit	2 tbsp. cheery cordial (liqueur)
1 C. sugar	Orange sherbet

Wash and hull strawberries; halve if large. Cut grapefruit in half lengthwise instead of crosswise; cut off all peelings and membrane and remove sections; mix with strawberies. Boil sugar and water together until syrupy; cool. When cool, add cherry cordial and pour over berries and grapefruit. Chill thoroughly. To serve, put scoop of orange sherbet in glass and cover with the fruit and syrup. A delectable combination. Serves 3-4.

Amelia M. Brown, Pittsburgh, Pennsylvania

Strawberry Delight

1 box white cake mix
1 box strawberry glaze (or prepared glaze)
1 quart fresh or frozen strawberries
1 large size Cool Whip (or any whipped topping)

Bake cake according to directions on package; cool cake in pan. Spread glaze over top of cake. Spread strawberries on top of glaze. Cover with Cool Whip. Refrigerate. Garnish with whole strawberries if desired. Makes 12 generous servings.

Lucille Johnson, Connelly Springs, North Carolina

Fruit Cocktail Cake Dessert

1-1/2 C. sugar	2 eggs
2 C. flour	1 tsp. vanilla
1 tsp. soda	1 No. 2 can fruit cocktail,
1/2 tsp. salt	juice and all

Put this all in a bowl and beat good. Put in a greased and floured 9x13 pan and bake 40-45 minuts at 350 degrees. Before baking, sprinkle top of cake with brown sugar and chopped nuts. After cake is baked, pour sauce over it.

Sauce:

1/2 C. sugar	1/2 C. canned milk
1/2 C. margarine	1 tsp. vanilla

Bring to a boil and cook to the count of ten. Pour on the warm cake and serve pieces with whipped cream or vanilla ice cream.

Betty Brennan, Faribault, Minnesota

Upside-Down-Rhubarb Cake

3 C. rhubarb, diced   1 C. mini-marshmallows
1 C. sugar

Combine and put into a well greased 9x13" pan. Cream together 1-1/2 C. brown sugar, 1/2 C. margarine, 1 egg, 1 tsp. vanilla, 1 C. buttermilk, 2 C. flour, 1 tsp. cinnamon or pumpkin pie spice, 1 tsp. salt and 1 tsp. soda. Pour into pan and bake at 375 degrees for 40-45 minutes. When done, invert onto serving plate and serve with whipped cream or vanilla ice cream.

Betty Brennan, Faribault, Minnesota

Apple Cake Dessert

1/2 C. margarine
2 C. sugar
2 eggs, beaten
2 C. flour
1 tsp. soda

3 tsp. cinnamon
2 tsp. nutmeg
1 tsp. salt
4 C. finely chopped apples
1 C. chopped nuts

Cream margarine; gradually add the sugar heating until light and fluffy. Add eggs; beat well. Sift all dry ingredients and add to creamed mix, stir in apples and nuts. Put in a greased and floured 9x13" pan and bake for 15 minutes at 350 degrees. Turn down heat to 300 degrees and bake for 45 minutes more. Serve with this sauce: Combine and cook until mix coats a spoon (1 C. sugar, 1/2 C. margarine, 1/2 C. light cream and 1 tsp. vanilla).

Betty Brenna, Faribault, Minnesota

 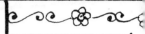

Graham Cracker Crumb Cake

This is rather open-textured, moist and tender. Serve hot, cut in rectangles, split and spread with plenty of butter.

1/2 C. flour
1 tsp. baking powder
1/2 tsp. baking soda
1/2 tsp. salt
1-1/2 C. graham cracker crumbs
1/2 C. butter or margarine, softened

2/3 C. granulated sugar
2/3 C. packed light brown sugar
3 eggs
1 tsp. vanilla
1 C. buttermilk
1 C. chopped black walnuts (optional)

Stir together flour, baking powder, soda and salt; mix with crumbs; set aside. In large bowl, cream butter and sugars, beat in eggs one at a time and vanilla; beat until fluffy. Add flour mixture to egg mixture alternately with buttermilk, beating just to blend. Stir in black walnuts. Spread in greased 9-inch square baking pan. Bake in preheated 350 degree oven for 40 mintues or until pick inserted in center comes out clean. Makes 10 servings.

Mrs. Maxine Hester, Sedalia, Missouri

Losaw's Whiskey Cake

1 pkg. Duncan Hines yellow or lemon cake mix
1 pkg. instant lemon pudding

5 eggs
3/4 C. olive oil
3/4 C. whiskey

Mix these ingredients together for about three minutes; keep moving the mixture from the sides. Then, mix by spoon:

1 C. chopped nuts (walnuts)
3/4 C. chopped maraschino cherries (not too fine)
3/4 C. peanut butter chips

Mix well and bake at 350 degrees for 1 hour in a 13x9-inch pan (greased and floured). Let stand 20 minutes then put on platter and frost.

Frosting: Mix 10 tbsp. butter, then add 1/4 C. or a little more of whiskey and 3 C. confectioners sugar. Mix until creamy. After cake is iced, decorate with 1/2 C. peanut butter chips and sprinkle 1 C. of coconut on top. Let set a few hours before cutting.

Mrs. Stanley Losaw, Phillipsburg, New Jersey

Chocolate Coca-Cola Cake

2 C. flour   2 C. sugar

Sift together in a bowl and set aside.

2 sticks margarine   1 C. coca-cola
3 tbsp. cocoa

Bring to a boil in a saucepan. Then add to sifted ingredients.

1/2 C. buttermilk   1/2 C. miniature
1 tsp. vanilla   marshmallows
2 eggs   1 tsp. soda

Mix together and pour into a well greased and floured pan (13x8x2). Bake 45 minutes in a 350 degree oven.

Cake Icing:

1 stick margarine   3 tbsp. cocoa
7 tbsp. coca-cola

Bring to boil. Then add: 1 lb. box powdered sugar and 1 tsp. vanilla. Put 1 C. miniature marshmallows on hot cake, let cool then spread icing on.

Karen Colmer, Mansfield, Illinois

Chocolate Refrigerator Cake

1 pkg. chocolate cake mix   12oz. lemon-lime soda
1-3oz. chocolate instant   2 envelopes Dream Whip
pudding   1-1/2 C. cold milk
3/4 C. oil   1-3oz. pkg. chocolate instant
3 eggs   pudding

Prepare cake mix along with package of pudding, oil, eggs and soda. Bake in an oiled and floured 12x9" pan at 350 degrees for 45 minutes. Cool. Beat Dream Whip and milk until very stiff. Add remaining pudding mix and beat. Spread on cake and refrigerate. There is more frosting than we like on our cake, so I spread remaining between graham crackers and dip in melted almond bark - refrigerate.

Mrs. Gerald Hesse, Sioux City, Iowa

Chocolate Sheet Cake

2 C. flour   Pinch of salt
2 C. sugar

Mix together and set aside.

1 stick margarine   4 tbsp. cocoa
1/2 C. oil   1 C. water

Mix together in a saucepan. Bring this mixture to a boil and pour over the flour and sugar mixture.

Add:
2 eggs, beaten   1/2 C. buttermilk
1 tsp. baking soda   1 tsp. vanilla
1/2-3/4 C. nuts, chopped

Stir. Pour out onto a greased cookie sheet (approximately 15-1/2x10-1/2 with 1 inch sides). Bake for 20 minutes at 400 degrees.

Frosting:
4 tbsp. cocoa   6 tbsp. milk
1 stick oleo

Combine and bring to a boil.

Add:
1 box powdered sugar.

Stir until smooth. Spread over sheet cake.

Karen Colmer, Mansfield, Illinois

Never Fail Chocolate Cake

2 eggs   2 tsp. vanilla
1 C. cocoa   2 tsp. soda
1 C. shortening   2 C. sugar
3 C. flour   1 C. hot water
1 C. sour milk

Put everything in bowl in order. Beat well and bake at 350 degrees for 35-45 minutes. Makes a large cake.

Faye M. Walter, Stowe, Pennsylvania

White Coconut Cake

4 eggs
1 box white cake mix or any
flavor you wish
1 box vanilla or coconut
instant pudding

1-1/2 C. water
1/4 C. oil
1 C. nuts
2 C. coconut

Mix first 5 ingredients together, beating well, then add coconut and nuts folding carefully. Bake at 350 degrees in a 9x12x2" pan 35 minutes or until cake is done.

Frosting:

1/2 C. margarine
1 tsp. vanilla
1/2 C. coconut

8oz. cream cheese
2 C. powdered sugar
Nuts on top

Melt margarine. Add cream cheese, powdered sugar; mix well. Add vanilla and coconut. Put nuts on top.

Theresa Nuoci, Lafayette, Colorado

Poor Man's Cake

1 C. sugar
1 egg
2 scant C. flour
2 tbsp. butter, melted

2/3 C. milk
2 tsp. baking powder
1 tsp. vanilla extract
1/3 tsp. salt

Beat egg and sugar together until light and fluffy; add the milk, then melted butter and extract. Sift the flour, salt and baking powder twice, add the liquid mixture to them and beat well. Bake in round or oblong cake pan at 325-350 degrees for about 45 minutes. Ice with favorite frosting.

Joyce Cunningham, Alliance, Ohio

Yum Yum Cake

4 eggs
2 C. sugar
1 C. corn oil

2-2/3 C. self-rising flour
1 C. milk

Beat eggs until fluffy then gradually add sugar, stir until mixed and add oil, stir real good and then gradually add flour, then pour milk a little at the time and beat mixture until it's smooth and fluffy. Spray 4 cake pans (average size) with Pam. Pour batter in pans evenly and bake at 325 degrees for 25-30 minutes or until knife inserted comes out clean. Cool layers.

Icing:

1 small box of instant chocolate pudding
1 small box of instant vanilla pudding
4 C. milk
2 C. crushed pecans
1 large Cool Whip

Mix in separate bowls each box of pudding according to directions on pudding box. Add one cup of pecans to each bowl of pudding mix and spread one kind of pudding on first layer of cake then spread Cool Whip on that, then put another layer of cake and spread with other flavor of pudding and top with Cool Whip. Do this until each layer has been iced, then take remaining Cool Whip and spread on top of cake. After cake has been iced, refrigerate.

Mrs. Marie Brown, Wilson, North Carolina

Oatmeal Cake

Pour 1-1/2 C. boiling water over 1 C. one-minute oatmeal; let soak 20 minutes. Cream together: 1/2 C. margarine, 1 C. brown sugar, and 1 C. white sugar. Add and beat well 2 eggs. Sift together: 1-1/2 C. sifted flour, 1 tsp. baking powder, 1 tsp. cinnamon, 1/2 tsp. salt and 1 tsp. baking soda. Add to creamed mixture with 1 tsp. vanilla. Beat well; add oatmeal mixture, beat again. Bake in greased 13x9" baking pan at 300 degrees for 45 minutes. Frost with cream cheese frosting.

Cream Cheese Frosting:

1/2 stick margarine   1/2 tsp. vanilla
3oz. pkg. cream cheese   1/2 box confectioners sugar

Mix together until smooth.

Joan LeViness, Winsted, Connecticut

Sausage Cake

1 lb. pork sausage
1-1/2 C. firmly packed brown sugar
1-1/2 C. sugar
2 eggs, lightly beaten
3 C. sifted flour
1 tsp. ginger
1 tsp. baking powder
1 tsp. pumpkin pie spice
1 tsp. baking soda
1 C. cold strong coffee
1 C. raisins
1 C. chopped nuts

In mixing bowl, combine meat and sugars; stir until mixture is well blended. Add eggs and beat well. Sift flour, ginger, baking powder and pumpkin pie spice onto a piece of waxed paper. Stir baking soda into the coffee. Add flour mixture and coffee alternately to meat mixture, beating well after each addition. Pour boiling water over the raisins and let stand 5 minutes; drain well and dry raisins in cloth. Fold the raisins and walnuts into the cake batter. Turn batter into well greased and floured bundt pan. Bake 1-1/2 hours at 350 degrees or until done. Cool 15 minutes in pan before turning out. NOTE: you can dust this cake with powdered sugar, or make a glaze of your choice, or serve it with a hard sauce or a lemon sauce. I use a warm lemon sauce and it's quite tasty. This cake sounds strange, but it really is delicious. It has a spicy flavor.

Betty Belair, Cumberland, Rhode Island

Pinto Bean Cake

1 C. sugar
1 stick of butter
2 eggs
2 C. of cooked pinto beans (mashed)
1 C. self-rising flour
1 tsp. cinnamon
1 tsp. salt
1/2 tsp. ground cloves
2 C. diced raw apples
1 tsp. vanilla
1/2 C. pecans
1 C. raisins

Cream sugar, flour and butter. Add eggs and mashed beans. Sift all dry ingredients into creamed mixture along with apples, raisins, nuts and vanilla. Mix well and pour into greased and floured tube pan. Bake at 350 degrees for 1 hour.

Frosting:

One box of confectioners sugar, 2 tbsp. of bean juice, 1 tsp. vanilla, 4 tbsp. butter, 2 tbsp. milk. Combine all ingredients and spread on cake.

Stephanie A. O'Dell, New York, New York

Yellow Pound Cake

2 C. plain flour
2 tsp. baking powder
1/4 tsp. salt
12 egg yolks

2 C. sugar
1 tbsp. orange juice
1 tsp. lemon rind
1 C. hot water

Heat oven to 350 degrees. Use 10 inch tube pan. Sift the flour, baking powder together, set aside while you beat the egg yolks. Stir until thick and creamy. Beat in sugar, then flour mixture; add the orange juice and rind, then the hot water. Beat until real smooth and put in pan and bake. Let this cool in pan before taking out.

Evelyn Thomas, Knoxville, Tennessee

Ooey Gooey Butter Cake

1 dry yellow cake mix
1 stick melted butter
2 eggs

Mix and spread in greased oblong pan.

8 oz. cream cheese
2 eggs
1 box powdered sugar

Mix and pour on top of other mixture

Heat oven to 350 degrees. Bake for 40-45 minutes.

Mrs. D. A. New, Lilbourn, Missouri

Crazy Cake

1-1/2 C. flour
1 C. sugar
1 tsp. soda

1/2 tsp. salt
3 tbsp. cocoa

Mix dry ingredients thoroughly in 8" cake pan, with a fork. Do not grease cake pan.

Add:
1 tbsp. vinegar
1 tsp. vanilla

6 tbsp. oil or melted shortening
1 C. warm water

Mix thoroughly with dry ingredients using a fork. Bake in 350 degree oven for 30 minutes.

Karen Colmer, Mansfield, Illinois

Lemon Egg White Cake

Beat 4 egg whites, 1/4 tsp. cream of tarter and 1 C. sugar very stiff. Spread in well greased 10" pie plate. Bake in 275 degree oven for 1 hour. Leave in oven until cool. Beat 4 egg yolks; add 1/2 cup sugar, and juice of one lemon. Cook on very low heat until thick, stirring constantly. When cool, fold in 1 carton stiffly beaten whipping cream (1 large carton of Cool Whip can be used also).

Take top off cake. It may break into many pieces, but save them to put on top of custard. Put custard on cake; top with pieces. Refrigerate overnight; cover with whipping cream when serving.

Mrs. Wilson (Eileen) Odle, Vero Beach, Florida

Festive Holiday Cake

2 C. granulated sugar	1 tsp. salt
1 C. cooking oil	1 tsp. baking soda
3 eggs	1 tsp. baking powder
8oz. can crushed pineapple	1 tsp. cinnamon
(juice pack)	2 C. finely chopped bananas
1-1/2 tsp. white vanilla	1-3/4 C. sifted powdered sugar
2 C. all-purpose flour	3 tbsp. orange juice
1 C. whole wheat flour	

Beat together the sugar and oil in a large bowl. Add eggs, one at a time, beating well after each addition. Blend in undrained pineapple and vanilla. Stir in flours, salt, baking soda, baking powder, and cinnamon. Blend into pineapple mixture well. Then stir in bananas gently. Turn into greased and floured 10" tube pan. Bake at 350 degrees for 60-70 minutes. Cool in pan for 10 minutes. Remove to rack. Prepare glaze: Combine the powdered sugar and orange juice. Drizzle over cake when it is cool. Serves 16.

Cynthia Kannenberg, Milwaukee, Wisconsin

Eazy Snack Cake

2 C. flour
1 tbsp. baking powder
1 tsp. salt
1/2 cup butter
3/4 C. sugar

1 tsp. vanilla
2 large eggs
1 carton (8oz.) of vanilla yogurt
1/4 C. angel flake coconut
1/2 tsp. cinnamon

Sift together flour, baking powder, cinnamon and salt. Cream butter, sugar, vanilla until light and fluffy. Beat in eggs, one at a time. Blend flour mixture into creamed mixture alternately with the yogurt. Stir in coconut. Pour into greased and floured 8" pan. Bake at 350 degrees for 45 minutes. Serve warm topped with thin slices of chedder cheese or serve with a scoop of sweetened whipped cream. Serves 8.

Cynthia Kannenberg, Milwaukee, Wisconsin

Misty Mountain Apple Cake

3 C. chopped peeled apples
1-1/2 tsp. salt
3/4 C. sugar
2 tsp. baking powder
3/4 C. golden raisins
2 eggs
1/3 C. chopped almonds

1/3 C. oil
3 tbsp flour
1/3 C. water
1 tsp. cinnamon
1/3 C. sugar
2-1/2 C. flour
1-1/2 tsp. vanilla

Combine apples, 3/4 C. sugar, raisins, nuts, 3 tbsp. flour and cinnamon. Set aside. Blend flour, baking powder and salt. Beat together: eggs, oil water, 1/3 C. sugar and vanilla. Gradually stir flour mixture until completely blended. Turn batter out on floured board and with floured hands, shape batter into a ball and divide into three equal parts. Roll out one piece to make a 9" square. Place it on an oiled 9" square pan. Cover with half the apple mixture. Roll out the second piece just like the first and place over apple layer. Cover with the rest of the apple mixture. Roll out third piece of dough and place on top. Make several slits on top layer to allow steam to escape. Bake at 350 degrees for 60-70 minutes. Frost while warm. Serves 9.

Frosting:

1 C. confectioner's sugar 1/4 tsp. vanilla
2 tbsp milk

Blend until smooth.

Lori Prange (age 14), Lincoln, Nebraska

Banana Creme Torte With Broiled Coconut Frosting

Cake:

1/2 C. butter
1-1/2 C. sugar
2 eggs
1 C. mashed bananas
1 tsp. almond extract

2-3/4 C. all-purpose flour, sifted
1 tsp. baking soda
1/4 tsp. salt
1/2 C. buttermilk

Cream butter and sugar. Blend in eggs, bananas and extract. Sift flour, baking soda and salt through sifter. Add buttermilk and blend. Pour batter into a greased 9" square or round pan. Bake at 350 degrees (325 degrees for glass pans) for 40 minutes. Cool 10 minutes then split into 2 layers.

Broiled Coconut Frosting:

1 C. brown sugar
2 tbsp butter
1/2 C. coconut

3 tbsp. cream
1 tsp. rum flavoring
Slivered almonds (optional)

Blend all ingredients. Spread over each slightly warm cake layer. Set under pre-heated broiling unit in oven and broil for a few minutes or until delicately brown and bubbly. Cool.

Banana Creme Filling:

1 pkg. banana instant pudding
1 envelope Dream Whip
1 C. cold milk

Whip with electric mixer until thickened. Let sit about 2 minutes. Spread between cake layers.

Applesauce Cake

1 C. sugar
1/2 C. shortening
1 egg
1-1/2 C. applesauce
2 C. whole wheat flour
1/2 C. raisins
1/2 C. walnut meats

3/4 tsp. soda
2 tsp. baking powder
1 tsp. cinnamon
1/2 tsp. nutmeg
1/2 tsp. cloves
1/4 tsp. salt

Cream shortening. Add sugar and cream. Add beaten eggs and applesauce. Sift together all dry ingredients and mix all together. Bake in loaf pan at 350 degrees for 45 minutes.

Pineapple Cake

2 C. flour
2 C. sugar
2 eggs
1 tsp. salt

1 tsp. baking soda
1 large can crushed pineapple undrained
1 C. chopped walnuts

Mix ingredients in order and bake at 350 degrees for 40 minutes.

Frosting:

1 stick margarine (room temperature)
1 (8 oz.) pkg. cream cheese (room temperature)
2 C. powdered sugar

Blend together until smooth.

Marge Kamenisch, Joliet, Illinois

Banana Loaf

1/4 C. butter
1 C. sugar
2 eggs

3 to 4 bananas (mashed)
1-1/2 C. flour
1 tsp. soda

Mix all ingredients well. Put in loaf pan and bake at 350 degrees for 40-50 minutes.

Mrs. Joyce Arnett, Winnipeg, Manitoba Canada

Cream Cheese Cake

1 - 8 oz. pkg. cream cheese
2 sticks butter or oleo
1-1/2 C. sugar
2 tsp. vanilla
4 eggs

2-1/4 C. flour with 2 tsp. baking powder
1 C. pecans
1 C. candied mixed fruit

Cream cheese, butter, sugar and vanilla well; add eggs, one at a time. Beat well. Gradually add 2 C. flour. Dredge nuts and fruit with 1/4 C. flour; fold into batter. Pour in oiled bundt or tube pan. Bake for 1 hour and 10 minutes at 325 degrees. Cool in pan for 5 minutes. Remove.

Elizabeth Swain Lawson, Delberton, West Virginia

Eggless, Milkless, Butterless Cake

Boil for 5 min.:
1 C. sugar
1/2 C. shortening
1/2 tsp. salt

1-1/2 C. water
1/2 C. raisins
1 tsp. each cinnamon, cloves
and nutmeg

Let cool and stir in 1 tsp. soda dissolved in 1 tbsp. water. Stir in 2 C. flour. Bake for 30 minutes at 375 degrees. This makes a good moist cake.

Jean Baker, Chula Vista, California

Sugarless Cream Cake

2-1/4 C. sifted cake flour
2-1/4 tsp. baking powder
1/4 tsp. salt
1/2 C. shortening
2 tsp. grated orange rind
1-1/4 C. Karo (Red label)

3 egg yolks beaten until thick
and lemon colored
1/2 cup milk
1-1/2 tsp. vanilla
3 egg whites
1 small pkg. chocolate pudding

Sift flour once; measure. Add baking powder and salt and sift together 3 times. Cream shortening with orange rind; add Karo gradually, beaten well after each addition. Add 1/4 of flour and beat until smooth. Add remaining flour in thirds alternately with milk in halves. Beat very well after each addition. For best results, beat cake very well at each stage of mixing. Add vanilla. Beat egg whites until they will hold up in moist peaks. Stir quickly but thoroughly into batter. Bake in two greased 8-inch layer pans in moderate oven at 375 degrees for 30 minutes or until done. Cool

Prepare pudding as directed on package, reducing milk to 1-2/3 cups. Cool.

Split layers in halves. Spread pudding between layers, arranging a cut surface of cake against a baked surface to avoid slipping of layers.

Sift powdered sugar on top of cake. If desired, sift sugar over lace paper doily to make design. Remove doily carefully.

Zenana Warren, Wauseon, Ohio

Chocolate Angel Food

1-1/2 C. egg whites	1-1/2 C. sugar
1/4 C. cold water	1 C. cake flour
1-1/4 tsp. cream of tarter	1/2 C. sugar
1 pinch of salt	5 tbsp. cocoa
	Vanilla

Beat egg whites, salt and water until foamy, then add cream of tarter. Beat until soft peaks stand up. Fold in 1-1/2 C. sifted sugar and then fold in cake flour, 1/2 C. sugar and cocoa which have been sifted together. Add vanilla. Bake at 325 degrees until it raises and sort of shrinks down again.

Lois Pritchard, Atkinson, Illinois

Coconut Cake Bars

Slice a pound cake 1/2 inch thick. Cut each slice into 4 strips. Spread three sides with butter and honey; roll in flaked coconut; place on greased cookie sheet. Toast in moderate oven (375 degrees) about 5 to 10 minutes or until delicate brown.

Anna Mae Pritchyk, Clarks Summit, Pennsylvania

Carrot and Zucchini Brownies

1/4 C. margarine or butter	1 tsp. baking powder
3/4 C. brown sugar or honey	1/4 tsp. salt
1 egg	1 C. grated carrots
1 cup flour	1 C. grated zucchini

Preheat oven to 350 degrees F. or 180 degrees C. Melt margarine or butter in a saucepan, add sugar or honey, stir until well blended. Remove from heat, beat in egg. Sift together flour, baking powder and salt. Beat flour mixture and carrot and zucchini into butter, sugar and egg mixture.

Pour into an 8x8x2 inch greased pan. Bake for 35 minutes. Cut into squares while slightly warm.

Mrs. Gordon Ede, Invermere, British Columbia

Snow Drop Cake (No Baking)

2-6oz. pkg. of Zwieback toast
2 envelopes of Dream Whip prepared according to instructions on package.
1/4 lb. powdered sugar
2 tbsp. granulated sugar

3 tbsp. rum (or vanilla extract)
6 oz. <u>unsalted</u> butter or margarine
1/4 lbs. finely ground walnuts (other nuts are okay)
1 to 1-1/2 C. milk
2 egg yolks

Beat egg yolks, butter and 1/4 lb. powdered sugar until smooth and creamy. Add 2 tbsp. rum extract and 1/4 lb. ground walnuts. Mix until smooth. Divide prepared Dream Whip into two equal portions. Mix one portion into cream, and save other portion for later.

Dissolve granulated sugar in milk and add 1 tbsp. of rum extract. Dip and turn individual toast, but do not soak. Lay toast to cover bottom of 4 qt. dish. Judging from the number of toasts used and the numbers remaining, divide the cream equally according to the number of layers expected. Spread portion of cream over dipped toast layer. Lay dipped toast on top of cream and cover again with portion of cream. Repeat if necessary until all of the toast and cream are used. Cover cake with the remaining Dream Whip. Decorate with fresh fruit, drops of jam or candy. Refrigerate before serving. Flavors blend to optimum in a day in the refrigerator. Serve directly from dish.

Julianna R. Heil, Winters, California

Poor Man's Icing

1 stick oleo
1/4 C. Crisco
1 C. sugar

3/4 cup warm milk
1 tsp. vanilla (or more if desired)

Cream oleo, Crisco and sugar until very creamy - add milk, small amount at a time or it will be very discouraging. Add vanilla and beat until very smooth. This icing will keep for as long a a week or more unrefrigerated. If you wish, you can substitute brown sugar and use maple flavoring. Using white sugar, it can also be substituted for Reddi whip type topping.

Ina Spencer, Pleasantville, Pennsylvania

Betty's Chocolate Cake

3 squares of semi-sweet
chocolate
1 C. hot coffee
2 C. sugar
1/2 C. margarine, melted
2 eggs

1 C. buttermilk
2-1/2 C. flour
1/2 tsp. baking powder
2 tsp. baking soda
1/4 tsp. salt
1 tsp. vanilla

Cook the 3 squares of chocolate in the 1 C. coffee; set aside. Cream well the sugar, margarine, egg and add the buttermilk; mix in all the dry ingredients and add the chocolate mix and vanilla, creaming good. This can be baked in layers, as cupcakes, in a 9x13" cake pan or even as a bundt cake. Layers bake 20-25 mnutes, 9x13" bakes 35-40 minutes, cupcakes for 20-25 minutes and bundt cake for 50 minutes. All in a 350 degree oven. Frost with your favorite frosting.

Betty Brenna, Faribault, Minnesota

Popcorn Cake

Pop enough popcorn to round an angel food cake pan. Put the popcorn into a bowl and toss with 8oz peanuts and 1 lb. gumdrops small ones. Then melt together: 1/2 C. margarine, 1/2 C. oil, 1 lb. marshmallows. Pour over popcorn and press into the angel food cake pan, chill. Invert onto a plate when set firm and cut into slices.

Betty Brennan, Faribault, Minnesota

Strudel Top Apple Pie

3 med. tart apples (about 1 lb.)
1 pkg. coconut pecan frosting
mix, divided
1/4 tsp. salt
1 tsp. cinnamon
1-1/2 tsp. lemon juice
1/2 tsp. lemon rind
1 tbsp. butter, approx.

Strudel Topping:

1/3 crust
1 C. frosting mix
1 tbsp. butter, softened

Pastry dough (double crust, reserve part)

Preheat oven to 425 degrees. Measure 1 C. frosting mix and set aside in medium bowl. (Roll out dough for bottom crust. Put remaining dough in bowl with frosting mix for strudel topping) Wash, pare, core and slice apples in large mixing bowl. Add remaining frosting mix, salt, cinnamon, lemon juice and rind. Toss until apples are well coated and ingredients are well mixed and distributed. Pour apples into pastry shell. Place small chunks of butter (about 1 tbsp.) on top of apples. Prepare strudel topping by cutting pastry, frosting and butter together until the consistency of rice. Sprinkle topping on apples. Be sure to cover completely, especially the edges. Bake at 425 degrees for 10 minutes. Reduce heat to 350 degrees and bake for 45 minutes, or until apples are soft when tested with fork.

Apple Custard Torte

2 C. flour
1 C. butter or margarine
2 tbsp. sugar
1/4 tsp. salt

5 med. sized apples
(Winesap or MacIntosh)
1 C. sugar
1/2 tsp. cinnamon

Mix the flour, butter, 2 tbsp. of sugar and salt together as you would pastry. Line bottom and sides of 9x13" pan. Cover with a thick layer of sliced apples, which have been peeled. Sprinkle with 1 C. of sugar and the cinnamon, which have been mixed together. Bake for 1 hour at 350 degrees.

Custard:

3 egg yolks
2 C. milk
3 tbsp. sugar

2 tbsp. cornstarch
1 tsp. vanilla

Beat egg yolks thoroughly, add milk, sugar and cornstarch. Cook in

-165-

top of double boiler until thick. Add vanilla and cool. Pour on top of baked mixture.

Meringue:

3 egg whites   1/8 tsp. cream of tartar
1/3 C. sugar

Beat egg whites until stiff. Slowly pour in the sugar while beating and add the cream of tartar. Spread on top of custard and bake at 350 degrees for 15 minutes or until brown.

Carme Venella, Laurel Springs, New Jersey

Million Dollar Chocolate Fluff Pie

Crust: 3/4 C. chopped toasted pecans
3 C. flaked coconut   1/2 C. butter, melted

Preheat oven to 325 degrees. Combine all of the crust ingredients. Press into the bottom and sides of a 10-inch glass pie pan. Bake 15 minutes. Cool on wire rack.

Filling:
4oz. German Sweet Chocolate   8oz. cream cheese, softened
2 C. miniature marshmallows   4 C. thawed frozen whipped
2 tbsp. sugar   topping
Dash salt   1/2 tsp. vanilla

Melt chocolate over a double boiler with the marshmallows, sugar, salt and milk; stir until melted. Remove from heat. Beat the cheese until smooth. Beat in the chocolate mixture; mix well. Blend in vanilla. Set aside to cool. Fold in frozen whipped topping. Spoon into cooled pie shell. Garnish with shaved chocolate or toasted coconut. Refrigerate overnight. Serves 8-10.

Cyndee Kannenberg, Brown Deer, Wisconsin

Pinto Bean Pie

1-1/3 C. margarine or butter   3/4 C. mashed, well cooked
1-1/2 C. firmly packed brown   pinto beans with very little
sugar (light brown)   seasonings
3 large eggs   1 tsp. vanilla
                                         1 unbaked 9" pie shell

Beat together butter and sugar until fluffy. Beat in eggs one at a time, then stir in the beans and vanilla. Turn the mixture into the pie shell and bake at 350 degrees for 45-50 minutes, or until lightly browned. Cool before serving. Just before serving, sprinkle with a light coating of sugar and cinnamon and add a dip of Cool Whip.

Joy Parrish, Stamping Ground, Kentucky

Pinto Bean Pie

1/2 C. white sugar
1 C. brown sugar
1/2 C. butter or margarine

1 heaping cup of mashed pinto beans
2 eggs, beaten

Blend sugars, eggs and butter until creamy. Add beans; blend well. Pour into 9-inch unbaked shell. Bake at 375 degrees for 20 minutes, then at 350 degrees for 25 minutes.

Carrie Wright, Buena Vista, Colorado

Sweet Potato Pie

Combine:
1-1/2 C. mashed, cooked
sweet potatoes
1/2 C. sugar
1/2 tsp. salt

1/2 tsp. nutmeg
1 tsp. cinnamon
1/4 tsp. cloves
2 eggs, well beaten
1/2 tsp. vanilla

Melt 1/4 C. butter in 1 C. milk. Pour gradually into potato mixture; stirring constantly. Beat gently until well blended and smooth. Turn into pastry lined 9-inch pie pan. Bake at 450 degrees for 10 minutes. Reduce heat to 350 degrees and bake 45 minutes, or until knife comes out clean.

Southern Sweet Potato-Pecan Pie

1 unbaked pie shell
1 large (303) can of yams,
mashed
1-1/2 C. evaporated milk
1 C. brown sugar
1 tbsp. melted butter
3 eggs beaten

1 tsp. ginger
1 tsp. cinnamon
1 tsp. nutmeg
1 tsp. salt
1/2 C. pecans, chopped
10-12 pecan halves

Heat milk, sugar, butter and spices; add in the yams and gradually add the eggs. Stir in the chopped pecans. Mix well. Pour into pie shell. Decorate top with pecan halves. Bake 40 minutes in a 425 degree oven. Cool 20 minutes before serving.

Mrs. Joy Parrish, Stamping Ground, Kentucky

Joy's Peanut Butter Pie

2/3 C. firmly packed brown sugar
1 C. sifted confectioners sugar
1 tbsp. instant coffee
1/4 C. cornstarch
1/4 tsp. salt
1-3/4 C. canned milk
1/4 C. prepared instant coffee

3/4 C. peanut butter (chunky style)
1 tbsp. butter, melted
3 egg yolks, slightly beaten
1 large pie shell, baked
3 egg whites
6 tbsp. granulated sugar

Mix brown sugar, confectioners sugar, instant coffee, cornstarch and salt in a large bowl; set aside. Combine the milk, liquid coffee, peanut butter and butter in a saucepan, gradually add in the egg yolks. Cook, stirring constantly until smooth and thick. Stir in cornstrach mixture and cook 4-6 minutes. Pour into the baked pie shell.

Beat egg whites until foamy, then gradually beat in the granulated sugar and continue beating until mixture forms stiff shiny peaks. Spread over the pie and seal the edges of the crust with the meringue. Bake at 425 degrees for 5-7 minutes, or until meringue is golden brown. Cool well before cutting.

Mrs. Joy Parrish, Stamping Ground, Kentucky

Sour Cream Apple Pie

2 tbsp. flour
1/8 tsp. salt
3/4 C. sugar
1 egg

1 C. sour cream
1/2 tsp. vanilla
2 C. chopped apples
Pastry

Sift flour, salt and sugar together. Add slightly beaten egg, sour cream and vanilla. Beat until smooth. Add to apples and pour into pastry lined 9" pie tin. Bake in a hot oven (425 degrees) for 15 minutes. Reduce heat to 350 degrees and bake for 30 minutes. Remove from oven and add:

Crumb Topping:

1/3 C. sugar
1/3 C. flour

1 tsp. cinnamon
1/4 C. butter

Blend together and sprinkle over pie. Bake at 400 degrees for 10 minutes.

Libia's Pineapple Creamy Pie

Crust:
3 egg whites
3/4 C. sugar
1 C. walnuts, finely chopped
12 soda crackers, unsalted,
crushed fine

Filling:
22 large marshmallows
1/2 C. pineapple juice
1 C. heavy cream, whipped
1 C. drained crushed pineapple

Beat egg whites, add sugar slowly. Beat well until stiff. Fold in nuts and soda crackers. Press into 9-inch pie pan and bake at 350 degrees for 25 minutes. Meanwhile, melt marshmallows in a double boiler in the juice from drained pineapple. Hold aside; let cool. Whip cream, then add crushed pineapple. Combine with the marshmallow mixture. Pour into cooled crust. Chill several hours.

Mrs. Libia Foglesong, San Bruno, California

Pecan Raisin Cream Pie

1 pkg. (8oz) cream cheese,
room temperature
1 pkg. coconut pecan frosting
mix

2 tbsp. corn syrup
1 C. raisins
3/4 C. milk
9" pastry crust, baked

Heat milk, corn syrup and frosting mix on medium heat until hot and smooth. Cool. Blend in cream cheese. Pour into pastry shell. Chill before serving.

Raisin Pie

1 C. raisins
3 eggs
1 C. sugar

1/4 lb. butter
1 tbsp. flour

Cook raisins in a small amount of water until tender. Separate egg yolks and whites. Mix sugar and flour with beaten yolks. Pour egg mixture into raisins and cook until thick. Pour into baked pastry shell and cover with meringue. Bake in moderate oven (350 degrees) about 12 minutes. Makes one 9-inch pie. 6-8 servings.

Meringue:

Beat egg whites until soft peaks form. Gradually beat in 6 tbsp. sugar and continue beating until stiff.

Walnut Pie

3 tbsp. butter, softened
3 eggs
1 pkg. coconut pecan
frosting mix
1/3 C. light corn syrup

1 tsp. vanilla
3/4 C. evaporated milk
1/2 tsp. salt
1 C. walnuts
Pastry for 9" pie

Preheat oven to 450 degrees. Combine all the filling ingredients and blend well. Pour into prepared, uncooked pie crust. Bake at 450 degrees for 10 minutes. Reduce heat to 350 degrees and cook for another 35 minutes.

Impossible Pie

2 C. milk
4 eggs
1 tsp. vanilla
1/2 C. flour

1/2 stick oleo
2/3 C. sugar
1/4 tsp. salt
1 C. coconut

Put all ingredients in blender and blend for 20 seconds. Pour into 10-inch pie plate. Bake 1 hour at 350 degrees or until knife comes out clean. Crust will settle to bottom, custard in center and toasted coconut on top.

Rosemary Kodunc, Gilbert, Minnesota

Torture Pie

3 egg whites   1/2 tsp. baking power

Beat until stiff. Add 1 C. sugar gradually and beat; add 1 tsp. vanilla. Crush 20 Ritz crackers and 3/4 C. fine pecan pieces; add to egg whites. Put in 9-inch pie plate and bake 25 mintues at 350 degrees. Cool. Slice 3 ripe bananas on top and frost with Cool Whip (medium size carton).

Mary M. West, Columbia, Tennessee

Fresh No-bake Peach Pie

Make a crust and bake and cool. Filling: 6 large peaches, sliced, sugared and sprinkled with fruit fresh to keep them from darkening. Let set until juice forms, pour juice into measuring cup. You need

2 C. of liquid; add water to get the needed amount. Put juice in saucepan, add 3 tbsp. cornstarch to liquid, stir and add 1/4 C. sugar, 1 tsp. almond extract and a few drops of yellow food coloring. Cook and stir continuously until liquid becomes thick and clear or glazed looking. Put small amount of glaze in bottom of cooled pie crust. Pour remaining glaze over peaches. Mix well, put glazed peaches in crust; refrigerate. Serve topped with whipped cream or prepared topping.

Mrs. Eleanor Shelley, Youngstown, Ohio

Peachy Custard Pie

1 can diced peaches, drained	1 C. Bisquick
1/4 tsp. cinnamon	1-1/2 C. milk
1/4 tsp. nutmeg	3 eggs
1/2 C. sugar	Pinch of salt
1 tsp. almond extract	

Preheat oven to 400 degrees. Grease 9-inch pie plate, put drained diced peaches in pie plate; sprinkle peaches with cinnamon. In a blender, put 3 eggs, 1/2 C. sugar, nutmeg, almond extract, milk, Bisquick and pinch of salt. Blend 1 minute. Pour blended mixture over peaches in pie plate. Bake for 35-40 minutes or until pie sets up and is lightly browned. Let set 10 minutes before cutting. Can be served warm or cold; refrigerate leftovers.

Mrs. Eleanor Shelley, Youngstown, Ohio

Carol's Sliced Pumpkin Pie

1 small pumpkin (peeled and sliced thin)	1/2 tsp. nutmeg
1 tsp. cinnamon	1 C. sugar
4 tbsp. water	3 tbsp. butter
	Few drops vanilla

Prepare pie crust for top and bottom. Dust the bottom with flour. Add the sliced pumpkin, sugar, and spices. Add vanilla to water and pour on pumpkin. Sift a small amount of flour over this. Dot with butter, cover with top crust. Bake at 350 degrees for 1 hour.

Carol Favreau, Brunswick, Maine

Fresh Rhubarb Pie

2 eggs
1-3/4 C. sugar
2 C. fresh sliced rhubarb

1 C. soda cracker crumbs
1/4 C. crushed pineapple, undrained
3 tbsp. butter

Combine sugar and eggs. Add rhubard, crumbs, pineapple. Mix thoroughly and pour into pastry lined pan. Dot with butter. Bake at 425 degrees for 45 minutes. Serve with your favorite whipped topping or ice cream.

Mrs. John Eudy, Des Moines, Iowa

Rhubard Pie

3-1/2 C. rhubarb
1-1/2 C. sugar
2-1/2 tsp. tapioca

2 eggs
Vanilla

Beat eggs good, sugar, tapioca and vanilla. Stir and then add rhubarb. Put this in pie crust, it's a two crust pie. Bake at 375 degrees.

Mrs. Lois Pritchard, Atkinson, Illinois

Rhubarb Torte

2 C. flour
2 tbsp. sugar

1 C. oleo or butter

Work oleo in real well until crumbly. Pat into a 9x13" pan. Bake at 350 degrees for 15 minutes.

6 egg yolks, beaten
1 C. half & half cream
1/2 tsp. salt

2 C. sugar
4 tbsp. flour
6 C. rhubarb, cut up small

Mix together. Pour this over crust while hot and bake at 350 degrees until custard is set - about 1 hour. Beat 6 egg whites until stiff. Add 12 level tbsp. sugar, 1 tsp. vanilla and beat until real stiff again. Spread over baked rhubard and brown in oven.

Karen Colmer, Mansfield, Illinois

Oatmeal Pie

1/4 C. honey
1/4 C. melted margarine
2/3 C. molasses
3 eggs

1 tsp. cinnamon
1 C. rolled oats
1/2 tsp. ginger

Mix and pour into a 9-inch pie shell and bake 1 hour at 350 degrees. For variation, add 1 C. crushed pineapple, 2/3 C. coconut and 1/2 C. raisins and decrease the oats to 2/3 C.

Joan LeViness, Winsted, Connecticut

Surprise Pie

1/2 C. sugar
1/4 C. butter or margarine,
softened
1 C. dark or light corn syrup
1/4 tsp. salt

3 well beaten eggs
1/2 C. shredded coconut
1/2 C. quick cooking oats
1-9 inch unbaked pie shell

Cream sugar and butter or margarine until fluffy. Add syrup and salt; beat well. Beat in eggs, one at a time. Stir in coconut and oats. Pour in pastry shell. Bake at 350 degrees until a knife inserted into off-center of pie comes out clean (about 50 minutes). Cool before serving.

Jo Wendt, Eau Claire, Wisconsin

Easy But Beautiful Fruit Tarts

1 pkg. (4-serving size) instant lemon pudding mix
2 C. cold milk
8 baked 3-inch tart shells (cooled)
2 C. canned mixed fruits (drained)
1 pkg. (3oz) strawberry or orange gelatin

Make pudding with milk as directed on package. Divide evenly into bottom of tart shells. Arrange drained fruit on top of pudding and chill well. Prepare gelatin as directed on package and chill until thickened. Spoon gently over fruit in tarts to create a glaze. Chill tarts until ready to serve. Can be garnished with whipped topping if desired or left plain. Makes 8 tarts.

Jodie McCoy, Tulsa, Oklahoma

Pineapple-Banana Tortlets

Slice 1 large banana and divide among 3 tart pans putting 4 slices on the side and bottom of pan. Sprinkle with 2 tbsp. coconut. Melt 1-1/2 tbsp. margarine and add 1 tsp. cinnamon, 1 tbsp. honey and 10oz crushed pineapple with juice. Mix 2 tsp. water with 1 tsp. arrowroot powder (or cornstarch). Add and cook until thick. Pour into pans and sprinkle with granola. Chill well. Makes 3.

Joan LeViness, Winsted, Connecticut

Meringue Shells

Separate 3 eggs while still cold. Bring egg whites to room temperature. Add 1/4 tsp. cream of tartar, dash of salt and 1 tsp. vanilla. Beat until frothy. Gradually add 1C. sugar; continue beating to very stiff peaks. Meringue should be glossy, not dry. Cover baking sheet with ungreased paper such as a grocery bag. Bake in 275 degree oven for 1 hour. Turn off heat and let shells dry in oven with door closed for about 1 hour; this makes them extra crisp. Fill with ice cream, fresh fruit or a cream filling.

Miss Adela Conejo, Seguin, Texas

COOKIES

Carma Bites

35 Kraft carmels	3/4 C. melted butter (only
6 tbsp. cream	butter)
1 C. flour	1 tsp. vanilla
1 C. oatmeal, raw	1-13oz pkg. chocolate chips
3/4 tsp. soda	1/2 C. chopped pecans
1/4 tsp. salt	

Mix flour, oatmeal, sugar, soda and vanilla. Add melted butter and mix well. Pat 1/2 or more of the mixture in a 9x13" cake pan. Save remainder of mixture for topping. Bake 10 minutes at 350 degrees. Now melt carmels with cream in a double boiler. Put chocolate chips and nuts on top of baked crust base. Cover with creamy carmels. Spread carefully and add rest of crumbs and put in oven and bake 10 minutes longer. Cool and cut in squares or bars.

Linda Lou Urich, Dows, Iowa

Pudding Cookies

2 C. sugar	2/3 C. evaporated milk
3/4 C. butter or margarine	

Bring mixture to boil; stirring often. Remove from heat. Add one 4oz. package Pistachio instant pudding and 3-1/2 C. quick oats. Mix well and let stand 15 minutes. Drop by tsp. on wax paper. Note: can use any flavor instant pudding and food coloring if desired.

Kathy Dietz, Grosvenordale, Connecticut

Cherry Squares

1 C. margarine or butter	1-1/2 C. sugar
4 eggs	2 tsp. vanilla
2 C. flour	Cherry Pie Filling

Cream butter or margarine. Add sugar, eggs, vanilla and flour. Mix well; it will be thick. Spread evenly on greased cookie sheet. Knife squares off (seven one way and six other way). In center of each square, use pie filling. Approximately 2 cherries in each. Bake for 40 minutes at 350 degrees. Cool. Sprinkle with powdered sugar.

Marge Camenisch, Joliet, Illinois

-175-

Chocolate Refrigerator Cookie Dessert

1 C. shortening or margarine
1/2 C. brown sugar
1-1/2 tsp. vanilla
2-3/4 C. sifted flour
1 tsp. salt

1/2 C. sugar
2 eggs
2 squares unsweetened chocolate
1/2 tsp. soda
1 pt. whipping cream

Mix together the margarine, sugars, eggs and chocolate. Add flour, soda and salt. Mix well with hands and press into a long roll about 2-1/2" in diameter. Wrap in waxed paper and chill overnight. Cut in thin (1/8" to 1/16") slices and place on an ungreased sheet. Bake at 400 degrees for 6-8 minutes. Let cool well. Makes about 6 dozen. Stack cookies side by side with sweetened whipped cream in between. Spread whipped cream over the top and sides of the roll. Chill 6-8 hours to let it absorb the moisture and become nice and soft. Slice diagonally. This freezes well.

Joan LeViness, Winsted, Connecticut

Lemon Coolers

1/3 C. confectioners sugar
3/4 C. cornstarch

1 C. butter
1-1/4 C. all-purpose flour

Mix these ingredients together. Roll cookie mixture into logs (2) and roll logs in 1 C. very finely chopped pecans until well coated. Cut in 1" pieces. Press with fork on ungreased cookie sheet. Bake at 350 degrees until slightly brown. Cool.

Icing:

1 C. confectioners sugar (sifted)1/2 stick butter
Lemon juice (to make a thick icing)

Combine confectioners sugar, butter and lemon juice. Ice cookies when cool.

Mrs. Stephanie O'Dell, New York, New York

Lemon Squares

Crust:
2 C. flour
1/2 C. powdered sugar

1 C. butter
1/2 tsp. vanilla

Mix and cut butter into flour mixture. Press into bottom of

buttered 9x13" pan. Bake at 350 degrees for 25 minutes. Meantime make filling.

Filling: Beat together:

4 eggs, beaten
2 C. granulated sugar
1/3 C. lemon juice
Rind of one grated lemon

Add:

1/4 C. flour
1/2 tsp. baking powder

Mix well. Spread over baked crust and bake again at 350 degrees for another 25 minutes. Sprinkle top with confectioners sugar. Cut into small bars. These are very rich. They freeze very well.

Mrs. Arlene Jackson, Niland, California

Overnight Cookies

Cream together:

3 C. brown sugar
1 C. white sugar
1/2 C. butter
1/2 C. lard

Then add:

4 well beaten eggs
1 tbsp. salt
1 tbsp. soda
1 tbsp. cream of tartar
6 C. flour

Mix and form into long loaf and let stand in refrigerator overnight. Slice 1/4" thick and bake at 350 degrees for 8-10 minutes or until brown.

Elsie Gingerich, Kokomo, Indiana

Frosted Gingerbread Nut Cookies

1/2 C. shortening	1 tsp. ginger
2/3 C. sugar	1 egg, unbeaten
1/2 C. molasses	1 tsp. soda
1/2 tsp. salt	2-1/2 C. enriched flour
1/4 tsp. cloves	1/2 C. sour milk
1 tsp. cinnamon	1/2 C. chopped nuts

Combine shortening, sugar, molasses, salt, spices and egg and beat thoroughly. Sift soda with flour. Add flour and sour milk to creamed mixture. Add nuts and mix thoroughly. Drop by teaspoonful on greased baking sheets. Bake in 350 degree oven for 12-15 minutes. Frost with Creamy Vanilla Frosting.

Creamy Vanilla Frosting:

1 tbsp. shortening	1/4 tsp. salt
1 tbsp. butter	2 C. sifted confectioners sugar
3/4 tsp. vanilla	3 tbsp. scalded cream (approx.)

Combine shortening, butter, vanilla and salt and blend. Beat in 1/2 C. sugar, add hot cream alternately with remaining sugar; beating vanilla after each addition. Add only enough cream to make a nice spreading consistency.

Arlene Krug, Cedar Rapids, Iowa

Pineapple Maple Bars
(Makes two dozen 2" bars)

	1/3 C. sugar
1 pkg. (8) crescent rolls	2 tbsp. cornstarch
1/4 C. maple syrup	1 egg, beaten
5 tbsp. butter or margarine,	1/4 C. coconut
divided	1/4 C. flour
1 C. pineapple (crushed with	3 tbsp. brown sugar
juice)	Chopped nuts, optional

Preheat oven to 350 degrees. Spread crescent rolls into greased 7x11" baking dish. Keep rolls in two long strips. Fill the bottom of the dish and 1-2" up the sides with rolls. Press seams well with fingers so there are no breaks in the crust. Prick dough lightly with fork, but not through. Melt butter. Mix 3 tbsp. with maple syrup. Pour butter and syrup over dough. Spread evenly over surface. Bake 10 minutes. Beat egg and strain. Mix pineapple, egg, sugar and cornstarch. Cook over medium heat, stirring frequently until mixture begins to thicken slightly. Remove from heat. Pour into crust. Mix coconut, remaining butter, brown sugar and flour until they are a mealy consistency and well combined. Sprinkle on top of bars. Bake 20 minutes.

Open Sesame Cookies

1 C. sesame seeds, toasted
2 large eggs
1-1/2 C. brown sugar

2/3 C. oil
2 C. sifted flour
1/4 tsp. baking powder
1 tsp. vanilla

To toast sesame seeds, spread on cookie sheet and place in 350 degree oven for about 4 minutes. Stir during this time and watch carefully so they don't burn. Beat eggs. Add oil, sugar and continue beating until blended. Sift together flour and baking powder. Combine with liquid ingredients. Mix until thoroughly blended. Stir in vanilla and sesame seeds (cooled). Drop dough by teaspoonfuls about 2" apart on greased cookie sheet. Bake at 350 degrees for 10 minutes or until browned, but still soft.

Raisin Duff

1/2 C. sugar
1 tbsp. butter
1/2 C. milk
1 egg

2 C. flour, approx.
1/2 tsp. cinnamon
3/4 C. floured raisins
2 tbsp. baking powder
1/2 tsp. salt

Cook raisins for about fifteen minutes or until they swell and water discolors. Drain and cool raisins saving liquid. Mix rest of the ingredients to make a stiff dough. Add the floured raisins until mixed. Spread dough in ungreased 9x13" pan. Pour the following syrup, while hot, over the dough and bake at 350 degrees until brown (45 minutes). The dough raises to the top and gooey part goes to the bottom.

Syrup:

Use liquid from raisins and add enough water to make 3 C. To this add 1/2 C. brown sugar and 1/2 C. white sugar. Cook until sugar is dissolved, adding 1 tsp. vanilla and 2 tbsp. butter. Pour over dough while hot and bake.

Juanita P. Fulton, Arcadia, Missouri

Lazy Cinnamon Buns

2 loaves frozen bread dough,
thawed
1 stick butter
1 C. brown sugar

2 small boxes vanilla pudding
(not instant)
2 tbsp. milk
1 tsp. cinnamon

Melt butter, sugar, pudding, milk and cinnamon on stove. Tear up one loaf of bread in pieces. Put in 9x13" pan. Pour mixture on top of bread. Take second loaf of bread; tear it up. Put on top and let rise 2-1/2 hours. Bake at 350 degrees for 30 minutes. Pour onto big tray; syrup will run over buns. Very good.

Faye M. Walter, Stowe, Pennsylvania

Toasted Marmalade Bread

1 loaf French bread
1/3 to 1/2 C. soft butter or
margarine

1/2 C. orange marmalade
Cinnamon

Cut bread in 1 to 1-1/2" diagonal slices. Spread with butter, then with marmalade generously. Sprinkle cinnamon over top. Place slices, marmalade side up, on ungreased baking sheet. Heat in hot oven (400 degrees) about 8 minutes, or until hot.

Anna Mae Pritchyk, Clarks Summit, Pennsylvania

My Mom's Apple Bread

2 C. all-purpose flour
2 C. chopped apples (I grate
half of my apples)
1 C. brown sugar
2 eggs

1/2 tsp. salt
1 tsp. baking soda
1 tsp. baking powder
1/2 C. shortening
1 tsp. vanilla
1 C. of nuts, if desired

Sift flour, baking powder, soda and salt. Cream shortening and sugar. Add eggs and beat well. Add apples, nuts and vanilla, stir in the flour mixture. Stir well and pour in a greased and lightly floured baking dish. Sprinkle with a topping of 1/4 C. sugar and 1-1/2 tsp. cinnamon mixed together. Bake for 1 hour at 350 degrees. Do not slice until bread is cool.

Mrs. Joy Parrish, Stamping Ground, Kentucky

Chocolate Chip Cheesecake

2 rolls chocolate chip cookie dough
2 (8oz.) pkgs. cream cheese

1/4 C. sugar
2 eggs
1 tsp. vanilla

Using a brownie pan (ungreased), take one cookie roll and pat down to cover bottom of pan. Mix cream cheese with sugar, eggs, and vanilla. Beat until smooth. Pour in pan. Take second roll of cookie dough and slice into thin slices, covering top of cheese mixture. Bake at 350 degrees for 35 minutes. Keep refrigerated. Note: Any roll of cookie dough will do instead of chocolate chip.

Betty Belair, Cumberland, Rhode Island

Waist Trimmers Cheesecake

2 eggs separated
1 C. skim milk
2 env. unflavored gelatin
1 C. sugar

1/4 tsp. salt
1 tsp. grated lemon peel
3 C. creamed cottage cheese
2 tbsp. lemon juice
1 tsp. vanilla extract

In blender, liquify cottage cheese; add vanilla, lemon peel and lemon juice. Pour into large mixing bowl. Combine gelatin, sugar and salt in a 2 quart saucepan and add beaten egg yolks and milk. Mix well. Cook over medium heat until thickened; stirring constantly. Cool. Add gelatine mixture to cottage cheese and blend well. Beat egg whites until stiff peaks form then blend into cottage cheese mixture. Mix well. Mixture will be runny until set. Pour into 3 ready-made graham cracker pie crusts or 16 ready-made graham cracker tart crusts. Refrigerate until set (2 hours). When ready to serve, top with frozen strawberries, blueberries or other favorite fruit.

Mrs. Stephanie A. O'Dell, New York, New York

Holiday Cheesecake

Crust:
1 C. graham cracker crumbs

3 tbsp. sugar
3 tbsp. margarine, melted

Combine crumbs, sugar and margarine. Press into bottom of 9" springform pan. Bake at 325 degrees for 10 minutes. Reduce oven temperature to 300 degrees.

Cheesecake:
3 (8oz.) pkg. cream cheese
3/4 C. sugar

1 tbsp. lemon juice
1 tbsp. lemon rind (optional)
3 eggs

Combine softened cream cheese, sugar, juice and rind, mixing until well blended. Add eggs one at a time mixing well after each addition. Pour mixture over crust. Bake at 300 degrees for 55 minutes then take out (top does not brown)

Topping:
1 C. dairy sour cream
2 tbsp. sugar

1 tsp. vanilla
Strawberry halves

Combine sour cream, sugar and vanilla. Carefully spread over cheesecake; continue baking for 10 minutes. Loosen cake from rim of pan, cool before removing rim of pan. Garnish with strawberry halves. Chill.

Jennifer Lewis (11 years old), Norwalk, Connecticut

Yogurt Honey Cheesecake

In blender, whip 2 eggs, 1 C. cottage cheese. Add 1/4 C. honey and 3/4 tsp. vanilla. Preheat oven to 350 degrees. Spoon into an 8" square pan or custard cups. Bake for 25 mintues. Mix 1/2 tsp. vanilla, 3/4 C. plain yogurt and 1 tsp. honey. Spread on cakes. Bake 10-15 minutes more. Chill well. If desired, make in a graham cracker crust.

Joan LeViness, Winsted, Connecticut

REFRIGERATOR & GELATIN DESSERTS

Chocolate Eclair Dessert

Butter a 9x13" pan (bottom and sides). Line bottom of pan with whole graham crackers. Beat 2 (3-3/4oz) pkg. instant French vanilla pudding with 3 C. milk. Add a 9oz. thawed carton of Cool Whip to the pudding and mix well. Pour one-half of mixture over layer of crackers, top with another layer of crackers. Pour balance of pudding over crackers and top with another layer of crackers (3 layers of crackers).

Topping:

2 oz. Bakers liquid chocolate	3 tbsp. milk
2 tbsp. soft butter	1 tsp. vanilla
2 tbsp. white syrup	1-1/2 C. powdered sugar

Beat well and pour over graham crackers. Refrigerate 24 hours - do not freeze.

Mrs. Jacquita Newberry, Mackinaw, Illinois

Champagne Salad

1 (8oz) pkg. cream cheese   3/4 C. sugar

Cream the above together thoroughly. Add the following:

1 (10oz) pkg. frozen straw-berries, thawed, undrained	2 bananas sliced
1 #2 can crushed pineapple, drained	1/2 C. chopped nuts
	9oz container Cool Whip, thawed

Spread in a 9x13" pan. Can use a smaller pan for a higher salad. Cover and freeze.

Mrs. Charles Boyer, Fremont, Ohio

Cranberry Salad

Cook 1 box or bag of cranberries in 2 C. water for 3-4 minutes. Add 1-1/2 C. sugar; then strain. Bring to a boil and pour over 3 boxes of orange jello; stir well. Add 1 C. cold water, 1 C. seeded grapes cut up, 1 C. diced apples (fine), 1 C. English walnuts, 1 large can crushed pineapple (don't drain). Mix well. Pour in long cake pan and refrigerate and serve.

Faye Walter, Stowe, Pennsylvania

-184-

E-Z Dream Salad

1 large carton (24oz) cottage cheese
1 (3oz) pkg. gelatin, any flavor
1 (9oz) container whipped topping
1 small can fruit cocktail
1 C. miniature marshmallows (optional)

Stir dry gelatin into cottage cheese.   Mix well with rest of ingredients.

Margie Pulick, Yonkers, New York

No-Cook Ice Cream

2 eggs
1 C. sugar or 1/3 C. honey
1/2 tbsp. vanilla

1 can canned milk (condensed)
1 milk can water

Mix until well blended and pour into shallow dish or pan (tin foil) and freeze until firm.   Variations - add bits of grated chocolate, fruits, coconut, chopped nutmeats, etc.

Margie Pulick, Yonkers, New York

Pineapple Blueberry Gelatin Dessert

1 large pkg. black raspberry jello
1 large can crushed pineapple, drained, reserve juice
1 can of blueberry pie filling
1 large container Cool Whip

Put jello in a small saucepan.   Measure reserved pineapple juice. You need 2 C. of liquid - use pineapple juice and add water to make 2 C.   Pour over jello in pan.   Put on stove; heat, stirring until jello melts.   Put in refrigerator in bowl until jello beings to gel.   Remove; add crushed pineapple and container of Cool Whip. Mix with mixer until light and fluffy.   Fold in blueberry pie filling.   Pour into large glass dish.   Cover with plastic wrap.   Refrigerate several hours until set.   Cut and serve.

Mrs. Eleanor Shelley, Youngstown, Ohio

Lemon Fluff

3 egg whites at room
temperature
1/2 tsp. cream of tartar
1 C. sugar
1 tsp. vanilla

1 pkg. crushed soda crackers
1/4 C. chopped nuts
1 large carton Cool Whip
1 pkg. lemon pudding mix

Grease a 9x13" dish or pan. Preheat oven to 350 degrees. In a bowl, put egg whites and beat until stiff. Add sugar gradually. Continue beating. Add cream of tartar and vanilla and beat until egg whites are stiff and look like marshmallow whipp then fold in crushed soda crackers and 1/2 of the chopped nuts. Spread this mixture in prepared pan or dish and bake until light brown. Remove from oven and cool. While it cools, make pudding according to package directions. Put pudding on cooled crust. Let pudding cool. Top with Cool Whip and sprinkle on nuts - refrigerate.

Mrs. Eleanor Shelley, Youngstown, Ohio

Grace's Green Galore

1 (12oz) pkg. marshmallows   1 C. milk

Melt in double boiler and cool.

1 pkg. chocolate wafers (crushed)   1 tsp. pure peppermint extract
1 pint cream (whipped)   Few drops green food coloring

Add peppermint and green food coloring to cooled marshmallow mixture and fold in whipped cream. Line bottom of 8x8x2" pan with half of wafer crumbs. Pour marshmallow mixture over this and cover with the remaining crumbs. Refrigerate overnight; cut into squares and serve.

Grace Sahli, Little Rock, Arkansas

Pineapple-Custard Mold

1/2 C. sugar
1 env. unflavored gelatin
1/4 tsp. salt
3/4 C. reconstituted nonfat
dry milk
2 beaten egg yolks
1/2 tsp. vanilla

1/2 C. evaporated milk
2 stiffly beaten egg whites
1 (8-3/4oz) can pineapple
tidbits
1/3 C. sugar
4 tsp. cornstarch
Dash salt
3/4 C. orange juice

In small saucepan, combine 1/2 C. sugar, gelatin and 1/4 tsp. salt. Combine milk and egg yolks; add to gelatin mixture. Cook and stir over low heat until mixture thickens slightly and coats metal spoon. Add vanilla. Chill until partially set. Meantime, pour evaporated milk into freezer tray. Freeze until edges are icy; whip to stiff peaks. Fold whipped milk and whites into gelatin mixture. Turn into 4-1/2 C. mold; chill until firm. To prepare sauce, drain pineapple, reserving syrup. In saucepan, combine 1/3 C. sugar, cornstarch and dash salt. Stir in reserved syrup and orange juice. Cook and stir until thickened and bubbly. Reduce heat; cook 1 minute. Cool slightly; stir in pineapple. Chill. Unmold gelatin. Serve with sauce. Makes 8 servings.

Jo Wendt, Eau Claire, Wisconsin

Friendship Salad
(13x9" pan)

Bottom layer:
1 box lemon jello

1 box lime jello
3 C. hot water

Dissolve gelatin. Put in pan to set. When partly set; sprinkle over and press in 1 can crushed pineapple (13-1/4 oz.) drained.

Second layer: Add water to pineapple juice to make 1-1/2 C. liquid. Add to liquid, then boil until thickened: 4 tbsp. flour, 4 tbsp. butter, 2 beaten eggs and 1/2 C. sugar. Cool. Then add 1 C. of Cool Whip. Slice 2 bananas over bottom layer. Spread second layer over bananas. Put into refrigerator to set.

Esther Blatter, McClusky, North Dakota

Ribbon Salad

1 (3oz) pkg. each of lemon, lime and cherry jello
3 C. boiling water
1-1/2 C. cold water
1/2 C. mayonnaise
1 can (1lb., 4-1/2oz) crushed pineapple
1 C. miniature marshmallows
2 pkg. (3oz. each) cream cheese, softened
1 C. whipped cream

Dissolve gelatin flavors separately, using 1 C. boiling water for each. Stir marshmallows into lemon gelatin; set aside. Add 3/4 C. cold water to lime gelatin; pour into a 13x9x2" pan. Chill until set, but not firm. Add 3/4 C. cold water to cherry gelatin; set aside at room temperature. Add cream cheese to lemon mixture; beat until blended. Chill until slightly thickened. Blend in mayonnaise, whipped cream and crushed pineapple. Chill until very thick; spoon gently over lime gelatin. Chill until set, but not firm. Meanwhile, chill cherry gelatin until thickened; pour over lemon gelatin. Chill until firm.

Karen Colmer, Mansfield, Illinois

Cranberry Fluff

1 can (303 or 2 C.) whole cranberry sauce
2 pkg. rasperry jello
1 pkg. Dream Whip
1/2 C. diced walnut meats
2-3 bananas (optional)

Prepare jello according to box directions. Use 1 C. of ice in place of the cup of cold water to speed setting time. Whip Dream Whip according to directions. When jello has begun to set slightly and get thick, beat in the Dream Whip and blend in cranberries. Add walnuts and sliced bananas. Mix well to distribute evenly throughout. Allow to set by placing back in the refrigerator and leaving for about 20-30 minutes.

Melonade Sherbet

2 C. watermelon pulp
1 can (6oz) frozen lemonade
concentrate

1 lemonade can water
2 egg whites, stiffly beaten
Dash of grated nutmeg

Put watermelon through ricer or sieve to make pulp. Combine concentrate, water and pulp, add nutmeg. Pour into freezing tray. Freeze to a mush. Remove from tray and add egg whites. Mix thoroughly. Return to tray and freeze until firm (about 3-4 hours); stirring once or twice during process. Yields approximately 1-1/2 pints. Cantaloupe can be used instead of watermelon. Watermelon is so pink, pretty and cool. Cantaloupe is golden and beautiful too.

Mrs. E. Mazerolas, New York, New York

Harvest Ice Cream Squares

1-1/2 C. graham cracker
crumbs
1/4 C. melted butter
1/2 C. brown sugar
1 tsp. cinnamon
1/4 C. sugar

1 (16oz) can solid pack
pumpkin
1/2 tsp. salt
1/4 tsp. ginger
1/4 tsp. cloves
1 quart vanilla ice cream,
softened

Mix crumbs with sugar and butter, press into bottom of 9" square pan. Combine pumpkin with brown sugar, spices and salt. Fold in ice cream, pour into crumb-lined pan. Cover with foil and freeze until firm. Cut into squares about 20 mintues before serving, top with whipped cream.

Mrs. Judy M. Sax, San Antonio, Texas

Three Sherbet

Juice of
3 lemons
3 oranges

3 C. sugar
3 C. water
3 bananas, mashed

Mix all together and place in ice cube tray in freezing compartment of refrigerator for several hours.

Mrs. William R. Long, Willow Grove, Pennsylvania

-189-

Frozen Salad

1 pkg. Dream Whip
1 can crushed pineapple, drained

1 can cherry pie filling
1 can sweetened condensed milk

Fold together and freeze. Also put in cupcake dishes for individual servings.

Arlene Krug, Cedar Rapids, Iowa

Lemon Fluff

1/2 C. boiling water
1 pkg (3oz) lemon jello
1 C. sugar

1 large can evaporated milk
1/4 C. lemon juice or the juice of 2 lemons

Dissolve lemon jello in boiling water. Add 1 C. sugar, lemon juice and whip with mixture. Chill until set. Whip milk and add to lemon mixture. Pour in pan that has been lined with graham cracker crumbs. Sprinkle a few cracker crumbs on top. Put in freezer until used.

Dena Park, Alcova, Wyoming

Frozen Graham Cracker Snacks

1/2 C. peanut butter (use creamy or chunky)
1-1/2 C. cold milk
1 pkg. (4 serving size) chocolate instant pudding mix
24 graham crackers or cinnamon crackers

Add milk slowly to peanut butter in a deep bowl and blend until well mixed and smooth. Add dry pudding mix and beat slowly about 2 minutes. Let stand 5 minutes. Spread chocolate filling about 1/2" thick on 12 of the crackers. Place remaining crackers on top making 12 sandwiches. Press together gently and smooth filling around edges with table knife. Freeze about 3 hours or until firm.

Jodie McCoy, Tulsa, Oklahoma

Lemon Ice
(6-8 servings)

1 large pkg. lemon jello
1 C. hot water
1 C. lemon/line soda pop

1 C, whipped cream, Dream Whip or Cool Whip
4 tsp. lemon juice
1 tsp. lemon rind

Heat water to boiling in saucepan. Sprinkle in jello and stir until dissolved. Add cold soda pop, lemon juice and rind. Let chill in fridge until egg white consistency. Fold jello mixture into cream. Chill in freezing compartment until frozen. Note: The whipped cream should keep the mixture from becoming icy. If not, remove from freezer, thaw until barely soft and whip before serving.

Noodle Strudle

Cook 1/2 lb. fine noodles; drain. While noodles are still warm, add 2 tbsp. lemon juice. Cream 1 (8oz) cream cheese with 3/4 C. sugar. Add 1 lb. small curd cottage cheese and 1/2 pint sour cream. Add 4 beaten eggs and mix with warm noodles. Pour into 9x12" pan. Sprinkle with topping.

Topping: 1/2 lb. butter (melted) with 1/2 C. sugar, 1 C. corn flakes (crushed). Sprinkle over noodles. Bake at 350 degrees for 1 hour.

Marge Camenisch, Joliet, Illinois

Raspberry/Rice Surprise

1 C. uncooked rice	1/2 C. sugar
3 C. boiling water	2 tbsp. honey
3/4 tsp. salt	1/4 tsp. almond extract
	1 C. cream, whipped

Cook rice in salted water until tender and fluffy. Blend in sugar, honey and almond extract. Chill. Fold in whipped cream.

Raspberry Sauce:

1 tbsp. cornstarch	2 C. raspberries
1/2 C. sugar	1 tbsp. lemon juice
1/4 C. water	

Mix cornstarch and sugar. Add cold water and stir until smooth. Add the raspberries and lemon juice. Bring to boil; reduce heat; simmer 5 minutes. Chill. Top each serving of rice with raspberry sauce. Makes 6 servings.

Rosemary Kodunc, Gilbert, Minnesota

Rice Pudding

1-1/2 C. rich milk	1/4 C. sugar
1 tbsp. melted butter	2 eggs, beaten
1/4 tsp. salt	1/4 tsp. ground coriander seed
1/2 C. raisins	1 tsp. vanilla
2 C. cooked rice	

Combine all ingredients and mix well, adding rice last. Put in a well buttered casserole, top with butter crumbs that have been mixed with a little sugar. Bake the pudding in a 325 degree oven until just set. Serves 4.

Fluffy Rice Dessert

Whip 1 C. cream until stiff. Add sugar and vanilla extract to taste (about 3 tbsp. sugar and 1 tsp. vanilla). Stir in enough cooked rice so that the rice is nicely coated (about 2 C. cooked rice). Drain and add 1 C. crushed pineapple. Mix well and refrigerate until ready to serve. Snack crackers go good with this.

Mrs. Henry S. Kubat, Owatonna, Minnesota

Cherry Pudding

1 C. sugar	2 C. flour
1/2 C. shortening	2 tsp. baking powder
Add 1 egg	1 C. milk

Mix thoroughly and add 1 C. drained cherries (raw). Bake in 350 degree oven for 45 minutes.

Sauce for Cherry Pudding:

Mix 3/4 C. sugar, 2 tbsp. flour, 1 drop almond flavoring and 1 C. cherry juice. Boil together until thick.

Mrs. Russell Hymes, Arenzville, Illinois

Leftover Coffee Parfait

2 env. unflavored gelatin	3/4 C. sugar
1/2 C. cold water	1/2 C. coffee flavored liqueur
3 C. cold leftover coffee	1 C. heavy cream

Sprinkle gelatin over cold water in top of double boiler. Place over simmering water and stir until gelatin is dissolved. Add coffee and 1/2 C. of the sugar; stir until sugar has dissolved. Remove from heat and add 1/4 C. of the coffee liqueur, pour into a shallow pan and refrigerate until firm. Whip cream with remaining sugar until stiff; fold in remaining liqueur. Cut chilled firm gelatin into small cubes. Spoon about half of these into the bottom of 6 parfait glasses, cover with some of the whipped cream, add a second layer of diced gelatin and top with remaining whipped cream.

Mrs. Judy M. Sax, San Antonio, Texas

Quick Devils Pudding

Mix up half package of devils food cake mix. Pour the batter into a well greased 9" square pan. Combine thoroughly 1 C. each chopped nuts and brown sugar with 1/4 C. cocoa. Sprinkle mixture over the cake batter. Pour 1-3/4 C. hot water over cake and bake at 350 degrees for 45 minutes. Cut baked pudding into squares while still warm. Top with whipped cream or ice cream.

Mrs. Eileen Odle, Vero Beach, Florida

-194-

Quick Cooking Pudding

1 C. water	Dash of salt
2 tbsp. flour	1/2 tsp. vanilla
1/4 C. sugar	1 egg
	1/2 C. dry milk solids

Place water in saucepan and bring to boil. Place sugar, flour, salt and cocoa (if making chocolate pudding) in sifter and sift until mixed. Add dry milk solids, egg and dry ingredients together in a medium bowl. Gradually stir in one half of the hot water and beat with a mixer until smooth. Add mixture to the hot water gradually; stirring constantly. Mixture will thicken rapidly. Add vanilla. Serve hot or cold as desired. Makes 3 servings.

Variations

Chocolate Pudding: Add 2 tbsp. cocoa and sift with the flour and sugar. Add 2 tbsp. more sugar to basic recipe.

Caramel Pudding: Substitute brown sugar for white sugar and add 1/4 tsp. maple flavoring syrup.

Coconut Pudding: Stir in 1/4 C. moist coconut after pudding is thickened.

Banana Pudding: Alternate layers of sliced bananas and pudding (1 banana).

Pineapple Pudding: Add 1/2 C. drained crushed pineapple after pudding is thickened or alternate layers of pineapple and pudding.

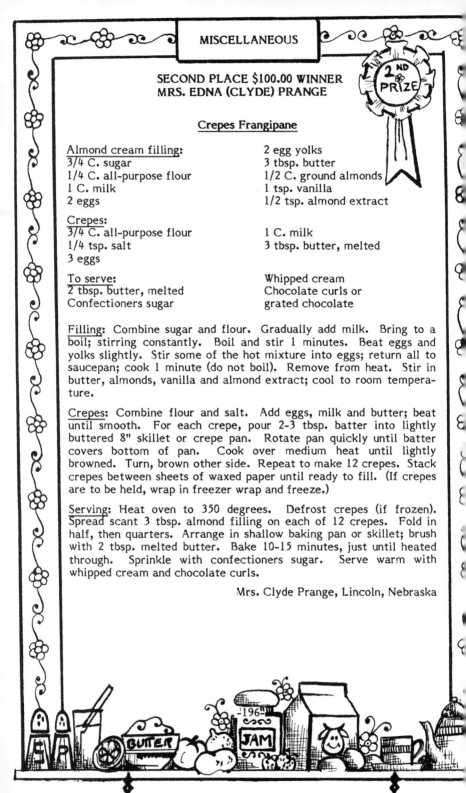

SECOND PLACE $100.00 WINNER
MRS. EDNA (CLYDE) PRANGE

Crepes Frangipane

Almond cream filling:
3/4 C. sugar
1/4 C. all-purpose flour
1 C. milk
2 eggs

2 egg yolks
3 tbsp. butter
1/2 C. ground almonds
1 tsp. vanilla
1/2 tsp. almond extract

Crepes:
3/4 C. all-purpose flour
1/4 tsp. salt
3 eggs

1 C. milk
3 tbsp. butter, melted

To serve:
2 tbsp. butter, melted
Confectioners sugar

Whipped cream
Chocolate curls or
grated chocolate

Filling: Combine sugar and flour. Gradually add milk. Bring to a boil; stirring constantly. Boil and stir 1 minutes. Beat eggs and yolks slightly. Stir some of the hot mixture into eggs; return all to saucepan; cook 1 minute (do not boil). Remove from heat. Stir in butter, almonds, vanilla and almond extract; cool to room temperature.

Crepes: Combine flour and salt. Add eggs, milk and butter; beat until smooth. For each crepe, pour 2-3 tbsp. batter into lightly buttered 8" skillet or crepe pan. Rotate pan quickly until batter covers bottom of pan. Cook over medium heat until lightly browned. Turn, brown other side. Repeat to make 12 crepes. Stack crepes between sheets of waxed paper until ready to fill. (If crepes are to be held, wrap in freezer wrap and freeze.)

Serving: Heat oven to 350 degrees. Defrost crepes (if frozen). Spread scant 3 tbsp. almond filling on each of 12 crepes. Fold in half, then quarters. Arrange in shallow baking pan or skillet; brush with 2 tbsp. melted butter. Bake 10-15 minutes, just until heated through. Sprinkle with confectioners sugar. Serve warm with whipped cream and chocolate curls.

Mrs. Clyde Prange, Lincoln, Nebraska

-196-

Santa Mouse Fudge

1 lb. butter	1 C. dry cocoa powder
1 lb. Velvetta cheese	1 tbsp. vanilla
4 lbs. powdered sugar, sifted	1/2 C. chopped toasted pecans

Melt butter and cheese together. Add sugar and cocoa and mix well. Stir in vanilla. Mix well. Stir in nuts. Place in a buttered 9x13" pan. Cool and cut into pieces. Makes 6-1/2 lbs.

Cynthia Kannenberg, Milwaukee, Wisconsin

Carmel Candy

2 C. white sugar	1 C. cream
1 C. brown sugar	1 C. butter
1 C. light corn syrup	1 C. evaporated milk

Cook over low heat to 248 degrees on candy thermometer; stirring constantly. Remove from heat; add 1 tsp. vanilla. Pour in well greased 8x8" pan. When firm, cut and wrap in plastic wrap.

Mrs. Russell Hymes, Arenzville, Illinois

Cornflake Candy

3/4 C. white sugar   3/4 C. corn syrup (light or dark)

Bring to boil; stirring constantly. Remove from heat and stir in:

3/4 C. peanut butter   4-1/2 C. cornflakes

Mix well and drop by spoonfuls onto wax paper. Let set until cool.

Glenna Mitchell, Merritt Island, Florida

Vanilla Cream Sauce

1-1/4 C. sugar
1 stick margarine   Cream together.

Add:
2 eggs, beaten   1 tsp. vanilla
1 pinch of salt   1/4 C. hot water

Cook in double boiler for 20 mintues until sauce consistency; stirring occasionally. Serve warm over gingerbread, raw apple cake or as a topping for ice cream.

Betty R. Turner, New Haven, Indiana

Popcorn Balls

Mix:
12 C. popped corn   1 C. shredded coconut
1 C. colored miniature   1 C. peanuts
marshmallows

Cook to soft ball stage the following:
1 C. white corn syrup   1/2 C. cream or half and half
1 C. sugar

Then add:
1 tbsp. butter   1 tsp. vanilla

Pour over popped corn, coconut, marshmallows and peanuts. Mix well. Let cool until it will form balls.

Mrs. Russell Hymes, Arenzville, Illinois

Mashed Potato Doughnuts

1/4 C. melted butter   4 C. flour
1-1/2 C. sugar   5 tsp. baking powder
1 C. seasoned mashed potatoes   1 tsp. nutmeg
2 eggs, beaten   1 tsp. salt
                                     1/2 C. milk

Cream butter and sugar. Blend in mashed potatoes. Stir in beaten eggs. Sift dry ingredients together and mix alternately with milk. Chill 2 hours. Roll out 1/2" thick on floured board. Cut out. Fry in deep hot fat (365 degrees) about 1 minute on each side. Drain on paper towels. Sprinkle with powdered sugar.

Hot Fudge

1/3 C. margarine	1/8 tsp. salt
6-8 T. cocoa or 2 squares	1 C. evaporated milk
unsweetened chocolate	1 tsp. vanilla
1 C. honey or 1-1/4 C. sugar	1/4 C. margarine

Combine. Stir occasionally until thick (10-15 minutes). Thickens more as cools. Yield is 2 C.

Coconut Quicke

1 stick margarine	1/2 C. chopped nuts
(room temperature)	1 C. flour

Mix and pat in bottom of 9x13" pan. Bake for 15 minutes. Cool.

Mix:
1 C. powdered sugar

1 (8oz) pkg. cream cheese
1 C. Cool Whip

Put over cooled crust.

Mix: 2 pkgs. instant coconut pudding with 3 C. milk until thick. Spread over cheese mixture. Top with Cool Whip. Chill.

Mrs. Frank Douvier, Freeport, Minnesota

BREAD MONEY SAVING IDEAS

Cereals and breads are great budget savers. Use hearty yeast and quick breads in meals to provide a filling supplement to other dishes.

BREAD PLANOVERS

o <u>Crumbs</u>: I keep one container with buttered bread crumbs made from buttered leftover toast and another from bread that was getting older and I dried in another container. The buttered crumbs are great for casseroles and Fruit Betty. The non-buttered is best for coatings for fried foods, etc. Add grated cheese and herbs for special taste effects. A blender makes crumbs very quickly, but if you don't have one, roll bread with a rolling pin to the desired fineness.

o <u>Croutons</u> can be made from day old breads by buttering and coating with spices/herbs or parmesan cheese. Cut into cubes and bake on low heat until dried. Store in air tight bag or container.

o Make into bread pudding or casseroles that call for "day-old" bread.

o Make into French toast.

o Use to make stuffing - stove top or the type that is placed inside of a roasted bird.

o <u>Mock macaroons</u>: remove crusts, quarter and dip "day-old" bread in sweetened condensed milk. Roll in coconut. Cook on broil until lightly browned.

No-knead Basic 3 Loaf

1-1/2 C. scalded milk	1-1/2 C. water
1/2 C. shortening	3 pkg. yeast
1/4 C. sugar	3 eggs
2 tbsp. salt	9 C. sifted all-purpose flour

Combine first 4 ingredients. Cool to lukewarm with water. Add yeast. Beat in eggs one at a time. Add flour, mixing until well blended. This will be softer than a kneaded dough. Shape into three loaves on well floured board. Place in well greased pans. Cover. Let rise until double. Bake at 375 degrees for 1 hour.

Variations:
Add 1/2 C. nuts for nut loaf.

Coffee Cake: Spoon into pan. Sprinkle with 1/2 C. brown sugar, 1/4 C. chopped nuts and 2 tbsp. melted butter.

Cinnamon roll: 2 tbsp. melted butter, 1/4 C. sugar, 1 tsp. cinnamon.

Pecan roll: Cover bottom of pan with 1/4 C. brown sugar, 1/4 C. corn syrup, 1 tbsp. butter and 1/4 C. nuts. Roll with 1/4 C. sugar and 1/4 C. chopped nuts.

Chile Bread

1/2 of 4oz can green chopped chilies
Garlic salt
1/2 C. grated cheddar cheese
1/2 C. grated monterey jack cheese
1/2 of the recipe for Bisquick pancakes

Preheat oven to 475 degrees and grease 8x8" pan. After greasing pan, put chilies evenly in bottom of pan. Sprinkle with garlic salt. Cover with cheeses; cover with pancake batter. Bake for 35 minutes. Let set 5 minutes before cutting.

Mrs. Dolie Bond, Carlsbad, New Mexico

Beer Bread

3 C. self-rising flour   1 can warm beer
2 tbsp. sugar

Grease and flour loaf pan. Combine and bake at 350 degrees for 1
hour. Fifteen minutes before time is up, remove loaf and butter the
top. Place a foil tent on top and return to oven.

Vivian Grew, McQueeney, Texas

Corn Cakes

1 C. corn meal   2/3 level tsp. salt
Boiling water   1 tbsp. sugar
4 level tbsp. flour   1 egg
2 level tsp. baking powder   Milk

Put corn meal in bowl and add enough boiling water to cover it. Let
stand for 5 minutes. Add flour, salt and sugar; stir to blend. Thin to
a batter with beaten egg and milk. Add baking powder and beat
well. Cook on a hot well greased griddle.

Joyce Cunningham, Alliance, Ohio

Delicious Scrappel

1/2 lb. sausage   4 C. water
1 tsp. instant chicken bouillon   1 C. yellow corn meal
granules

Brown sausage lightly. Drain off excess fat, but not all of it. In a
pan, put 3 C. of water and bring to a boil, add the sausage to the
boiling water. Add the instant chicken bouillon granules; let simmer
10 minutes. Meanwhile in a bowl, put corn meal, add 1 C. of cold
water to corn meal and let stand 5 minutes; then stir. Add the corn
meal mixture to the sausage mixture. Sir thoroughly; cover and
simmer 5 minutes. Stir occasionally. Grease a loaf pan. Pour into
loaf pan. Cool. Slice when cold and flour each slice. Fry until
golden brown in skillet. Serve hot as is or with maple syrup.

Mrs. Eleanor Shelley, Youngstown, Ohio

Crunchy Granola

4 C. rolled oats
1-1/2 C. shredded coconut
1/2 C. wheat germ
1 C. sunflower seeds
1 C. sesame seeds
1/2 to 1 C. honey

3/4 C. oil
1 C. slivered almonds
1 C. raisins
Small can mixed nuts
6 oz. pkg. chocolate chips
1 C. peanut butter (nutty)
1 C. brown sugar

Combine all the dry ingredients in large mixing bowl. Measure oil and add honey to oil. Pour over dry ingredients. Mix thoroughly with hands (if desired). Spread thin layer in baking jelly roll pan. Bake one hour; stirring often at 350 degrees. Cool. Stores in airtight container for weeks. Use with milk like a cereal or pack some to take anywhere you go.

Linda Lou Urich, Dows, Iowa

SECTION V

MISCELLANEOUS

SYRUP

JELLY

MISCELLANEOUS
Sauces, Dressing, Jelly, Punch, Syrup

Basic White Sauce Mix

2 C. dry milk	Cut margarine into mixture
1 C. flour	until crumbly. Cover and store
1 C. margarine	in refrigerator.

Sauce:
- Thin   1/4 C. mix plus 1 C. water
- Medium   1/2 C. mix plus 1 C. water
- Thick   3/4 C. mix plus 1 C. water

Gradually stir water into mix. Cook over low heat; stirring constantly. Season with salt, pepper and herbs, etc. of choice.

Add broths, tomato juice or vegetable juices for all or part of water.

Cheese: Add 1/2 to 1 C. grated cheese and stir until blended.

Curry: Add 1 tsp. curry powder to thickened sauce.

Chicken: Add 1/4 to 1 C. chopped chicken, 1 tsp. or 1 cube chicken bouillon, 1 tsp. dried parsley, 1/8 tsp. garlic salt and 1/8 tsp. poultry seasoning, if desired.

Mushroom: (Or other vegetable) 1 (4oz) can mushrooms. Use liquid plus water to bring liquid to 1 C.

Gravy

1 C. liquid (broth plus water or milk)	2 tbsp. flour or 1 tsp. corn-starch
1-2 tbsp. drippings or fat	Salt and herbs to taste
	Bouillon for taste if needed

Flour Method #1: Stir flour into drippings. Blend. Add liquid and other ingredients and cook until thickened.

Flour Method #2: Blend flour into cup with about 1/4 C. cold liquid until smooth. Add remaining ingredients. Heat until thickened.

Corn Starch: Blend cornstarch into about 1/4 C. of cold liquid until smooth. Add remaining ingredients. Heat until thickened.

Fruit Sauce

1 C. juice of desired fruit
3/4 C. sugar

1 tsp. cornstarch
1 tsp. flavoring or extract

Mix cornstarch with 1 tbsp. water. Blend ingredients. Heat until smooth and thick.

The Best Spaghetti Sauce

1 large onion, chopped
1 green pepper, chopped
Garlic
1 lb. ground beef
1 env. Spatini (or other spaghetti sauce mix)
1 can tomato paste
1 can (28oz) crushed Italian tomatoes

1/4 C. red wine
1 tsp. oregano
1 tsp. salt
1/2 tsp. pepper
1 tsp. sugar
1 tsp. basil
1 tbsp. parsley
1 tsp. chili powder
Dash red hot pepper

Brown in oil: onion, green pepper, garlic and ground beef. Add rest of ingredients. Simmer, covered for 2 to 2-1/2 hours. (If desired, sausages can be added)

Caroline M. Awalt, Huntington, Connecticut

Spaghetti Sauce

2 tbsp. Italian herbs
1/2 tsp. garlic salt
2 tsp. sugar
1/2 to 1 lb. ground beef, pork or leftover chopped meat

2 cans (8oz) tomato sauce
1 can (16oz) whole tomatoes
(blended until almost smooth)
1 C. water
1 onion finely chopped

Brown onions and meat (if not precooked). Combine remaining ingredients. Blend. Cook for 20-30 minutes on low heat.

Homemade Barbeque Sauce

3/4 C. melted margarine
3 small onions, chopped
1-1/2 C. packed dark brown
sugar
1 (4oz) bottle liquid smoke
2 (26oz) bottles tomato catsup

1 (24oz) jar prepared mustard
2 tbsp. garlic powder
1 (7oz) bottle worcestershire
sauce
3/4 C. bottled lemon juice
5 C. water

Saute chopped onion in margarine in Dutch oven or large kettle. Add brown sugar and mix well. Add all of remaining ingredients and bring to boiling; then reduce heat and simmer about 30 minutes. Makes approximately 4 quarts. Store in refrigerator.

Jodie McCoy, Tulsa, Oklahoma

Good Sauce for Meat

Thin down 1/2 C. - 1 C. of cherry preserves or any kind of marmalade, jam or jelly with 4 T. port or apple wine. Heat, simmering for 5 minutes. Serve hot or at room temperature on any kind of meat.

Mrs. Charles Boyer, Fremont, Ohio

Blue Cheese Dressing

4oz. Blue Cheese
3/4 C. mayonnaise
1 C. sour cream

2 tbsp. dry sherry, white
wine or lemon juice
1/4 tsp. black pepper
1/4 tsp. garlic salt

In a bowl crumble blue cheese with a fork. Add remaining ingredients; blend well. Store in pint jar in refrigerator.

Mary Miller, Honeoye Falls, New York

Aunt Mary's Salad Dressing

1/2 C. sugar
1 tbsp. flour
1/2 C. vinegar

1 tsp. mustard
1 or 2 eggs

Boil altogether until thick. Let cool. Add 1/2 C. cream (plain or whipped evaporated milk) when you want to use it.

Arlene Krug, Cedar Rapids, Iowa

Blender Salad Dressing

Mayonnaise:
2 tbsp. lemon juice
1/2 tsp. salt

1 tsp. prepared mustard
1 egg
1 C. salad oil

Whirl at high speed with 1/4 C. oil until blended. Add remaining oil gradually.

Chutney: Add 2-4 tbsp. chutney. Use on fruit salad or fruit bread.

Anchovy: 6 anchovy fillets or 2 tbsp. paste. Use on dressed fish, vegetables, green salad.

Egg: 1 hard cooked egg and 1/2 tsp. instant onion. Use on fish, vegetables or green salad.

Green Goddess:
3 anchovy fillets
1 tbsp. chopped green onion
2 tbsp. chopped parsley

1-1/2 tsp. tarragon
1-1/2 tbsp. chives (chopped)
1-1/2 tbsp. tarragon vinegar

Curry: Reduce amount of mustard and add 1 tsp. curry. Good on articokes, rice, meat or seafood salads.

Dilled Sour Cream

1 C. sour cream
2 tbsp. vinegar
1 tbsp. minced onion
1 tbsp. sugar
1/2 tsp. salt

1/4 tsp. dry mustard
1/4 tsp. monosodium glutamate
3/4 tsp. dill seed
1/8 tsp. garlic powder
1/8 tsp. pepper

Combine and chill at least 30 minutes.

Sour Cream Blue Cheese

1 C. sour cream
1/2 C. crumbled blue cheese
Salt and pepper

1 tbsp. chopped onion
1-2 drops worcestershire
1 tsp. lemon juice

Combine, mix well and chill.

Basic French Dressing with Variations

3/4 C. salad oil
1/4 C. vinegar
1 tsp. salt

1 tbsp. sugar
1/2 tsp. paprika
1/4 tsp. dry mustard
Pepper

Mix to blend all ingredients.

Continental: Add 2 tbsp. catsup, 1 tsp. celery seed, 1 tbsp. chopped chives and 1 tbsp. chopped parsley.

Roquefort: 1/4 C. crumbled cheese

Lemon: 1/2 pkg. lemon gelatin dissolved in 1 C. hot water. When set, beat into dressing. Chill until firm. Beat until light and fluffy. Serve with fruit. Substitute grapefruit juice for vinegar.

Mexicana: 1 hardcooked egg (finely chopped), 2 tbsp. worchestershire, 1/2 tsp. chili powder, 1 tbsp. grated onion and 1 clove garlic (remove before serving).

Herb: 2 tbsp. chopped parsley, 1/8 tsp. thyme and 1/2 tsp. oregano.

Low Calorie Blender Salad Dressings

Blue Cheese:
1/2 pint yogurt
3 tbsp. blue cheese

1/2 tsp. salt
Whirl until smooth (in blender).

Bearnaise:
1 C. cottage cheese
3 tbsp. lemon juice

3 tbsp. white wine
1 or 2 egg yolks

Blend. Put in double boiler with 1 tsp. salt, cayenne, pinch dry mustard. Cook until heated. Good on poached eggs, vegetables, fish and meat).

Holiday Appetizer Cheese Torte

2 beaten eggs
2 tbsp. flour
1/2 tsp. seasoned salt
1/3 C. milk

4oz. can chopped green chilies
1/2 lb. grated cheddar cheese, sharp
1/2 lb. grated monterey jack cheese

Mix everything together well. Place in a well greased flat 8x12" pyrex dish. Bake at 350 degrees for 35 minutes. Cut into tiny squares. These also reheat well. Serve with crackers.

Cynthia Kannenberg, Milwaukee, Wisconsin

-211-

Bean Dip

Drain about 2 C. of cooked pinto beans and put in blender. Add juice of 1/2 of a lemon, 1 minced clove of garlic, 2 tbsp. mayonnaise, 1/4 tsp. tabasco and salt and pepper to taste. Blend until smooth. Serve as a dip for crisp raw vegetables or corn chips.

Jean Baker, Chula Vista, California

Cheese Spread

1 (8oz) pkg. cream cheese, softened
2 tsp. ground black pepper
1/4 tsp. garlic powder

1/4 tsp. seasoned salt
1/4 tsp. hickory smoked seasoned salt

Mix all ingredients well. Store covered in refrigerator for 1 hour. Let set at room temperature to spread on crackers.

Mary Hicks, Hickory, North Carolina

Rhubarb Jelly

5 C. rhubarb
(cut up fine)

4 C. sugar
1 pkg. strawberry jello

Cook rhubarb and sugar until rhubarb is done. Pour jello in and stir until all is dissolved. Put in container and freeze.

Elsie Gingerich, Kokomo, Indiana

Oven Homemade Apple Butter

18 C. applesauce
8 C. sugar (white)

1 C. vinegar
2 tsp. cinnamon
1 tsp. ground cloves

Mix all together in large roaster pan. Put in 350 degree oven for 3-1/2 to 4 hours. Stir every hour. Pour in jars and seal.

Faye M. Walter, Stowe, Pennsylvania

Sugar Syrup Punch

4 C. sugar
4 C. water   Boil until clear
4 pkg. kool-aid

Punch: 1 C. syrup
                3 C. cold water

Party Punch: 2 C. sugar syrup
                8 C. water and ice
                1 (6oz) frozen can orange juice
                1 (6oz) frozen can lemonade
                7-Up (optional)
                Pineapple-grapefruit juice (optional) or juices pour-
                ed from canned fruits.
                Add water to taste.

Cafe Maple Syrup

2 C. white sugar   Dash salt

Dissolve in 1 C. hot coffee in saucepan. Heat to boiling and boil 1
minute. Stir in 1/2 tsp. maple flavoring. Remove from heat and
serve hot over pancakes, waffles, etc.

                            Glenna Mitchell, Merritt Island, Florida

INDEX

Almond	37, 70, 77, 126, 158, 159, 205
Angel Food Cake	162
Apples	4, 40, 58, 69, 85, 139, 141-146, 149, 155, 158, 159, 165, 168, 181, 184, 212
Applesauce	142, 143, 146, 159
Apricot	140, 146
Apricot Preserve	140
Arrowroot	8, 174
Artichoke Jerusalem	102
Asparagus	17, 117
Bacon	21, 25, 34, 47, 50, 66, 85, 100, 103, 109, 112, 113, 127, 132
Banana	125, 138, 157, 159, 160, 170, 174, 184, 187, 188, 189, 195
Barbeque	25, 38, 134, 209
Barbeque Salad	134
Bean (general)	4, 16, 18, 29, 31
kidney	20, 47, 51, 102, 111
pork/beans	38, 47, 52, 113

chili	112
butter	47
lima	112
green	53, 64, 126, 132
navy	111
great northern	108, 111
pinto	111, 155, 166, 167, 212
Bean Sprouts	53
Beef (general)	29, 48, 57, 58, 102, 131
ground	3, 31-52, 54, 61, 103, 104, 106, 107, 112, 208
round steak	21, 22, 23, 25
hamburger	31, 32, 36, 38, 41, 42, 47, 50, 52, 53
meatballs	40, 41, 44, 54
roast	21, 22, 24, 27, 28, 29
chuck	24, 51, 111
sirloin	25
short ribs	26
stew meat	28, 30
corned beef	28, 30
Berries blueberry	140, 141, 146, 182, 185
strawberry	9, 140, 141, 148, 173, 182, 183, 184
raspberry	192
cranberry	184, 188

Biscuit & biscuit mix	49, 62, 76, 86, 95, 97, 101, 143, 147	Casseroles	21, 27, 29, 37, 38, 39, 41, 46, 50, 53, 56, 60, 61, 63, 64, 65, 77, 80, 82, 86, 93, 94, 97, 99, 104, 105, 107, 114
Bologna	102		
Bouillon	10, 11, 21, 28, 30, 37, 51, 56, 69, 74, 76, 86-89, 107, 128, 130, 133, 203, 207		
		Catsup-Ketchup	10, 22, 33, 34, 35, 36, 39, 40, 43, 47, 55, 63, 72, 83, 88, 99, 101, 125, 132, 209, 211
Bread	181, 203, 204		
Broccoli	17, 76, 114, 124	Cauliflower	125
Broth	10, 21, 26, 30, 65, 77, 80, 84, 85, 87, 116, 207	Celery	22, 24, 29, 30, 36, 37, 48, 50, 51, 53, 55, 56, 57, 60, 61, 63, 67, 69, 76-80, 82, 83, 84, 86, 87, 89, 91, 95, 104, 116, 126, 131, 132, 133, 135
Brownies	162		
Buttermilk	5-7, 9, 119, 149, 150-152, 159, 164		
Cabbage	3, 39, 41, 42, 52, 54, 68, 99, 124, 131, 133	Cheese (general)	11, 12, 19, 37, 38, 40, 50, 61, 77, 79, 87, 107, 109, 110, 117, 118, 207
Cakes	139, 150-165	american	37, 44, 63, 67, 76, 116, 127, 197
Candy	197		
Cantaloupe	189	blue	209, 210, 211
Caramel	195	brick	114, 116, 117
Carrots	24, 25, 29, 30, 34, 35, 48, 51, 54, 57, 60, 62, 63, 68, 79, 85, 97, 124, 125, 129, 131, 135, 162	cheddar	36, 37, 41, 43, 51, 62, 64, 65, 76, 90, 96, 97, 105, 107, 127, 129, 158, 203, 211
		cheeze whiz	114
		cottage	5, 35, 106, 115, 119, 182, 183, 185, 192, 211

-216-

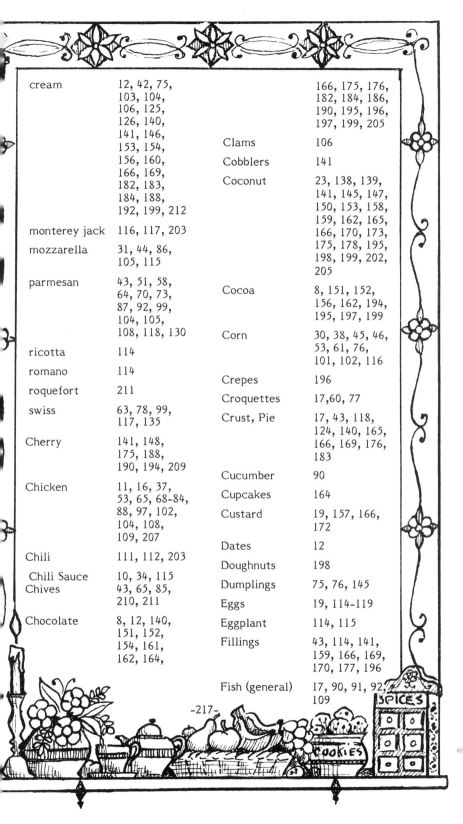

cream	12, 42, 75, 103, 104, 106, 125, 126, 140, 141, 146, 153, 154, 156, 160, 166, 169, 182, 183, 184, 188, 192, 199, 212
monterey jack	116, 117, 203
mozzarella	31, 44, 86, 105, 115
parmesan	43, 51, 58, 64, 70, 73, 87, 92, 99, 104, 105, 108, 118, 130
ricotta	114
romano	114
roquefort	211
swiss	63, 78, 99, 117, 135
Cherry	141, 148, 175, 188, 190, 194, 209
Chicken	11, 16, 37, 53, 65, 68-84, 88, 97, 102, 104, 108, 109, 207
Chili	111, 112, 203
Chili Sauce	10, 34, 115
Chives	43, 65, 85, 210, 211
Chocolate	8, 12, 140, 151, 152, 154, 161, 162, 164, 166, 175, 176, 182, 184, 186, 190, 195, 196, 197, 199, 205
Clams	106
Cobblers	141
Coconut	23, 138, 139, 141, 145, 147, 150, 153, 158, 159, 162, 165, 166, 170, 173, 175, 178, 195, 198, 199, 202, 205
Cocoa	8, 151, 152, 156, 162, 194, 195, 197, 199
Corn	30, 38, 45, 46, 53, 61, 76, 101, 102, 116
Crepes	196
Croquettes	17, 60, 77
Crust, Pie	17, 43, 118, 124, 140, 165, 166, 169, 176, 183
Cucumber	90
Cupcakes	164
Custard	19, 157, 166, 172
Dates	12
Doughnuts	198
Dumplings	75, 76, 145
Eggs	19, 114-119
Eggplant	114, 115
Fillings	43, 114, 141, 159, 166, 169, 170, 177, 196
Fish (general)	17, 90, 91, 92, 109

catfish	93	Macaroons	202
tuna	94-97	Manicotti	104
perch	90	Marinade	20, 26
flounder	90	Marshmallow	12, 149, 151, 164, 166, 169, 185, 186, 188, 198
scallops	92		
salmon	97, 98		
Frankfurters/ hot dogs	101, 102, 110	Melon	140, 189
Fritters	101, 122, 144	Meringue	166, 168, 169, 174
Frosting/Icing	150-155, 158-160, 178	Muffins	66, 138
Fudge	197, 199	Mushrooms	10, 11, 25, 28, 43, 44, 62, 70, 71, 73, 80, 84, 99, 100, 103, 104, 105, 107, 115, 117
Gelatin	133, 134, 173, 185, 187, 188		
Gingerbread	177		
Glaze	148, 157	Noodles	29, 38, 46, 53, 78, 86, 88, 94, 102, 105, 107, 124, 192
Goulash	115		
Grapefruit	148, 211		
Gravy	19, 100	Nuts	12, 16, 70, 126, 158, 159, 196, 197, 205
Ham	63-67		
Hash	17	Oats	173
Hot Dogs	See Frank-furters	Oranges	12, 72, 161, 189
Icing	See Frosting	Oyster Plant	128
Ketchup	See Catsup	Patties	32, 45, 47, 57, 65, 77, 112, 124
Lamb	99		
Lasagna	105, 107	Pastry	62, 165, 169, also see Crust
Lentils	16		
Lettuce	51, 80	Peas	29, 35, 52, 53, 76, 79, 81, 85, 93, 95, 97, 112, 132, 133
Liver	82, 100		
Macaroni	12, 18, 99, 103, 104, 107, 108, 133		
		Peaches	9. 140, 141, 142, 147, 170, 171

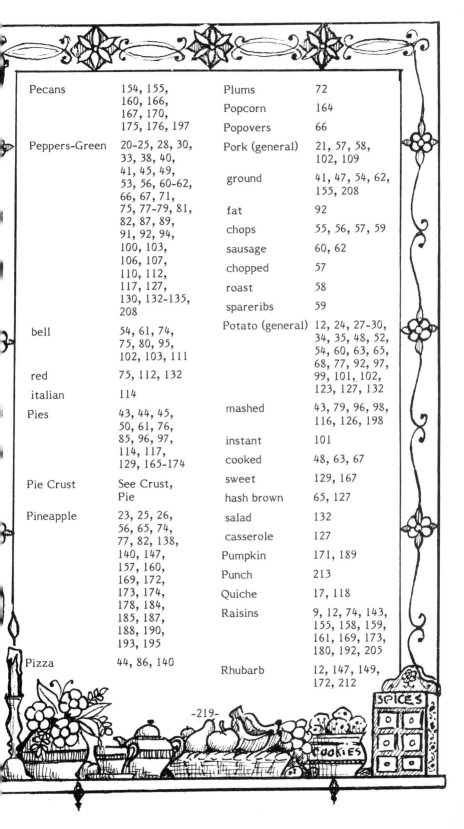

Pecans	154, 155, 160, 166, 167, 170, 175, 176, 197	Plums	72
		Popcorn	164
		Popovers	66
Peppers-Green	20-25, 28, 30, 33, 38, 40, 41, 45, 49, 53, 56, 60-62, 66, 67, 71, 75, 77-79, 81, 82, 87, 89, 91, 92, 94, 100, 103, 106, 107, 110, 112, 117, 127, 130, 132-135, 208	Pork (general)	21, 57, 58, 102, 109
		ground	41, 47, 54, 62, 155, 208
		fat	92
		chops	55, 56, 57, 59
		sausage	60, 62
		chopped	57
		roast	58
		spareribs	59
bell	54, 61, 74, 75, 80, 95, 102, 103, 111	Potato (general)	12, 24, 27-30, 34, 35, 48, 52, 54, 60, 63, 65, 68, 77, 92, 97, 99, 101, 102, 123, 127, 132
red	75, 112, 132		
italian	114		
Pies	43, 44, 45, 50, 61, 76, 85, 96, 97, 114, 117, 129, 165-174	mashed	43, 79, 96, 98, 116, 126, 198
		instant	101
		cooked	48, 63, 67
Pie Crust	See Crust, Pie	sweet	129, 167
		hash brown	65, 127
Pineapple	23, 25, 26, 56, 65, 74, 77, 82, 138, 140, 147, 157, 160, 169, 172, 173, 174, 178, 184, 185, 187, 188, 190, 193, 195	salad	132
		casserole	127
		Pumpkin	171, 189
		Punch	213
		Quiche	17, 118
		Raisins	9, 12, 74, 143, 155, 158, 159, 161, 169, 173, 180, 192, 205
Pizza	44, 86, 140		
		Rhubarb	12, 147, 149, 172, 212

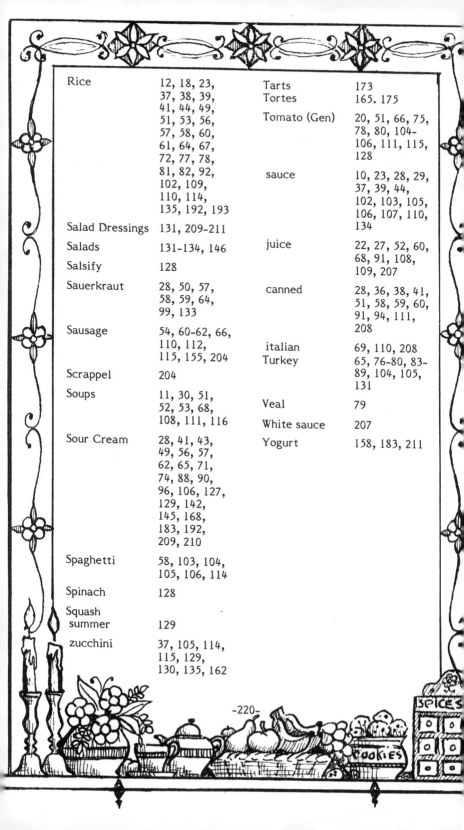

Rice	12, 18, 23, 37, 38, 39, 41, 44, 49, 51, 53, 56, 57, 58, 60, 61, 64, 67, 72, 77, 78, 81, 82, 92, 102, 109, 110, 114, 135, 192, 193	Tarts	173
		Tortes	165. 175
		Tomato (Gen)	20, 51, 66, 75, 78, 80, 104-106, 111, 115, 128
		sauce	10, 23, 28, 29, 37, 39, 44, 102, 103, 105, 106, 107, 110, 134
Salad Dressings	131, 209-211	juice	22, 27, 52, 60, 68, 91, 108, 109, 207
Salads	131-134, 146		
Salsify	128		
Sauerkraut	28, 50, 57, 58, 59, 64, 99, 133	canned	28, 36, 38, 41, 51, 58, 59, 60, 91, 94, 111, 208
Sausage	54, 60-62, 66, 110, 112, 115, 155, 204	italian	69, 110, 208
		Turkey	65, 76-80, 83-89, 104, 105, 131
Scrappel	204		
Soups	11, 30, 51, 52, 53, 68, 108, 111, 116	Veal	79
		White sauce	207
Sour Cream	28, 41, 43, 49, 56, 57, 62, 65, 71, 74, 88, 90, 96, 106, 127, 129, 142, 145, 168, 183, 192, 209, 210	Yogurt	158, 183, 211
Spaghetti	58, 103, 104, 105, 106, 114		
Spinach	128		
Squash summer	129		
zucchini	37, 105, 114, 115, 129, 130, 135, 162		

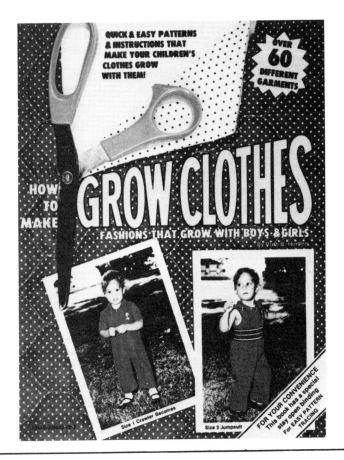

HOW TO MAKE GROW CLOTHES. . .Fashions That Grow With Your Kids by Ruth B. Hinden

The original guide to Saving Time & Money on your children's clothing. If your kids outgrow their clothes. . . You must get this book. Complete with Patterns & Instructions for over 60 garments. ONLY $5.95. A really great gift. ORDER NOW! (Shipped from our Las Vegas Warehouse.)

A basic book on knit fabrics SEWING KNITS helps you select the right fabric for the right project, prepare and cut the fabric properly as well as giving the various methods of making a "knit seam". Learn how to make a basic T-shirt from a multi-size pattern and then do many different neckline finishes. Fit and sew knit pants like a pro, make sweaters and swimsuits, apply exposed zippers, do easy bound buttonholds, Chanel trim and much, much more. This book is a must for knit lovers.   Just $5.95

MACHINE EMBROIDERY
YARN STITCHERY
by Verna Holt

This is really TWO BOOKS ONE! Now you can make be: tiful "hand-made" creations your sewing machine. Compl step-by-step instructions w dozens of diagrams a delightful color photos. ONl $7.95 While Supplies La (Shipped from our Atlar Warehouse.)

LET'S CALL IT QUILTS
Verna Holt

Verna Holt does it again! takes the time consuming, very rewarding old-world ar hand quilting & turns it int quick & easy sewing mach process. NOW you can turn beautiful quilts in no time at instead of the many hours takes for hand quilting. ON $8.95. (Shipped from our At ta Warehouse.) Call it quilts hard work & do it the easy w

If you are sewing for the man in your life, or want to, then SEWING KNITS MENSWEAR is for you. It covers the knit sports coat in depth, featuring the use of fusible interfacings and the tailoring know how for fitting, pockets, collar application, facings, sleeves and linings so that finished coat looks like it came off the rack of an expensive men's store. Instructions are also given for knit pants, sports shirts and the vest along with tips to speed your sewing along and make it easier. $4.95

The Most Complete Sewing Book We've Ever Seen! Whether you're a beginner or a seasoned sewer, SEW SMART can have you sewing like a Pro in no time. Learn to pick the right needles, threads & fabrics for the professional look. Learn to duplicate expensive designer fashions with Ultra Suede, inexpensively! Just about everything you need to know about sewing is in this BIG 272-page Masterpiece. ONLY $12.95, While Supplies Last.